MOTHERWELL

Champions of Scotland

1931-32

DESERT ISLAND FOOTBALL HISTORIES

CLUB HISTORIES	ISBN
Aberdeen: A Centenary History 1903-2003	1-874287-49-X
Aberdeen: Champions of Scotland 1954-55	1-874287-65-1
Aberdeen: The European Era – A Complete Record	1-874287-11-2
Bristol City: The Modern Era – A Complete Record	1-874287-28-7
Bristol City: The Early Years 1894-1915	1-874287-74-0
Cambridge United: The League Era – A Complete Record	1-874287-32-5
Cambridge United: 101 Golden Greats	1-874287-58-9
The Story of the Celtic 1888-1938	1-874287-15-5
Colchester United: Graham to Whitton – A Complete Record	1-874287-27-9
Coventry City: The Elite Era – A Complete Record	1-874287-51-1
Coventry City: An Illustrated History	1-874287-59-7
Dundee: Champions of Scotland 1961-62	1-874287-72-4
Dundee United: Champions of Scotland 1982-83	1-874287-71-6
History of the Everton Football Club 1878-1928	1-874287-14-7
Halifax Town: From Ball to Lillis – A Complete Record	1-874287-26-0
Hereford United: The League Era – A Complete Record	1-874287-18-X
Huddersfield Town: Champions of England 1923-1926	1-874287-66-X
Ipswich Town: The Modern Era – A Complete Record	1-874287-43-0
Ipswich Town: Champions of England 1961-62	1-874287-56-2
Luton Town: The Modern Era – A Complete Record	1-874287-05-8
Luton Town: An Illustrated History	1-874287-37-6
Matt Busby: A Complete Man U record 1945-1971	1-874287-53-8
Motherwell: Champions of Scotland 1931-32	1-874287-73-2
Norwich City: The Modern Era – A Complete Record	1-874287-67-8
Peterborough United: The Modern Era – A Complete Record	1-874287-33-3
Peterborough United: Who's Who?	1-874287-48-1
Plymouth Argyle: The Modern Era – A Complete Record	1-874287-54-6
Plymouth Argyle: 101 Golden Greats	1-874287-64-3
Portsmouth: From Tindall to Ball – A Complete Record	1-874287-25-2
Portsmouth: Champions of England – 1948-49 & 1949-50	1-874287-38-4
The Story of the Rangers 1873-1923	1-874287-16-3
The Romance of the Wednesday 1867-1926	1-874287-17-1
Stoke City: The Modern Era – A Complete Record	1-874287-76-7
Stoke City: 101 Golden Greats	1-874287-55-4
West Ham: From Greenwood to Redknapp	1-874287-19-8
West Ham: The Elite Era – A Complete Record	1-874287-31-7
Wimbledon: From Southern League to Premiership	1-874287-09-0
Wimbledon: From Wembley to Selhurst	1-874287-20-1
Wimbledon: The Premiership Years	1-874287-40-6
Wrexham: The European Era – A Complete Record	1-874287-52-X
WORLD CUP HISTORIES	
England's Quest for the World Cup – A Complete Record	1-874287-61-9
Scotland: The Quest for the World Cup – A Complete Record	1-897850-50-6
Ireland: The Quest for the World Cup – A Complete Record	1-897850-80-8
MISCELLANEOUS	
Red Dragons in Europe – A Complete Record	1-874287-01-5
The Book of Football: A History to 1905-06	1-874287-13-9
Football's War & Peace: The Tumultuous Season of 1946-47	1-874287-70-8

MOTHERWELL
Champions of Scotland 1931-32

Series Editor: Clive Leatherdale

Alex Smith

DESERT ISLAND BOOKS

First published in 2003
by
DESERT ISLAND BOOKS LIMITED
89 Park Street, Westcliff-on-Sea, Essex SS0 7PD
United Kingdom
www.desertislandbooks.com

British Library Cataloguing-in-Publication Data
A catalogue record for this book is available from the British Library

ISBN 1-874287-73-2

Printed in Great Britain
by
Biddles Ltd

Photographs in this book are reproduced by kind permission of:
John Swinburne, Keith Brown, Mrs J McCubbin, Paul Pettigrew, and
The Motherwell Heritage Centre (page 65, bottom; page 72, bottom)

~ Contents ~

~ Preface ~

Sadly, I never enjoyed the good fortune to see any of the legends that won the League Championship in 1932 but I had been regaled throughout my earlier years with stories and anecdotes about 'the finest exponents of Scottish football'.

As an engineering apprentice in Motherwell the highlight of each morning was the tea break at the smiddy fire in the blacksmith's shop, listening to blacksmith Joe Fraser eloquently running through the main attributes of that great Well team which shattered the 'Old Firm' and everyone else in the league as they cantered to a famous milestone in the history of not only Motherwell Football Club but also of Scottish football itself.

This was the very first time since 1903-04 that any club other than Rangers or Celtic had won the League Championship. Joe Fraser's favourite player varied from day to day as he extolled the footballing virtues of each and every one of his heroes of fifteen years earlier.

'Alan Craig,' he would say, 'would stroll through each game and never a hair out of place. He was an immaculate centre-half. Wales and Telfer were the team's inspiration in the engine room. They both had vision and passing ability but unless you can win the ball then you can't play and they were both tenacious tacklers as well. Then there was Geordie Stevenson – a total genius. He was the finest player that I have ever seen!

'Out on the wing was Bobby Ferrier with that wicked left foot. He could swerve a ball past a goalie at either the near or far post. Thirty goals from the wing – we'll never see that equalled. Wullie McFadyen missed more than he scored but still holds the record number of goals with 52 in a season. 'Poacher' Murdoch and the silky McMenemy supplied the ammunition and McFadyen finished it off. At the back we had big Allan McClory, Dowall and the hardman – Ben Ellis – what a team.'

Alex Smith has focused our attention on our great heritage, ... Thanks Alex!

John Swinburne MSP (Director, Motherwell FC)

~ AUTHOR'S NOTE ~

Motherwell FC's story deserves telling. Past glories fade too easily unless kept bright in the retelling. Motherwell's 'shining moment' in footballing history is the ten years from the mid-1920s until the mid-1930s. The remarkable Championship win of 1931-32 is that moment's pinnacle.

The bare fact of that League win can be found in record books but the story behind it is one of a painstaking manager, John 'Sailor' Hunter, and the men he blended into a superb footballing machine. It was a team of friends – some went on holiday together, they knew each other's families well, they helped each other out in times of trouble and adversity.

Professional footballers, however, were comparatively well off at that time. Motherwell's glory years coincided with real hardship and suffering in the Depression of the 1920s and 30s. Their subsequent decline came as conditions improved, until the football and world scene changed forever with the coming of the Second World War. Much of 1930s life we would now find quaint or hopelessly old-fashioned, and yet today's football fan could still empathise with his or her ancestors' passion and commitment to their team. This was true for sides now unfamiliar to us, such as Leith or Bo'ness, and for Celtic, Rangers or the Well.

In telling the story I have used terms and spellings from the time. Therefore, 'fans' was becoming common but a 'striker' was someone who went on strike; 'centre-forward', or often just 'centre', was the forward who went through the middle to score goals. Hamilton were the 'Acas'.

I couldn't have written this book without the help of others. My thanks are due to Pauline and Jamie Nimmo and Marie Mitchell for their help and encouragement. Ben Ellis's daughter, Mrs Nita McCubbin, provided photographs and wonderful stories. Jim McKeen did sterling work on statistics. Keith Brown and Dave Wardrope freely gave material. Richard McBrearty at the Scottish Football Museum was always helpful. John Swinburne helped with photographs and was kind enough to write the Preface. Clive Leatherdale, the book's editor and publisher, gave guidance and advice that kept me on the straight and narrow.

ALEX SMITH, August 2003

DEDICATION: This book is dedicated to Alec and Phil Smith and all those who were there and have now gone.

Introduction

~ CHAMPIONS OF SCOTLAND ~

Tension ran high among the three thousand supporters who had come to Fir Park on Saturday, 16 April 1932. As they waited impatiently for the the teams to reappear for the second half the talk undoubtedly centred on two footballing topics. The first was whether Motherwell could beat Cowdenbeath in this, their penultimate game of the season, take the two points, and so leave second-placed Rangers with the stiff task of having not only to win all of their last four games, but also to do so by improbably large goal margins. Otherwise Motherwell, still with that one further game left, in two weeks' time, would be Champions of Scotland. The Lanarkshire club played their football in the midst of an industrial heartland and drew much of their support from workers in local coal mines and iron and steel works. The town itself was once nicknamed 'Steelopolis' and the football team appropriately became known as 'The Steelmen'.

As Motherwell went into this penultimate game, the top of the Scottish First Division in this 38-game programme showed they and Rangers well in front of their nearest challengers, Third Lanark (who had already completed their programme) and Celtic:

	P	W	D	L	F	A	Pts
Motherwell	36	28	6	2	113	31	62
Rangers	34	26	4	4	112	36	56
Third Lanark	38	21	13	4	91	81	46
Celtic	36	18	10	8	88	49	44

If Motherwell were now to defeat Cowdenbeath, it would mean that Rangers would need to win all of their remaining four matches in order just to match Well on points. General opinion held that these games would be hard going for the defending champions. They had yet to face Clyde, Hamilton, Airdrie and Kilmarnock. The only one of these that seemed likely to pose little threat to Rangers was that against Hamilton, the only one of the four due at Ibrox. Clyde had already taken a point at Ibrox the previous November, and at their own Shawfield ground in Rutherglen they had notched up eight of their ten league victories to date.

Airdrie had won nine times so far at Broomfield and had managed to hold Celtic to a 1-1 draw there only the week before. As for Kilmarnock, they were strong enough to be Rangers' Cup final opponents on this very day. On the other hand, the game that remained for Motherwell after today seemed a much easier task in comparison: again it would be Clyde providing the opposition but, crucially, the game was to be at Fir Park. Motherwell hadn't lost a league game at home since Hearts had won there away back in September 1929.

Given that one of the magnetic features of football is its recurring unpredictability, then the possibility had to be considered that Well might just lose to Cowdenbeath and Rangers reap all eight points still available to them. In those days, rather than goal difference, the league differentiated teams finishing on equal points by means of goal average. This was calculated by simply dividing the goals scored by the goals conceded. So it was that much talk concerning the league finish centred not just on the maximum possible number of points that the Ibrox team could achieve, but also on their goal average compared to Motherwell's. Thus, Rangers' goal average stood at 3.111 whereas Motherwell's much healthier figure was 3.645. If the Well could register a win today it would further improve their standing, provided Cowdenbeath did not score.

The second topic concerned Willie McFadyen, the Fir Parkers' bustling centre-forward. (Willie's surname has appeared in print in different forms; here we are using the version as listed in the official Electoral Register of the time.) McFadyen needed only to score one more goal to overtake the Scottish League record set by Celtic's Jimmy McGrory back in season 1926-27 – an incredible 49 goals. McGrory had in fact beaten the previous record of 43, set by Hugh Ferguson, Motherwell's legendary centre-forward, in season 1920-21. Worryingly, however, there had been no McFadyen goals for a month past. There was much irony in the fact that Willie's last strike, his record-equalling counter, had come against Jimmy McGrory's club and in front of the Celtic support at Parkhead. In the interim he had missed a couple of games due to a knee injury he had picked up in that Celtic match. He had then returned against Partick Thistle at Firhill, a game that had unfortunately ended in a no-scoring sharing of the points.

Cowdenbeath proved themselves to be no pushovers as Motherwell's opponents, and had surprised many by the stubborn fight they had made of the first half. Despite their mid-table position and memories of a 5-1 drubbing Well had dished out back in October at their own Central Park ground, they were making progress difficult. It was in fact difficult to know what face they would show. Two weeks beforehand they had gone down 1-7 at home to Rangers; the next week they'd trounced fourth placed Kilmarnock by the same score.

Now, in brilliant sunshine and kicking against the swirling wind, the Fifers had thwarted the Motherwell forwards, particularly McFadyen. Willie had been his usual eager-running self and, although clearly desperate to get a goal to break the record, he had been unselfish and put balls out to his outside men when called for. When inside-left George 'Stevie' Stevenson had driven a smart hook-shot into the net the referee immediately blew to disallow it. In his eagerness to snatch up any crumbs, McFadyen had dashed forward then ended up standing on the goal-line and so was clearly offside.

The teams reappeared after the break to find that, apart from some small isolated groups, the crowd had migrated almost entirely behind the Cowdenbeath goal, obviously in eager anticipation or in dogged hope. Their move seemed a wise one as Motherwell pressed from the kick-off. The game had started at 3.15pm and it was not until just before 4.20pm that the built-up nervous tension in crowd and players was broken. Johnny Murdoch out on the right wing had been popping in dangerous crosses, as had team-mate Bobby Ferrier from the left. As Murdoch swung the ball in, Ferrier was on the spot to send it past Edwards in the Fifers' goal. In a scene probably more akin to modern celebrations, Bobby found himself swamped by his colleagues, not the more subdued congratulations usual of the time. It was indeed an indication of the relief felt and the importance of the breakthrough – the championship was now in sight.

The small but noisy crowd had barely stopped cheering when John McMenemy, Well's cultured inside-right, dribbled passed Campbell and let loose a shot that the goalkeeper seemed to have covered until left-back Russell spun the ball into his own net as he tried to block. Joy was now unbounded. With the Steelmen well on top, the result seemed secure. Rangers would need a considerable tally of winning goals in their last four matches, three of which they had to play before Well's last game, against Clyde at Fir Park.

The attention of the crowd at Fir Park now centred on their increasingly anxious centre-forward and his attempts to register a goal. All his fellow forwards attempted to set up one up for him. Manager Hunter's prize asset was his whole team which, at its best, worked like a well-oiled machine. Within that machine, however, the most precious parts were out on the left wing in the shape of George Stevenson and Bobby Ferrier. The phrase 'Stevenson and Ferrier' had become so repeated that it was now household. The two names in one phrase reflected the closeness of the partnership that these two players had developed over the course of eight years. The abundant skills of the one complemented those of the other. Stevie's classy inside play blended seamlessly with the craft and guile shown by winger Ferrier, playing now in his fourteenth season at Fir Park and reaching the pinnacle of his professional career. Offers and interest from English clubs for one or the other, or for both, run like a thread through Motherwell's glory years. The club's board gained hearty commendations in the Scottish press for holding out against the lure of English gold; they were said to have turned down the offer of a blank cheque.

Cowdenbeath's collapse had lasted all of ten minutes and had allowed Well to snatch their two-goal lead, but the minutes had flown past and still McFadyen hadn't scored. As the final seconds ticked relentlessly away, Well continued to press and George Stevenson gathered the ball for one last effort. He let go a powerful shot that rose until it smacked against the crossbar. As the ball flew down off the lower edge, it dropped just as Willie McFadyen thrust forward his forehead. The ball spun off and away from the reach of goalkeeper Edwards and into the net. Willie had his 50th goal of the season and the old record was broken. As the back-slapping Motherwell players trotted back up the field, referee Reilly blew the final whistle.

If any quick mental calculations were then attempted, with pencil and paper and a knowledge of long division, they would show Motherwell's revised goal average had improved to 3.742. This meant that Rangers would need to win all their four remaining games and in the process score 23 goals without loss to overtake Well's average as it now stood. The arithmetic possibilities were no doubt intriguing for those who were able to work them out. Nevertheless, the press were in no mood to quibble, portraying Motherwell as good as actual Scottish Champions, risking the pitfalls that football's unpredictability can bring. The *Daily Record* had even trumpeted: 'Motherwell All But Champions' on the morning of the Cowdenbeath game.

Despite the sunny day, manager John 'Sailor' Hunter may well have been wearing his accustomed black bowler hat or perhaps his more fashionable soft fedora as he watched his Motherwell team take on Cowdenbeath. As Well laid siege in the second half he must have glowed with satisfaction and pride in a team that he had largely formed, from what was commonly termed 'promising juniors'. He was later reported to have remarked, 'I never saw a keener game in all my life.' This is going some for a man who had then been in football for over 36 years. Not known as a man for the throwaway line, however, we have to presume he meant what he said and that the tension had certainly got to him as well. Success had been a long time coming, as he was now in his 22nd year at Fir Park. The side that he eventually moulded was one that would finish in the league's top three for eight successive seasons. Rangers had set the early pace in season 1931-32 but when Well climbed to the top in October they stayed there till the finish.

That same day the great Rangers machine was being held to a 1-1 draw by gutsy Kilmarnock in the final of the Scottish Cup at Hampden. The following Wednesday, however, the Glasgow giants would enjoy an easy 3-0 replay victory and so lift the trophy for the seventh time. It was largely because of their Cup campaign, which included a quarter-final defeat of Motherwell at Ibrox, that Rangers now faced a backlog of league games to win. There was no doubting their keenness to beat Well to the title. If they were to do so they would equal the achievement of their city rivals, Celtic, who had racked up a record sequence of six championships in a row between 1904 and 1910. By the same token, the Celtic club and its supporters were more than keen to see Motherwell hold off the Ibrox challenge in order to preserve their record. Their own side would eventually finish this season third, but well off the pace. Rangers were also determined to claim the League title in this particular season and so boast the honour of winning the 'double' (the League Cup competition would not be introduced until after the Second World War). They had managed to achieve the feat twice previously, in 1928 and in 1930. The fact that Celtic had three 'doubles' to their credit only added further spice to the affair.

The last time a club other than the big two of the Old Firm had won the Scottish League had been back in season 1903-04, when Third Lanark were champions, just before Celtic began their long run. Motherwell's triumph would in fact only briefly interrupt Rangers, who were to win three in a row after the Steelmen. Not until the Second World War had been and gone, and the nation was working its way to peacetime normality, would the Old Firm monopoly again be broken. The honour of doing so would fall to Hibernian in 1947-48. Thus, in a period spanning 43 years, only Motherwell were able to break the spell of the Glasgow giants.

Most people's experience of the early 1930s is through old photographs, newsreels and (sometimes silent) movies, almost invariably in black and white. Our perception of the world then tends to be in similar monochrome mental images. And yet, the sky then was often blue, the grass was green and footballers' strips were as colourful as they are today. Motherwell's shirts had been in claret and amber, unique in Scotland, since 1913. This was a time when ordinary people desperately needed some colour in their lives. The worldwide economic slump that had taken hold in 1929 had now reached its worst point. Unemployment was rife throughout the country but was particularly intense in areas of heavy industry, such as the Lanarkshire towns of Motherwell, Wishaw and Bellshill, as well as the surrounding villages. By 1934 the Government would step in and designate all of industrial Lanarkshire as one of six 'Distressed Areas' of Scotland, entitled to obtain grants to carry out public works and so offer some relief for the chronic unemployment. If he could afford a shilling (5p) admission money, a man could forget about his troubles for a while and hopefully be entertained with the colourful spectacle of a football match. There is an irony in the fact that, at this time of so much hardship and personal suffering amongst the working people of Lanarkshire, the local senior football teams performed so well – to the extent that they have never repeated their feats of these years in the League or Cup. This was also Hamilton Academicals' best period; Airdrie were chasing and snapping at the Old Firm before neighbours Motherwell took over their mantle. Albion Rovers, too, over in Coatbridge, flourished in these dark times.

Having played a Cup final, followed on the Wednesday by a victorious replay, Rangers now had to buckle down to League business. Saturday would take them to Shawfield against Clyde, then to Broomfield on the Monday to face Airdrie, quickly followed by the luxury of that home fixture against Hamilton, and finally by a trip away to Kilmarnock to finish their season. Six crucial games crammed into two weeks perhaps served to emphasise the old cry that having points in the bag was preferable to trying to catch up. This fixture congestion was a tough ending to a season made hot for Rangers for so long by Motherwell. In addition, the Gers would have been only too aware of their inferior goal average, that added a further burden to their attempt at overhauling Motherwell. It is worth considering whether that Rangers' quarter-final Cup win over Well was not in effect a blessing in disguise for the Steelmen. The Ibrox side ended up adding more league games to their backlog whereas Motherwell were free to pursue their league programme. It is intriguing to ponder what might have happened if it had been the Lanarkshire side who had gone on to the semi-finals instead.

The importance of Rangers beating Clyde was therefore paramount in trying to keep the Ibrox club's momentum going to the very end. Seven days after Well had beaten Cowdenbeath, Rangers ran out at Shawfield knowing that not only were they tackling the first of a series of crunch games, but also the only League opponents they had not succeeded in defeating so far. A stiff first-half breeze behind Clyde was used to the home side's advantage and in 36 minutes Clyde were awarded a free-kick. Right-winger McGurk got on to the ball and shot home from close range. Rangers did not lose heart and on the hour centre-forward Sam English was brought down in the area. Marshall strode forward and converted the penalty-kick to set up a nail-biting finish, with Rangers piling on the pressure for the last fifteen minutes. However, when the final whistle blew that vital point had been dropped. The mathematics now confirmed what the fans and the papers had been saying for a while now: Motherwell were Champions.

Rangers' subsequent collapse against Airdrie at Broomfield on the Monday hardly mattered. Their tired side was bolstered by the introduction of several reserves for the Hamilton game, which was won 1-0, and Kilmarnock were beaten 4-2 at Rugby Park. It was too little, too late. The point dropped at Shawfield merely underlined what Motherwell supporters and sympathisers had felt after that dramatic second half at Fir Park on 16 April. John Hunter's bunch of 'promising juniors' had at long last been the side that had burst the Old Firm monolith. It had been a long time in the making, but as things turned out, it could so nearly have been repeated by the Steelmen. This is the story of Motherwell, Champions of Scotland.

Chapter 1

~ FOUNDATIONS ~

Hopes were high when Alpha and Glencairn, the growing industrial town of Motherwell's two foremost sides of the day, amalgamated in 1886 to form Motherwell FC. The local *Motherwell Times* felt that the merging of the former rivals would make 'Motherwell FC second to none in the West of Scotland as a country club'. As Association Football developed and became further embedded in Scottish popular culture, 'country' or provincial clubs would find the big city clubs grow in financial strength and playing power. The Scottish Football League was established in 1890 with a ten-club set-up, and three years later a Second Division, also of ten clubs, was established. Motherwell, newly turned professional, were unanimously voted among their number.

Playing at Dalziel Park, a centrally situated but poorly drained and often rutted ground, Motherwell finished fourth in that inaugural season of 1893-94, then in second place in the following year. In the days before the advent of automatic promotion and relegation, elevation was in the hands of the votes of First Division clubs, and Second Division champions Hibernian were invited into the top league.

Motherwell were forced to quit their substandard field because of building requirements and in 1895 they moved further away from the town to ground leased from Lord Hamilton of Dalzell at his Fir Park estate. The team went through a poor spell as form plummeted and twice finished bottom of their division. After the turn of the century the club enjoyed a resurgence and achieved second place again in 1902-03. Playing still in their blue shirts and popularly known as 'The Well', they were awarded eleven votes and Lanarkshire neighbours Airdrie, who had finished above them as champions, just eight, but that was enough for both clubs to be voted aboard an elite division expanded from twelve clubs to fourteen.

The Scottish Cup at that time was organised on a regional basis for all but the top division sides in its early rounds, due to the large number of entries it attracted. In 1895 the lesser sides had to participate in a Scottish Qualifying Cup with the last sixteen teams left in then being eligible for the Scottish Cup proper. Motherwell reached their first national final when they travelled to the Second Hampden Park (the second incarnation of Queen's Park stadium in Mount Florida) in 1897, but Kilmarnock (who had finished third in the Second Division) had an easy 4-1 victory to lift the Qualifying Cup. In 1901-02 Motherwell again reached the Qualifying final and led Stenhousemuir 1-0 at half-time, only to lose two goals in the second period. In their final season in the Second Division, Well's third Qualifying final appearance again saw them face Stenhousemuir who had won the trophy twice previously. The team from Larbert won 2-0 before 10,000 at Celtic Park but Motherwell protested that one of their opponents was already cup-tied. A replay was ordered and Motherwell duly won their first national trophy by 2-1 a fortnight later at Ibrox. In the Scottish Cup itself, Motherwell's best was to reach only the second round during their first sixteen years in the competition.

The going in the top division was tougher than expected and little headway was made by Motherwell. The luxury of not having to participate in the Qualifying Cup was countered by a brief Scottish Cup campaign, ended by Leith Athletic in the second round. Motherwell finished next to bottom in the First Division, with fellow newcomers Airdrie only three points better just above them. Despite the poor finish, the Motherwell board in 1904 decided to turn the club into a limited liability company, its annual turnover having doubled over two years. Team selection at this period was in the hands of a committee, with a trainer and an assistant left to take charge of training and on-field practicalities. Within a short space of time two secretary-managers had been tried but without achieving much success. The post was later filled by one of the retiring directors.

Season 1904-05 was a disaster and bottom place in the division meant having to seek re-election to it and participation in the Qualifying Cup again. Well and Morton were successfully re-elected, while Falkirk and Aberdeen were voted up from Division Two, despite finishing second and seventh respectively. Reprieved, Motherwell established themselves as something of a mid-table outfit until form slumped in 1911 and they finished in penultimate place. Well managed to reach the third round of the Scottish Cup that year, paired against near neighbours Hamilton at Douglas Park on 3 March. The Lanarkshire Tram Co ran a tram per minute over the Clyde to Hamilton but sadly the 17,000 crowd saw Well fall 1-2. After the game the Motherwell directors communed in the Commercial Hotel (later the Hamilton Town Hotel) in Hamilton's Townhead Street for the important task of appointing someone to lead the team. The mood must have been somewhat low key: out of the Cup and back to a low position in the League. A list of 70 applicants for the manager's post was produced and a short list of twelve then drawn up.

The man finally settled on by the directors was the fresh-faced 36-year-old John 'Sailor' Hunter. The new man did not exactly receive a warm welcome: the sceptics greeted Hunter's arrival with complaints that the two previous managerial appointments had been less than satisfactory. John Bryson Hunter had been born near Paisley and entered football with Westmarch XI, a Paisley junior side. His 'Sailor' nickname apparently came from the rolling way he had of walking. Writing in 1927, perhaps with a touch of hindsight, old Rangers goalkeeper Harry Rennie recalled: 'He was one of the cleverest and brainiest forwards of the day, … he was dribbling very close and sailing in at an angle …'

Hunter had certainly been a strong and incisive attacker, progressing to recently relegated Abercorn in 1897-98 and making twenty appearances in his two years there before being signed by Liverpool. He helped the Merseyside club to their first ever League championship in 1901 as part of a side known to be 'durable and consistent rather than brilliant' (Butler: *Official Illustrated History of The Football League*). Returning to Scotland in 1902, Hunter joined Hearts as an inside-left and gained a losers medal against Rangers in the 1903 Scottish Cup final. He was back down south only a year later with Arsenal, where he made 22 appearances for the Gunners in season 1904-05. His next stop was Portsmouth in the Southern League, where he turned out 38 times for Pompey before heading back north once more. Signing for Dundee, he became a prolific goalscorer while at Dens Park, as the *Scottish Referee* noted of him: 'Hunter excels in snapping up chances near goal; he passes beautifully on the run, and is a past master as a "header".'

A solitary international cap came John Hunter's way at this time when he led the Scotland attack against Wales at Wrexham in 1909, the Welsh team winning 3-2. In a remarkable Scottish Cup final against Clyde the following year, Dundee were down 0-2 with only six minutes remaining, but a goal from Hunter, then another from team-mate Langlands two minutes later, earned a replay. After a no-scoring return match, Dundee won the second replay 2-1 for their only Cup win, John again being a scorer. Hunter moved on again next year, this time to Clyde, but at the season's end he decided to pitch his hat into the ring for the post of Motherwell's secretary-manager. Thus it was that Well gained a man, modest in his bearing and attitude but with a great deal of footballing experience crammed into a comparatively short period of time. Not only that, John Hunter had been a player of some class and had tasted success as both a winner in the Football League and the Scottish Cup.

Manager Hunter's start at Motherwell was inconclusive in the short term with a draw, a loss and a win at the start of the new season. In the longer stretch it was a similar story, with the side veering between a highest ever seventh place and the nether regions of the league. Interestingly, when they reached that seventh position, Well were the only side able to wrest full points away from eventual champions Celtic that season. Manager Hunter obviously had regard for his younger players, as witnessed by the reserve side winning the Reserve League championship of that year.

Motherwell also ditched their old blue shirts in favour of the rarer claret and amber, their new tops based on those of Bradford City, winners of the FA Cup just two years before. It was felt that there would be less occasion for colour clashes than the common blue had entailed.

The long drawn out summer of 1914 was shattered by news of the outbreak of war and although many imagined that it would be a short and glorious affair, it developed into a horrific and bloody struggle over the next four years. Life at home went on and included football. The SFA controversially decided to proceed with the Scottish League but to put the Cup into abeyance. It was during the course of the conflict that John Hunter brought in players who would make telling contributions to the development of Motherwell as a footballing force. The last line of defence had been unsettled since Colin Hampton, once capped for the Scottish League, had gone to Chelsea in April 1914. After a series of unsatisfactory replacements, Jock Rundell was signed from junior side Larkhall Thistle. Jock made his debut in goal on a day in April 1916 when Well lost *two* games, played one after the other due to fixture congestion and wartime rules. Celtic historians are rightly proud of the fact that their side won two games that day, but the 'victims' of the champions-to-be were Motherwell in fourteenth place and Raith struggling in twentieth. Well's other conquerors were Ayr, but despite this inauspicious start the stocky Rundell would make another 270 league appearances as part of an improving side.

Season 1916-17 brought an instant solution to another problem position when local lad Hugh Ferguson made his debut at centre-forward and grabbed both goals in Well's first game, followed two weeks later by a hat-trick against Dundee. Hughie was another junior, snapped up from Parkhead, who settled in well and quickly became a favourite with the fans at Fir Park because of his goal exploits. Ferguson would lead the club's scoring charts for every season until the year he left, notching up a total of 282 league goals. It was due in no small measure to Hughie's goals that Motherwell finished in the top five of the league over the next four years, up to 1920-21, as the nation came to terms with the aftermath of war. Although they finished fourteen points adrift, Motherwell even managed third spot in 1919-20, behind Rangers and Celtic. The monopoly of the two Glasgow giants had been well established by this time and the memory of Cathkin side Third Lanark's championship win back in 1904, when Motherwell were top division newcomers, was becoming rapidly dimmer.

Another acquisition from Parkhead Juniors was Willie Rankin, coincidentally the same height and weight as Hugh Ferguson at 5ft 7in and weighing 11st 7lbs. Performing mostly at inside-right, Rankin was modest as a goalscorer, largely acting as provider for Ferguson. His cultured style, however, was nurtured by manager Hunter and when he left the club some thought him the best player they had ever seen at Fir Park. Rankin gained several League caps but never a full international for Scotland. A year after Rankin arrived, John Hunter brought in a young left-winger, Bobby Ferrier, to replace Birmingham's Billy Morgan, who had come to Scotland for war work in munitions production. Ferrier's skills were early apparent as he regularly demonstrated how he could dribble past opponents, juggle the ball in the air and project deadly accurate crosses.

Hughie Ferguson's goal tally in 1920-21 rose to 42, a new Scottish record for the First Division. Unfortunately, even with Ferguson still rattling in the goals, the side slipped again into mid-table mode during the first half of the 1920s. The Scottish Cup, however, did offer some hope of glamour, especially during a time of rapidly rising unemployment and depression in the heavy industries, such as steelworking, engineering and mining, that sustained so much of the population of central Scotland and Lanarkshire in particular. Motherwell reached the quarter-finals of the Cup for the first time in 1921 when, without Ferguson, Renton were first eliminated 3-0. Well had needed Ferguson, a week at Seamill Hydro health resort on the Ayrshire coast, plus three games to finally overcome Ayr by 3-1 at Celtic Park after two 1-1 draws. In the quarter-final against Partick Thistle they also drew twice, 2-2 then 0-0 at Firhill with 25,000 looking on before the Glasgow side eventually got the better of them by 2-1 at 'neutral' Ibrox. In 1921-22 the quarter-final stage was again reached, where Morton managed to scrape home by 2-1 at Fir Park.

The following year Well went one better when they reached the semi-finals, meeting Celtic at Ibrox. Motherwell had never really been known as a Cup side but their two recent quarter-final ties had begun to change that. Although Celtic were favourites, they hadn't won the trophy since 1914, the last year before war had put the Cup into storage. Motherwell's side lined up: Rundell; Little, Newbigging; Greenshields, Brown, Stewart; Lennie, Rankin, Ferguson, Reid, Ferrier. Heavy rain had just subsided as the game kicked off before 75,000 at Ibrox and only one minute later Well were a goal down. Captain Craig Brown had stumbled and allowed Cassidy to run through to score. The Motherwell wing-halves were putting in crosses meant for Ferguson, but Celtic's Cringan was in fine form and mopped up whatever came his way. Well's Brown incurred an injury and was glad to hear the whistle for the break; in the second half Lennie and Dick Little also picked up knocks. Celtic pressure led to a scrimmage, and a free-kick just outside the area was turned in by McAttee for the winner. Celts went on to win the trophy by beating Hibs, and despite their exploits Motherwell found themselves at the season's end with another in a continuing series of financial losses.

A run of eight games unbeaten was put together early on in 1923-24, but disruption to the first team led to later points-leakage. The situation wasn't helped by financial constraints, which meant the abandonment of the reserve side, not for the first time. This year was notable, however, in that it heralded the first appearance of two further Motherwell greats. On 6 October at Ayr's Somerset Park a no-scoring draw was the ironic setting for the debut of one of Motherwell's and Scotland's greatest ever goalscorers: Willie McFadyen was played at outside-right in this, his first game for Motherwell and subsequently turned out there or at inside-right, or at centre-forward now and again – although that of course was Hugh Ferguson's berth. It would be seven games before McFadyen actually scored and a deal longer before he became a first-team regular. Even then, he was not always an automatic choice for the forward line, never mind centre-forward. Willie had actually been signed from Wishaw in 1921 but had then been 'farmed out' to Bo'ness and Clyde. Manager Hunter's new inside-left, George Stevenson – destined to become one of the club's all-time greats – made his debut in the middle of a run of five straight defeats, away to Third Lanark at Cathkin Park in December. Thirds won 2-1.

The side was again an unsettled one in 1924-25, especially in the half-back line and in defence. Goalkeeper Jock Rundell gave way to a tall and lanky 23-year-old from Armadale, Allan McClory, and although the side slipped down the table McClory kept several losses to single-goal deficits. This, together with an 8-0 thumping of fellow strugglers Third Lanark at Fir Park, was just enough to save the club from relegation. Well, Ayr and Thirds all finished with 30 points but the Steelmen's goal average was good enough to keep them up, automatic promotion and relegation having now been established. Whatever the feelings of relief felt by the Motherwell club and its supporters, there was ongoing and unsettling talk of Hugh Ferguson leaving for an English club and the wonder was that the club had managed to hold on to him this long. There was further rumour that both Rangers and Aberdeen coveted his signature. At this low time, Bobby Ferrier put in a transfer request but the club turned it down despite reports that Blackburn Rovers were prepared to part with a healthy £2,000 for him. There was no maximum wage operating in Scotland, apart from in wartime, and top division players might earn in the region of £8 or £9 weekly, plus bonuses. (At this time a semi-skilled worker might earn less than £2 per week.) Although the economic climate was still in the doldrums, the club was able to record its first profit since 1921.

Sadly for Motherwell, Hugh Ferguson played his last game for them at the end of October 1925 and received a touching farewell from the crowd at Motherwell railway station and then the workmen at Colville's Steelworks where 21 fog-horn blasts saluted his train as it puffed by on its way south. Ferguson scored goals freely for his new club, Cardiff, the most outstanding of which was the single goal which won them the FA Cup in 1927, gaining them the distinction of being the only side outwith England ever to have won the trophy. Cardiff's substantial outgoing transfer fee of £5,000 had been more than repaid.

One inheritor of Ferguson's mantle was Willie McFadyen, although he was still played mainly at inside-right or even at half-back before eventually becoming settled at centre-forward. Writing in 1924 the *Motherwell Times* had been unflattering but prophetic: 'McFadyen will come a bit at centre. He isn't quite a Hugh Ferguson and probably never will be, but still he will get the goals.' The narrow escape of the previous season appeared to have stung the club as the side proceeded to string victories together. 1925-26 marked a change in the offside rule in that now only two defenders instead of three were required to play their opponents onside. Goals flew in as defences struggled to adjust. The old system of 2-3-5 (two full-backs, three half-backs and five forwards) was to change with Arsenal leading the way, to a 3-3-4 set up where the centre-half was withdrawn from his attacking midfield role to become another back, a 'stopper'. To compensate in midfield, one of the inside-forwards dropped back to play a deeper role.

McFadyen scored a respectable sixteen League goals that season, 1925-26, gathered in the main from his outings at centre-forward, a position more often filled by Willie Tennant, who managed eleven goals, one fewer than Bobby Ferrier out on the left wing. The league match against Celtic at Fir Park was given over to Ferrier as his benefit and Motherwell marked it with a 2-1 win, although the man of the moment failed to score. Due mainly to the transfer money received for Ferguson, Well registered the fifth largest profit in Scotland and in the League reached fifth position, above Rangers and a single point behind St Mirren.

For ten days in early May 1926 around ten million British workers took part in the General Strike in support of the miners' wage claim. The miners themselves held out for six months and in places like Lanarkshire this meant knock-on effects for rail transport which depended on coal and of course for steel production. Soup kitchens made a reappearance in Motherwell and attendance at football matches also suffered. By October, at least one of Lanarkshire's senior clubs had to dip into its own pocket to meet the League's guarantee for visiting clubs. As the *Motherwell Times* put it: 'For the great bulk of the people there is a superabundance of holiday with no funds upon which to enjoy the vacation.' At Fir Park, while collections were taken up for the 'Distress Fund', Motherwell FC's large profit allowed manager Hunter the luxury of being able to run a reserve side once again, to good effect as it turned out during season 1926-27.

After a mediocre start, a ten-game unbeaten run brought a 32-goal harvest. However, the centre-forward berth was still proving difficult to fill after Ferguson's departure, and McFadyen, Banks, Tennant, Cameron and even George Stevenson all shared the task. Consequently it was Bob Ferrier who topped the scoring list with nineteen goals from the wing. Bobby's partnership with inside-man Stevenson had been developing over the past three years to the extent that it was becoming one of the most feared and admired in the country. Both local and national newspapers had been asking who might break the monopoly of the Old Firm, which had seen them lift the League title every year since Thirds' win in 1904; Celtic had taken thirteen and Rangers nine. The most likely candidates were the strong-going Airdrie, St Mirren, Hearts and perhaps Motherwell. Rumours flew around the district that Well were looking to sign Patsy Gallagher, the legendary ex-Celt known as the 'Mighty Atom' but it came to nothing. It did seem, though, as if a ready-made successor to Ferguson was to be found in young Willie Tennant, a polished centre who notched up eighteen goals in the space of just ten autumn games. Sadly he then picked up a string of injuries that curtailed his appearances and his season's tally remained at eighteen.

When McFadyen grabbed all four in the 4-0 romp at Dunfermline in November 1926 Well had gone second behind Rangers, whose goal average was better. However, league leadership was secured the following week with a 5-2 home win over St Johnstone. Motherwell stayed in top place until the following January, with only a brief drop to second in December. As both Celtic and Rangers had games in hand, the meeting with Rangers at Fir Park in late January was a crunch match. The record 32,000 crowd crammed into the ground saw the Ibrox side run out easy 4-1 winners: 'Perhaps the idea of a big game was too much for their nerves, but that indeed would be a poor excuse for League aspirants,' bemoaned the *Motherwell Times*. Well's main struggle now was to edge out Celtic and five more wins was enough to do so. The final table read:

1926-27	P	W	D	L	F	A	Pts
Rangers	38	23	10	5	85	41	56
Motherwell	38	23	5	10	81	52	51
Celtic	38	21	7	10	101	55	49

This runners-up season was to mark the beginning of Motherwell's glory years when, over the course of eight successive seasons, they would offer the only sustained challenge to the Old Firm and never be out of the top three.

Surprisingly, for such a high-flying team, there had been a dearth of international caps at Fir Park by this point. Stevenson did represent the Scottish League against the Football League, putting in a successful performance despite the unaccustomed inside-right role he was given. Motherwell fans felt that both Stevie and Ferrier were more than capable enough for full Scotland caps and could imagine their exciting partnership in claret and amber being reproduced in Scotland blue. Sadly for both Ferrier and for Scotland it was never to be. Bob had been born in Sheffield and, although his father was a Scot, according to the rules of the time he was unable to represent his father's country. Keeper McClory was another of international standard, capped once so far by Scotland and twice by the Scottish League; along with Stevie and left-half David Thackeray (picked for the Scottish League in 1927) McClory was also attracting the interest of some top English clubs.

A tour of Spain in the summer of 1927 began with two games for the King of Spain Cup sponsored by King Alfonso to promote football in his country. Well overcame fellow tourists Swansea 4-3 before meeting Real Madrid. A Swansea man who was at the Real game thought that George Stevenson was the hero of the day but added that the 'whole team were in exhibition mood and treated the Madrid people to a nice game'. Motherwell beat Real 3-1 to bring the stylish trophy back to Fir Park. Two games for the Barcelona Cup followed and before 22,000 Well held Barcelona to a 2-2 draw before beating Swansea again and earning their second piece of Spanish silverware. Ferrier, John Hunter and director Taggart were presented to King Alfonso himself. Subsequently, Well's only loss came against a Bilbao Select, although they defeated Celta Vigo twice before travelling to Paris for a 5-0 win over Red Star Olympique, four times winners of the French Cup.

What influence this tour might have had on the players is difficult to say but several demanded better terms or transfers before and during the following season. Manager Hunter had to work hard along with his board in order to persuade their star men to stay on. Sunderland, Everton, Leicester and Huddersfield were some of the latest sides to express interest. The board, said the *Motherwell Times*, 'realise that points are more than pounds sterling – meantime.' An unnamed director's public statement must have given little heart to Motherwell supporters: 'But the offers are very tempting, and as trade is bad in the district and gates consequently poor, the time may soon come when we shall have to release one or more players. As long as we can carry on without loss, so long will we hold to our players.'

With Ferrier as captain, Well resumed their winning ways on the field and by September 1927 were second behind Celtic with a game in hand, although Rangers were closing in on them. Anticipation of the meeting with Rangers built up daily and 30,000 gathered at Fir Park but little classy football was seen, and the points were shared in a hard battle. Celtic were conquered 2-1 at Celtic Park and easy wins over Dunfermline 5-0 away, Clyde 5-0 and Hamilton 5-1 at Fir Park were unfortunately spoiled by losses away at Aberdeen and Falkirk. 'Has Motherwell's Chance Gone?' asked the local *Times*, and despite going top after a midweek win at Airdrie, several subsequent draws answered 'yes'. Both Rangers and Celtic finished strongly, making up ground from their games in hand and falling only to Motherwell who enjoyed a famous 2-0 win before 50,000 at Ibrox. Celtic, already beaten by Well in Glasgow, were bettered by 3-1 in April at Fir Park, with long-time patrons, Lord and Lady Hamilton of Dalzell, in attendance. Rangers finished as clear champions, while Celtic pipped Well for second spot on goal average.

1927-28	P	W	D	L	F	A	Pts
Rangers	38	26	8	4	109	36	60
Celtic	38	23	9	6	93	39	55
Motherwell	38	23	9	6	92	46	55

The club had fixed up a tour of Argentina for the close season but fond memories of the jaunt to Spain were quickly dispelled by opening defeats. A correspondent writing from Argentina hoped the Scots could redeem themselves so that at least, 'local Britons will be able to pass their junior clerks and office boys without having to look the other way.' A McFadyen hat-trick helped beat Rosario 4-3 and five of the remaining seven games were won to restore some pride; they included 3-0 victories over an Argentina FA side, then an Argentina-Uruguay Select. Brazil held Well to a 1-1 draw before the final game saw the Scottish team fall 0-5 to a Brazil Select.

With Thackeray gone to Portsmouth for £3,500, Motherwell brought in John McMenemy from Celtic for a bargain £1,100. Profits came not only from foreign tours and the rare transfer out, but also from away gate money which, apart from stand takings, was shared. Gate money taken from those who paid to stand on the terracings was shared between the two participating clubs. First Division clubs had to pay the visiting side a guaranteed minimum of £100, so it often happened that a poor home crowd meant the host club would be out of pocket. It was, of course, more expensive to sit in the grandstand, normally two shillings (10p) at Fir Park during this period, although Cup games might cost 3s 6d (17½p) or even 5s (25p) for a reserved seat at some grounds. This income from the stand was kept by the home club in both League and Cup matches – a fact that was regretted by Sailor Hunter when Motherwell were thus unable to share in the Ibrox Park stand takings, at 5s per seat, in a Cup-tie that set a new ground record of 88,000.

Attendance figures as reported in the press were merely estimates, as the Scottish League did not provide reporters with official figures. It seems that these estimates did not generally include the stand. Figures given for Scottish Cup attendances were 'official' and comparatively more accurate.

Motherwell's home gates had dwindled and were on a par with clubs much lower in the League than themselves, but the prevailing economic climate was exerting a definite effect locally. Results over the season were inconsistent and ten draws did not help matters. In the quarter-finals of the Scottish Cup Celtic were held 0-0 at Parkhead but the replay was lost 1-2. Bobby Ferrier was again the top scorer with 29 goals, many of which he netted spectacularly by running in along the by-line and letting rip from a tight angle. Well ended 1928-29 in third place and only one point behind Celtic in second but Rangers had won their third successive title at a canter:

1928-29	P	W	D	L	F	A	Pts
Rangers	38	30	7	1	107	32	67
Celtic	38	22	7	9	67	44	51
Motherwell	38	20	10	8	85	66	50

When Hearts won 2-0 at Fir Park on 7 September 1929, Well had collected what was by now for them a mediocre five points from five games. The significance of the result would grow in subsequent weeks, months and years as it turned out to be the last time Motherwell would lose in the League at Fir Park for over three years. This was a season driven greatly by the left-wing pair of Stevenson and Ferrier. Bobby excelled himself, again topping the club's goal chart with his best ever 30 counters from 37 starts on the left wing. His hat-trick in the 7-2 rout of Cowdenbeath was bettered in the last League game of the season when he netted four times in a 9-0 drubbing of Queen's Park, ironically in a game that doubled as a benefit for Willie McFadyen, who did not score.

A stylish young left-half, Willie Telfer was picked up from juniors Blantyre Celtic and quickly found his place in the first team, forming a mid-line with Hugh Wales and Alan Craig that was to figure prominently for the remainder of the season and indeed for many seasons to come. Although Well lost twice to Rangers, they achieved the double over Celtic, winning 2-1 at Fir Park, then by 4-0 at Parkhead and so completing their League programme with a run of seven wins and the highest goals total in the division, finishing second in the process:

1929-30	P	W	D	L	F	A	Pts
Rangers	38	28	4	6	94	32	60
Motherwell	38	25	5	8	104	48	55
Aberdeen	38	23	7	8	85	61	53

Motherwell's Fir Park had taken its name from the plantation in which it was located, and part of which had been leased to the club in 1895 by landowner Lord Hamilton of Dalzell. By the 1930s the richly wooded estate of Dalzell House to the south contrasted starkly with the northern aspect of street upon street of two-storied tenement housing, its stone blackened by years of nearby industrial activity. On the ground's west side a small wooden grandstand, enlarged in 1921 and capable of holding around 1,000 'standites', offered the only cover, although it did also provide shelter to the narrow enclosure area immediately in front.

Spectators stood on 'terracing' constructed from numerous cartloads of earth and ashes built up over the years; the first such areas were at the eastern side adjacent to the school, and then behind the northern end known variously as the Town, Toll Street, Taggart's, or Knowetop goal. This banking had been terraced by cutting in steps which were then faced with strips of wood. To the south, behind the end known as the Estate goal, had been a curling pond that had prevented further development there for many years. Now it too had been acquired and covered with tons of dumped earth, ashes and 'clean refuse' to form a high banking that would only be fully terraced in February 1932.

Season 1930-31 kicked off optimistically for Well as the national press asked the recurring question: if anyone was to topple the Old Firm, who would it be? Motherwell were held to be most likely. It was November before they suffered their first loss, 1-2 to Dundee at Dens Park, but three more away defeats gave Rangers the advantage. A crunch game at Celtic Park was tamely lost 1-4 before two more points were dropped at Cowdenbeath, which consigned Well to third place. Again they boasted the highest goals tally, this time helped by McFadyen's 24 from only nineteen starts:

1930-31	P	W	D	L	F	A	Pts
Rangers	38	27	6	5	96	29	60
Celtic	38	24	10	4	101	34	58
Motherwell	38	24	8	6	102	42	56

On Christmas Day 1930, Hunter dropped 'handyman' Dowall in favour of McFadyen at centre-forward for the game away to Partick. By so doing, he brought together for the first time what would become the renowned forward line of Johnny Murdoch, John McMenemy, McFadyen, Stevenson and Ferrier. Well won 3-0 and the local *Times* verdict was that a 'superior' forward line had won the day.

In manager Hunter's twentieth year at Fir Park it looked as if the Scottish Cup was to be a fitting reward. Bathgate and Albion Rovers were dispatched before Hibs were beaten 3-0 in front of a record Easter Road crowd of 33,300. Another record was set at Cowdenbeath when 18,673 saw Well edge through 1-0. A goal by right-winger Johnny Murdoch was enough to see off St Mirren in the Ibrox semi-final, setting up a final with Celtic at Hampden Park on 11 April. The Hampden slopes were packed with 105,000 spectators as Stevie gave Well the lead in only seven minutes, followed just thirteen minutes later by one from McMenemy.

The Cup looked safe as Well continued to hold off Celtic in the second half. The irrepressible McGrory grabbed one back with only nine minutes remaining, but some presumptuous Well fans had started the journey home when, with two minutes left on the clock, Bertie Thomson tore down the wing and sent over a hopeful cross. Alan Craig thought he heard the shout of 'Go for it, Alan!' He did, but it was intended for keeper Allan McClory. Craig instinctively jumped and the ball glanced off his head and into the net. Referee Craigmyle thought that the prostrate Craig was hurt and asked if he would be all right. Alan replied with a groan: 'I've done it now!' (H Taylor: *Scottish Football Book, 1956-57*). Craig would take twenty years to get over his Cup error. The Motherwell side never really recovered and in the Wednesday replay before 98,588 fans they lost 2-4 and the Cup dream was gone. The standards had been set, however, and the foundations laid for yet another challenge.

Chapter 2

~ Uncrowned Kings ~

(May–September 1931)

The handsome sum of £300 which the Motherwell board had awarded to manager Hunter to mark his twentieth year at the club would not have lessened his pain and disappointment at losing the chance of lifting the Scottish Cup. A month before the Cup drama played out at Hampden Park, the Scottish League title had looked like a distinct possibility, not to say probability, in the eyes of the *Motherwell Times*: 'With only 5 laps to go Motherwell are favourably placed for winning the League and achieving the greatest triumph any Scottish provincial club has won for a generation.' Two draws and the surrendering of both points to Cowdenbeath (three points for a win only arrived 50 years later) meant that one half of a historic 'double' had disappeared. The local paper nevertheless kept faith in the team: 'If the main honours again elude them, it is safe to predict that Motherwell will sustain their challenge to the giants for a few seasons to come.' There was a great deal of national sympathy for the nearly-men, christened the 'uncrowned kings of Scottish football'.

The Union-Castle Line vessel 'Windsor Castle' carried Motherwell's South African tour party on the long voyage from Southampton, arriving in Cape Town on 18 May. The squad won fourteen of the fifteen games they played during a stay of 44 days, which involved over 5,300 miles of rail travel. Three 'Test Matches' were played against representative South African teams. The second of these, before 29,000 Johannesburg spectators, resulted in a new goal record in a representative South African match when Willie McFadyen scored six in Well's 8-0 win. Willie would go on to amass a personal total of 30 from his side's 57 scored on the tour. Two years later, correspondents were still extolling Motherwell's praises and ranking them as the best touring side ever to have visited South Africa. Additionally, it was claimed that football in that part of the world had benefited from attempts to assimilate Well's playing style, employing 'scientific' methods rather than reliance on speed. Attracting almost 70,000 spectators, Motherwell's three Tests alone had covered the club's expenses.

However, it was not only as a source of income that this and Well's previous tours to Argentina, Spain, and France could be seen, but also as valuable experiences in sampling other football cultures. Whereas a South African writer later wrote that the tour had been 'One big football lesson' for the country, on the other hand the Well team and its manager were also learning, even if the press might not readily admit it. Sailor Hunter, on his return from Argentina three years before, denied reports in a Buenos Aires newspaper which had printed a 'faked' interview in which he allegedly claimed that Motherwell were there to teach the Argentines how to play. On the contrary, he had much to say in praise of his hosts: 'Their ball control is simply magnificent, and they are alert as deers [sic]. ... The sooner it is realised that we are not the salt of the earth in matters of football the better.'

Similarly, there were two sides to the matter of players being together for so long, at sea and during the weeks of the tour itself. They would 'grow sick of each other and also risk injury on foreign fields', one writer wagered. Certainly, one player agreed that the sea voyages were not to his liking. However, there was also the possibility that players could forge stronger bonds with each other and as a team, facing novel surroundings so far from home.

Before setting off on the tour, Hunter had been anxious that a hard season challenging for the League, as well as a traumatic Cup campaign, would tell on his men. Fifteen games on often grassless pitches was also hard going. When their ship had called in at the island of Madeira on the way home they had learned the Scottish League fixtures for the start of the new season, the manager being dismayed to see that they were scheduled to play two games a week for the first four weeks. He had hoped to give his squad as much rest as possible before the new season began.

Back home in Scotland the summer had been poor and, although the smoke that normally hung over the Motherwell area had lessened due to the holiday break, the skies stayed stubbornly dull. The team had travelled up from Southampton by rail, some disembarking at Carstairs to journey to Lanarkshire by bus, while the rest carried on to Glasgow. Hunter went on to his usual annual holiday with his family in Blackpool.

When they reassembled for their initial training sessions, the players looked 'fit and bronzed' and the local *Times* reporter was prompted to gaze into his crystal ball: 'History may well record that the Motherwell team, on their way to the winning of the Cup or the League, took the long trail to South Africa, and finding new strength and inspiration in the waters of the Atlantic Ocean, returned recuperated and renewed of purpose to cut a sure trail to the Cup or League.'

By this time, Hunter's carefully crafted side was largely composed of those 'promising juniors'. The term 'junior' refers to the level of organisation in Scottish football, rather than an age grouping. Whereas senior clubs were members of the SFA, the juniors – formed predominantly from teams playing on public grounds – were members of the SJFA, established in 1886. There had also been a few bigger buys – in addition to John McMenemy from Celtic, Murdoch had come from Airdrie and reserve back Sandy Hunter from Hamilton – but it was those who had cost least who were still attracting keen interest from England. George Stevenson could easily fetch over £8,000 it was said, and Spurs were even rumoured to be considering an offer that would break the record £10,340 that Arsenal had paid for Bolton's David Jack.

Meanwhile, manager and board held what they had, despite the oft repeated cry: 'They will surely sell their players now!' The press knew where Motherwell's financial steel lay, as 'Caledonia' wrote in the *Daily Mail*: 'The biggest clubs in Scotland have come to regard the Fir Park club as one of the League assets. Motherwell's visits to their grounds are now established attractions.' The club's profit of £4,681 from the previous season was largely due to improved away gates, as their home drawings continued to fall. (The home club still had to guarantee the visiting side £100 in the First Division.) Opposition supporters were not only eager to see the high-flying Steelmen but also keen to see their own side bring them down to earth.

The well-turned-out player of the time sported a kit that would be generally familiar to the modern eye, but differences in material and technology would be apparent on closer inspection. The Motherwell shirt of the 1930s had a claret band around the chest on an amber background, with claret bands around the elbows; sometimes the cuffs and neck were claret too. There was also a later version with the colour combination reversed. The shirt was of the rugby type with a button neck, none too comfortable when wet, and was without badge or emblems – or even a number on its back – not to mention any form of logo or advertising. The white heavy cotton Motherwell shorts were long and baggy.

It was a disappointing 10,000 crowd which turned out at Hampden Park for the opening League fixture against Queen's Park on the second Saturday in August. A Tottenham representative sat in the stand and Motherwell were prompted to issue a 'nothing doing' statement, adding that it was a happy family at Fir Park and they resented distracting influences which could disturb the equanimity of the team. Naturally, this did not put a stop to transfer talk. Despite a typically swirling wind blowing around Hampden's sunken bowl, Well eventually took control and Willie McFadyen must have impressed the man from Spurs when he scored four in his side's opening 5-1 win.

The second League Saturday brought champions Rangers to Fir Park, looking for this season to yield their sixth title in a row to equal that record set by Celtic. The game was obviously an early test, too early some thought, between the two teams most likely to succeed in the long chase for the League. The Ibrox side had easily disposed of Dundee by 4-1 on the first Saturday, but Gers manager Bill Struth had complained in the *Daily Record*: 'Already we have a few men in the stocks,' and he kept his line-up quiet as long as he could. Motherwell would have to do without Bobby Ferrier who had picked up a tendon injury in his heel at Hampden. Handyman Willie Dowall was brought in and, although a big and sturdy player and a willing worker, he could appear awkward at times and certainly lacked the finesse that Ferrier brought to the left wing.

At this time the press thought rather optimistically that Fir Park could accommodate 40,000 spectators, about the population of the town of Motherwell. Thankfully, only 25,000 turned up for the Rangers game. In what was a hectic and no-holds-barred first half, George Stevenson had to withstand some rough treatment, particularly from Rangers' right-half McDonald. James Fleming, out on what was for him the less familiar right wing, opened the scoring for Rangers. It was the versatile Willie Dowall who set up the equaliser for Well: tearing in from the touchline, he raced past two defenders and laid the ball off for Murdoch to drive in with his left foot. Well took control in the second half and the unmarked Dowall shot home to take the lead as Rangers claimed offside. From the restart, Stevie gathered the ball and taking it past 'several' opponents blasted into the net from twenty yards out. Rangers refused to collapse despite this double blow in the space of two minutes. As play see-sawed, Ben Ellis, Well's Welsh full-back, put the shackles on Fleming, and Rangers' keeper Dawson had to make some fine stops at the other end. Although Rangers managed to pull one back through centre Smith, Motherwell's 'left triangle' of Telfer, Stevenson and Dowall worked the ball in for Murdoch to nonchalantly nod in his second to give Well a 4-2 victory.

Having defeated their main rivals, Well became early table-toppers. Somewhat bizarrely, Chairman Tom Ormiston invited the pressmen back to his home — The Moorings in the town's Hamilton Road. There to welcome them were Mrs Ormiston and the family, who gave their guests a tour of the garden before wining and dining them in sumptuous fashion. Ormiston made a speech of appreciation for the way the press covered his team, reminding the assembled reporters that he was 'in the pictures and [knew] the value of publicity' – and of the 'feel-good factor' we might add today.

At Ayr on the Wednesday following, Well were made to fight all the way for the points in a bad tempered scrap. After Ayr's half-back McCall was sent off for rough play, stones were thrown onto the field from the crowd, prompting Ayr chairman AC Moffat to appeal for calm. The following month the Scottish League, a trifle optimistically, ordered the club to secure convictions if possible. The League Management Committee had earlier discussed the question of whether to allow clubs to admit the unemployed at reduced prices. Those who had already been doing so were instructed to stop forthwith and charge all adults, including servicemen, the standard one shilling (5p) ground admission. While they were at it, the League proceeded to reprimand clubs for encouraging the current craze of autograph hunting. As soon as the players appeared on the field, crowds of young boys, autograph books clutched in their hands, would jump the perimeter walls and rush on from all over the terracing to obtain their heroes' signatures.

A tactical worry for Hunter at this period was his right-back position. There, John Johnman was known as a 'do or die' defender – not showy, but one of the most wholehearted players who ever donned a Motherwell jersey. He had been at the club since 1923 and turned out in most defensive positions in that time before settling at right-back. He had picked up an injury, but perhaps the verdict on him was 'good, but not now good enough'. Motherwell, and also Newcastle, made enquiries about Dundee United's right-back, Bill Taylor, but eventually, in September, versatile Willie Dowall would move into the right-back position and James Mackrell, ex-Falkirk, was signed as his cover in October.

The side that now faced Kilmarnock at Rugby Park in August was considered full strength, with the return of Ferrier. Bob's presence wasn't enough to prevent Well losing 0-1 to a Killie side who seemed to emulate the tactics of their county neighbours and rivals Ayr from a few days before. They 'mixed it' to the extent that a rattled Well found their polished play was to no avail. A midweek draw over at Lanarkshire rivals Airdrie saw the debut of young John Blair, signed from junior side Yoker Athletic. Blair was tried out in the right-back berth as Well slipped to sixth place.

Willie Dowall again had to demonstrate his adaptability when asked to stand in for the injured Murdoch on the right wing against Aberdeen. Young Blair replaced Alan Craig (suffering from a sore throat) at centre-half, while Johnman returned at full-back. The Dons had held Celtic 1-1 the week before, but were easily overcome by a McFadyen hat-trick at Fir Park in weather that now was oppressively hot. John McMenemy ran the show for Well, demonstrating in his swerving runs and the pinpoint accuracy of his passes that he was a worthy heir to the skills of his father, Celtic legend James McMenemy. John's ability to keep a cool head was severely tested on the following Tuesday evening at St Mirren's Paisley ground. Young Tom McKenzie debuted for Well at left-half, not his natural side, and Dowall switched positions again, this time to centre-forward. The *Glasgow Herald* thought it the finest contest seen at Paisley for some time and general opinion held that the Steelmen had ridden their luck in securing their 1-0 victory, Dowall having connected first time with a cross from Ferrier.

The footballs used at the period were of a type still recognisable, with groups of panels at right angles to each other or with interlocking T's and with a laced-up slit giving access to the internal bladder. Its leather was without plastic coating, of course, and although manufacturers had been advertising 'waterproof' balls even back in the 1880s, the reality was that when wet and muddy they became heavier as the game went on. Heading a heavy, wet ball full on the forehead would not have been a pleasant experience, particularly if the lacing was the point of contact.

By the 1930s, football boots had developed only slightly from the previous decade, when 80 per cent of British teams wore the 'Hotspur', made by Manfield of Bournemouth. 1930s' boots were not as high as the earlier type but still high enough to afford some ankle protection. There were now six or seven rows of eyelets instead of the previous eight or twelve; the top eyelets were often left unlaced to prevent them being too tight and to allow the boot's tongue to drop forward, giving more room for flexibility. They were still heavy and practically doubled their weight when wet; the dubbin that was lovingly rubbed on to protect them did not allow the leather to 'breathe'. The general practice of wearing shin-guards underneath the woollen socks would seem to have been a wise precaution. New boots were notoriously hard to 'break in' and some players apparently resorted to wearing them in the bath to soften them, then allowing them to dry on the feet to help mould them to fit.

Teamwise, something of a right-wing crisis now materialised, as Murdoch and his obvious replacements, Dowall and Tom Douglas, all had taken knocks. It was Douglas, though, who would replace Murdoch for several forthcoming games, the first being yet another local derby, this time across the Clyde at Hamilton's Douglas Park. The Acas' half-backs successfully marked Stevie and Ferrier, and it wasn't until late in the game that McFadyen managed to elude Hill, his shadow, and open the scoring. However, another derby brought only another draw, as well as another knock for Douglas when Acas' Watson accidentally headed him full in the face.

Fifteen miles away, at Ibrox, the injury sustained by Celtic's young goalkeeper, John Thomson, as he dived full length in front of Rangers' centre Sam English, was to prove tragic. Thomson died later that day in the city's Victoria Infirmary. At the next fixture at Fir Park, a Lanarkshire Cup semi-final against Armadale, the flag flew at half-mast, the players wore black armbands, and a two-minute silence was observed by spectators, who stood with heads uncovered (the cloth cap, or 'bunnet' being almost universal on the terraces at this time).

Clark of Brechin was given a trial at right-back but he proved to be no better than reserve Sandy Hunter, and although Well made a bid for Clark it did not come up to Brechin's expectations and the deal died. In what would be his only first-team appearance of the season, Sandy filled the problem position against Falkirk at Fir Park but found that he had little to do as Well's outstanding trio of McMenemy, Stevenson and Ferrier dictated the game. Two minutes silence had again preceded kick-off and it seemed to dampen the whole tenor of the afternoon with the 8,000 crowd understandably subdued. Even when a foul by Sandy a full yard outside the box saw the Bairns awarded a penalty, Motherwell, led by captain Ferrier, only 'protested quietly'. When referee Watson changed his mind after consulting his linesman, Falkirk in their turn 'refrained from making a fuss when the spot kick was cancelled', reported the *Evening Times.* Although praising how 'Ferrier used his Cinquevalli-like left foot to good effect', the *Sunday Mail* wondered: 'How McFadyen missed scoring with some of the chances presented is very difficult to explain.' At least Willie managed one in the 4-1 canter. The 'Cinquevalli' tag had apparently first been given to Ferrier by 'Waverley' (originally John Dunlop) of the *Daily Record.* It was the stage name of a renowned juggler from the late Victorian and Edwardian eras who had performed for royalty in London. He juggled not only billiard balls but also cues, hats, umbrellas, steel balls, suitcases, chairs, just about anything that wasn't fixed down. He died in 1918, the year Ferrier signed for Well.

Rangers, meanwhile, were keeping their noses in front, having dropped points only to Motherwell (2-4) on that second day of the season and to Celtic (0-0) in the tragic derby game. Three points behind them, with a game in hand, sat Motherwell and Kilmarnock.

Having enjoyed a successful try-out at right-back in the reserves (who played in the Scottish Alliance League), Dowall was given the shirt against Third Lanark on 16 September and would go on to miss just one game in that position over the rest of the season. On that occasion, Dowall had to forsake his new berth and move up to lead the line when Well had two men away with the Scotland squad. Thirds would sadly go out of business in 1967 but they had been a strong force in Scottish football, twice winning the Scottish Cup as well as that last League title before the Old Firm run began. In 1931 they had regained their First Division status and had performed well, standing fifth as the game started at 6.05pm, ten minutes early on a wet and miserable Wednesday evening. In an exhibition of powerful yet delicate football, Motherwell put them to the sword. Inside half an hour McFadyen had his hat-trick and Ferrier drove in a rocket shot before the break. McFadyen's positioning and Ferrier's crosses and corner-kicks were so finely judged that four of Willie's eventual five goals were from headers. Despite the 6-0 scoreline, Dowall and Ellis had been busy at times with the latter clearing one off the line.

That easy home win had been witnessed by yet another poor crowd at Fir Park. A year before, with Well's home crowds seeming to decrease in inverse proportion to the team's success on the field, the *Motherwell Times* surmised that 'the public have no time even for a winning team unless engaged in a game of vital importance'. The correspondent blamed a League that wasn't competitive enough, as the public wanted to see 'a full-blooded match with something at stake', and there were too few of these. In the opinion of the *Daily Record*, these were days of negative football with an attitude of 'hold what you have'. Motherwell couldn't win – if they played to their 'well-oiled machine' form, the very antithesis of negative football, then it wasn't enough of a contest. The Lanarkshire football public had precious little spare cash and were not prepared to spend it on foregone conclusions, but they would rather wait for the juicier games and the glamour of the Scottish Cup.

When Well travelled to Shawfield to meet Clyde, Douglas came in again for the injured Murdoch, while young Tom Wyllie led the line and McFadyen went to outside-left, as Stevie was with Scotland for the international against Ireland at Ibrox. Clyde made a decent game of it, even though they were 0-3 down with only a quarter of an hour left. Set to lose their unbeaten home record, they rallied with two late goals, the last in the final seconds, to put a better gloss on the final score. Clyde full-back Danny Blair was also at Ibrox with Scotland. To the disappointment of travelling Well supporters, old favourite Willie Rankin, now at Shawfield, hadn't been included in the Clyde eleven.

George Stevenson's appearance in a Scotland shirt was his eighth so far, not to mention seven outings when representing the Scottish League. Now, against Ireland, he put up a fine display and scored what was described as a 'brilliant' goal. Well's other Scottish internationalists at this point were goalkeeper Allan McClory, centre-half Alan Craig, Johnny Murdoch and, for Wales, Ben Ellis. Bobby Ferrier and Alan Craig had also been capped for the Scottish League and, during this season and beyond, further honours would come to Well's star men.

'Stevie', as Stevenson was affectionately known, had now been almost eight years at Fir Park. Signed as an 18-year-old from Ayrshire junior side Kilbirnie Ladeside, he had actually begun his football with juveniles Lochwinnoch Viewfield. The year before, Stevie had had a trial with Bury and he had also interested Liverpool, but right-half Hugh Wales's father was then a scout for Motherwell and he recommended the lad. Trainer Andy Donaldson then spoke to George's father after a junior game at Kilbirnie, and manager Hunter took up the pursuit as testified by the board minutes for May 1923: 'Permission was granted to the Secretary to approach and fix up Stevenson of Kilbirnie Ladeside and Johnman of Carluke if at all possible at a reasonable wage.' The signing itself apparently took place in a pub run by George's pal's father! Just before his arrival at Fir Park, young George was first seen locally when Kilbirnie, in their amber and black strip, played a Scottish Junior Cup-tie at nearby Newarthill. As we've already seen, the raw youth made his inauspicious debut for Well in December that year and played in the side that narrowly escaped relegation the following season.

At 5ft 9in and weighing 11st 7lbs, Stevie was of ideal build for the feints and swerves that made up much of his play. Where 'Waverley' had compared Ferrier to a juggler, Stevenson was likened by that correspondent to ballet dancer Anna Pavlova! Stevie's father had also played for the hometown juniors of Kilbirnie and had gone on to join Sunderland in the early 1890s. George's brother John served several clubs, including Ayr, Aberdeen, Nelson, St Johnstone and Bury, and the brothers opposed each other on occasion. Another younger brother, Willie, was a promising outside-right who also played for Kilbirnie.

International honours first came Stevenson's way when he was picked for the Scottish League in 1927 against the Football League. As there was no shortage of fine inside men at this time in the Scottish League, George was only third choice for the inside-right berth and was only informed that he would be turning out in the game, at Leicester, as the train carrying the squad was pulling out of Glasgow Central. Although often played at inside-right in the full Scotland side, to partner Rangers' Archibald, he was felt to be a 'natural' and so able to adapt well in this unaccustomed position. Against England at Hampden in March 1931, the forward line had read: Archibald (Rangers), Stevenson (Motherwell), McGrory (Celtic), McPhail (Rangers), Morton (Rangers). George eluded his marker, Huddersfield's Campbell, to open the scoring for Scotland against the Auld Enemy in their 2-0 victory.

Stevenson's skill on the ball, his positional sense, coupled with a strong shot from either foot made him a perfect partner for Bobby Ferrier in Motherwell's attack. Unfortunately, due to Ferrier's birth in England, their partnership – renowned throughout British soccer – would be seen in Scotland's blue only in their four Scottish League appearances together. And yet, even great players have their critics and some thought that Stevie dwelled too long on the ball at times. In addition to his footballing poise and skills, he was also dapper in appearance – his neat dark hair combed back in the typical 'short back and sides' style of the day – and became known as 'Gentleman George'.

The *Sunday Mail* featured a weekly article on various topics for 'Young Folks' and in late September 1931 ran a novel one under the banner: 'George Stevenson's New Game … For Perfecting Forward Play'. In that article, in simple terms, was George's (or his ghost writer's) cultured but straightforward footballing philosophy:

'"It is essential that an inside forward should have a perfect understanding with his half-backs as well as his colleagues in the forward line," began George Stevenson, Motherwell's clever inside left who put up such a brilliant display against Ireland last Saturday … "When you give your outside man a pass you should always be up to get it back again, and it is often a good idea to open up the game by sending across a long, swinging pass to the opposite wing.

"Always keep cool and collected, because a lot depends on the method of an inside man. Cultivate slipping the ball to your other inside man; it is a playing game. There is a great deal in the art of passing, and a common defect of today is the retiral of the player after he has passed the ball. Follow up the play, and by keeping your position your location is known to your colleagues.

"It is no use giving a man the ball if he is not in a proper position to receive it. … When your side is in possession get away from your opponents, and when the enemy are in possession stick to them like leeches."

'[Stevenson] added that small-sided practice games, 3v2 or 5v4 would improve passing skills, the extra man side having the ball and seeing how long they could retain possession. "Be methodical in your play, … If a player uses the correct part of his foot in shooting, he ought to be able to tell within a few inches where he is going to put the ball. To achieve this, however, one must learn to keep both eyes on the ball. A momentary glance should leave a photograph on the mind of the position of the defender and the goal, then keep both eyes on the ball in kicking it. … As a parting hint, I would like to advise young footballers to practise anything with a ball, as there is always something being learned".'

George's ideas about training sound rather more modern in tone than the daily regime, typical for its day, under trainers Donaldson and Walker at Fir Park: sprinting, then long distance running and some ball practice to finish.

Leith Athletic no longer feature in the Scottish League but on 26 September 1931 they provided Motherwell's next opposition. Nicknamed the Zebras from their black and white striped shirts, they had gained promotion to the top division just the season before but had struggled and finished seventeenth from twenty. So far this term they had still to find any consistency and although both Hearts and Dundee had fallen recently at their Marine Gardens park, the Edinburgh side were hovering in the bottom quarter of the table. Only later in the season would they become the First Division's whipping boys, an opportunity for the opposition to improve their goal average. Their major failing when they met Well at this time was said to be their lack of finishing power. Motherwell, meanwhile, started the match in joint second place with Kilmarnock, a single point behind Rangers.

The game got off to a quiet start, enlivened in the seventh minute when Willie McFadyen headed in Douglas's cross, followed by another from the centre-forward when he nipped in to score after a Leith defender miskicked in front of goal. A surprise counter by Athletic's Nicol stemmed from some uncharacteristic hesitation between Dowall and Ellis at the back. Leith goalkeeper Bryce, however, remained the busiest man afield, bringing off two superb saves from McMenemy but having to admit defeat when Douglas put Well 3-1 ahead before half-time. A miskick by McMenemy in front of an open goal broke kindly for McFadyen to grab his hat-trick and he went on to send home a pinpoint Ferrier cross for his fourth. Bob Ferrier, who had seen a lot of the ball, wound his way past two defenders and crossed for Douglas to score another before Stevenson got his name on the scoresheet, netting from close range. Stevie and McMenemy were now in exhibition mode but Ferrier was becoming over-anxious in his desperation to score one himself, twice hitting the side-netting before the final whistle. Despite losing seven, the Leith goalkeeper had performed heroics: 'Had it not been for the first half brilliance of Bryce in the Athletic goal, the Well would have swamped the Port team,' claimed the *Sunday Mail.*

Willie McFadyen's four had put him further out in front as the leading scorer in Scotland with twenty goals now, six in front of Celtic's McGrory. McFadyen's haul had also served to take his side to the top of the League, with Well now equal on points with Rangers, who had dropped a precious point to Hearts, while Killie were losing at Partick.

Motherwell's superior goal average (both had lost thirteen goals so far, but Well had scored 40 to Rangers' 35, the goal averages being 3.077 compared to 2.692) now put them in pole position and all seemed set fair for their best tilt at the championship yet. Manager John Hunter's patient acquisition of 'promising juniors', leavened with a sprinkling of experienced seniors, had gelled into a formidable side now reaching the peak of its power. Phrases used by various reporters of the time to describe the side at its best in action – 'well-oiled machine', 'clockwork precision', 'machine-like precision' – serve to affirm that it had been team-work that had sent Motherwell to the top of the Scottish League.

Chapter 3

~ Out in Front ~

(October–December 1931)

Most of the headlines being generated by Motherwell, the new League leaders, concerned their goalscoring achievements, led of course by scorer-in-chief Willie McFadyen. More unobtrusively, heartening progress was being made back in defence where 'play-anywhere' Willie Dowall had made three outings at right-back, looking more and more the part with each game he acquired under his belt. The *Motherwell Times* had hopes that 'there is just a possibility he will supply the missing link that Motherwell have been hunting for in the past'.

While Well travelled to Greenock to meet Morton in the League, Windsor Park in Belfast saw the Irish League beat their Scottish counterparts 3-2, the first Irish win in 28 years. Nevertheless, there had been a period in the first half when, according to the *Sunday Mail*, George Stevenson had 'delighted', playing as he was in his familiar inside-left position. Despite the defeat, it was more than likely that the Scottish selectors had been impressed sufficiently to accord Stevie further honours in the full Scotland side. His club faced a Morton side which had been poor away from home but were proving much more formidable on their own Cappielow ground, losing only to Hearts and narrowly at that, so far this season. The League leaders though, appeared to be on top form, losing only to Kilmarnock in their seven away matches from the opening twelve. That had also been the only time they had failed to register a goal. The visit of Motherwell was the occasion of the opening of Morton's new stand, several Town Provosts and football officials having been specially invited to attend.

The ceremonials completed, Motherwell began the game with Tom Wyllie standing in for the absent Stevenson. Well struggled and a mistake by Ben Ellis allowed Morton to open the scoring. Although McFadyen brought matters level five minutes later, Black put Morton back in front at that psychologically important point just before the break. When Well reappeared, their forward line had been rejigged by Hunter, right-winger Douglas swapping positions with Wyllie, who hadn't really been gelling with Bob Ferrier on the left. Ellis was obviously trying to atone for the error that had led to the opening goal; as Ben was clearing balls to safety with more than his usual venom, some Morton wags shouted at the eager Welshman please not to hurt their new stand!

Only eight minutes remained when Alan Craig went in to tackle Johnny Shankley (brother of Bill, or Willie as he was then known. The 'e' from Shankley was dropped after the Second World War). With Craig's arms swinging wildly he handled the ball in the box. Despite his protestations, which earned him a lecture from the referee, a penalty was awarded and Morton outside-left Graham whacked the ball high and seemingly net-bound. Allan McClory's long arms, however, allowed him to stretch and palm it away and clear. The omens had been favourable: this was in fact the third successive Saturday that Morton had missed a penalty. Just three minutes later Douglas crossed from his new position for McFadyen to equalise a second time and so rescue a precious point from what had seemed only recently to be a certain defeat. Well, nevertheless, dropped a place as well as a point, Rangers having trounced Cowdenbeath at Ibrox to go back to the top. Celtic were now only two points behind in third, following a 3-2 win at Kilmarnock, and they also had a game in hand. Motherwell had notched up 42 goals so far, and with McFadyen scoring 22 of them, the Scottish individual scoring record looked increasingly possible. The record holder, Jimmy McGrory, had also scored a double and so remained six behind McFadyen.

Only 4,000 showed up for promoted Dundee United's visit to Fir Park, an expected easy victory for Well materialising in their 5-0 win. George Stevenson made a welcome return after being sorely missed against Morton, appearing to be in 'merry mood' as he waltzed past opponents at will. Wriggling through into the box, George was brought down and McFadyen scored with the resultant penalty to complete another hat-trick. Although Douglas also scored twice, he wasn't finding it particularly easy to match the missing Murdoch's positional awareness, his inside partner McMenemy being unaware of exactly where Tom was at times. Celtic had unexpectedly dropped a point at home to Clyde and Rangers had been playing Queen's Park in the final of the Glasgow Cup, with the result that Well's two points enabled them to resume top spot in the table.

Heart of Midlothian had built up a reputation as a 'popular' side among Scots football fans and their meetings with the equally popular Motherwell were nurturing a reputation for competitive and attractive football. Hearts were indeed the last side to have come to Fir Park on League business and actually have won, but that was away back over two years before. Again Well were to display superb teamwork with an understanding shown not only between the forwards, but also between them and their half-backs pushing up behind, being a joy to behold. Watching closely in the stand was Arsenal's renowned manager Herbert Chapman, rumoured this time to be taking another look at McFadyen. Willie scored only once and that was from the penalty spot after Herd of Hearts had palmed away a Ferrier shot with goalkeeper Harkness stranded. Ferrier wasn't to be denied, however, and from a typically tight angle he squeezed the ball home for Well's second. Well had survived a sticky spell of early Hearts' pressure with the two 'Alans', McClory in goal and the rock-like Craig in the middle of the defence, standing firm. Tom Douglas, though, had again looked uncomfortable out on the right wing and good lead-up work by his colleagues had come to nothing.

The talk of the day was focused elsewhere, as news filtered through of a sensation at Ibrox. Well supporters were gladdened to hear that Queen's Park, beaten 0-3 last week in the Glasgow Cup by Rangers, had gained their revenge with a 1-0 win during which the Ibrox men had squandered two penalties. With Celts going down at Dundee in their first defeat of the season, Motherwell supporters might have felt a little cement was spread around their side's top placing, for they were now three points ahead of Rangers, who still had that game in hand.

The Steelmen now travelled east, out to Fife to face Cowdenbeath, undoubtedly full of confidence but perhaps with a slight niggle that this had been the side whose win last season had finally put paid to their title challenge. The Fifers, for their part, had cause to remember their 0-1 defeat at the quarter-final stage of the Scottish Cup, when Motherwell had scraped through at Central Park. Johnny Murdoch was now back on the right wing but Well were put to the test in the first 30 minutes and at half-time 1-1 was a fair reflection on play. Well quickly gained control after the restart and two McFadyen goals preceded a spectacular effort from Stevie before Willie completed yet another hat-trick. Portsmouth were the latest club to watch McFadyen and their representative had been looking on keenly at Central Park.

Perhaps as a consequence of their South African tour, some Well men, as well as Celtic's, went to Glasgow's west end on the Wednesday to see the Springboks rugby team at Anniesland. It was a pity that another major sporting event – the Wales and Scotland soccer international – coincided the following Saturday with Motherwell's fixture against Celtic. It meant that four of the best players from these two clubs would be missing, on duty for their country at Wrexham. Wales would in fact have taken Ben Ellis, too, if Motherwell had been able to spare him. As it was, Well would have to go into this crucial game without two of their most influential play-makers, George Stevenson and John McMenemy. Stevie turned out at inside-right for Scotland and, first-timing a volley, notched up a fine goal in the Scots' 3-2 victory. Celts' Bert Thomson and Jimmy McGrory also played, while Well's McMenemy travelled as a reserve.

The Motherwell directors met on the evening of Tuesday, 27 October at Fir Park to choose the side for the visit of Celtic. Ex-Falkirk James Mackrell was brought in at right-back to allow Dowall to play at centre-forward, while McFadyen was shifted to inside-right and Douglas replaced Stevenson on the other side. With autumn now fading steadily into winter, kick-off was advanced to 2.45pm, the gates opening an hour beforehand. With Well's new full-backs facing Celtic for the first time, the visitors' pressure told and Charlie Napier grabbed the first two goals of the game. The enthusiastic Dowall claimed a 'goal' when his 12½ stone frame barged the ball, as well as Joe Kennaway, Celtic's debutant goal-keeper, on the goal-line, but referee Leishman waved it away.

Kennaway, born of Scots parents in Montreal, had only arrived in the country by ship the day before. He conceded his first goal in Scotland when Ferrier and McFadyen did the hard work, letting Douglas in to blast high into the roof of the net. In the second half Motherwell reshuffled their front rank: Dowall moved out to the right wing, Murdoch came inside and McFadyen resumed his centre-forward berth. Again it was Ferrier and McFadyen's teamwork that allowed Dowall to flash past the defence for the equaliser – 2-2. Without the cultured play-makers, the outcome had been a pulsating match full of thrills, contested at a rousing pace that kept the packed terraces enthralled for all of the 90 minutes. But Well's lead over Rangers was back to only two points.

In the event, Tom Douglas had played his last game for the Steelmen and went south to the English top division, but his new club, Blackpool, were struggling. In Motherwell, club chairman Tom Ormiston had stood for the local parliamentary constituency at short notice and been elected as the Unionist member for Motherwell and Wishaw. The club received further honour when John McMenemy was selected for the Scottish League against the Football League at Celtic Park, but there was surprise at the omission of George Stevenson. He was named as one of the reserves along with teammates McClory, Telfer and McFadyen. Because Partick Thistle also had goalkeeper Jackson in the Scottish side, not to mention a travelling reserve, the League postponed their fixture with Motherwell. Celtic and Rangers, with several men involved, also had their matches postponed. (By contrast, when the full Scotland international team was in action, under the auspices of the SFA, the normal League programme generally went ahead.) Although he was criticised as 'more than a trifle too deliberate', McMenemy improved during the course of the League international, the Scots winning 4-3 before the 51,000 crowd at Parkhead.

John McMenemy had plenty of footballing pedigree to live up to. His father James was the Celtic legend christened by the Parkhead supporters as 'Napoleon'. James, too, had been an inside-right and had made 456 League appearances for his club and been capped twelve times for Scotland, as well as appearing in two Victory Internationals at the end of the Great War. James had been the brains of the Celtic forward line that had helped achieve the record six League titles in a row at the start of the new century; he also boasted seven Scottish Cup medals in his collection.

His sons obviously had football in their blood. Young John began his career with Glasgow junior sides St Anthony's and St Roch's before Celtic manager Willie Maley signed him for his father's old side. While mostly in the reserves, John made an appearance at inside-left in Celtic's Scottish Cup final team of 1927 and gained a winner's medal as they easily overcame East Fife 3-1. A season afterwards John approached Mr Maley to ask for improved terms but received short shrift and was informed: 'Your father Jimmy never asked that.' John apparently replied, 'I am a professional footballer and I must do the best for myself.' However, Maley had the last word: 'All right, you can do that with someone else.' With £3,500 received from Portsmouth for Davie Thackeray, the Motherwell directors were looking to spend some of it to strengthen the side and Hunter was instructed to negotiate with Celtic for John McMenemy and right-winger Paddy Connolly, who had scored in the 1927 final.

As it transpired, Motherwell obtained Johnny Murdoch for the right wing but still pursued McMenemy, Hunter being allowed all of £750 to clinch a deal. Celtic demanded £1,100 and this was finally agreed to by the Fir Park board. Celtic received £950 while John got £150 for himself. John made a happy debut for Well aged just twenty at Falkirk in October 1928 as his new side trounced the Bairns 7-0. He played at inside-left in this and his next game, standing in for Stevenson, but then moved to the inside-right position, where he would provide such subtlety and craft that many would do him the ultimate honour of saying he had inherited the mantle of his father, Celtic's Napoleon. At 5ft 9in tall and weighing 11st 7lbs, McMenemy was a compact figure who could thread through inch-perfect passes for his fellow forwards. The *Daily Record* sketched him: 'Clever footworker, fine sense of position and direction, has helped much [sic] Willie McFadyen to reap his big crop of goals.'

Known as an extrovert type off the field – his gap-toothed smile and slicked-back hair with centre parting hinting at a lively personality – McMenemy was also a 'natty dresser', wearing the fashionable clothes of the day, including wide trousers with razor-sharp creases. John took care of his appearance and tried to maintain the 'immaculate' look to the extent that some supporters claimed his strip didn't need laundering, even on the muddiest pitch. McMenemy's selection for the League international was a partial success, his instructions appearing to limit his play to supporting deep alongside the half-backs. Still, it was felt that he could win further Scotland honours, and, in common with so many other of his colleagues, he was attracting interest from south of the border.

Transfer talk flew thick and fast at this time, Well's stars being linked with a host of English top division sides. Motherwell themselves were at one point thought to be interested in the legendary but unsettled Scottish internationalist Hughie Gallacher of Chelsea. Hughie had only recently and reluctantly felt that he had to leave Newcastle, where he had been something of a hero, scoring a record 143 goals for the Magpies. Chelsea wanted an exchange or cash for their mercurial Bellshill-born goalscorer, who would stay at Stamford Bridge before eventually moving on to Derby. Other Well targets were closer to hand in the shape of defender 'Puggy' Allan and forward Willie Moffat of near neighbours Hamilton. The Acas were in financial trouble and would perhaps be willing to sell; their recent game against Dundee United had only attracted 1,000 to Douglas Park.

The rain fell in torrents before the Steelmen met Dundee at Dens Park on 14 November, with the result that the ground was heavy and unsuited to the cultured type of play the Well had been perfecting. Where a 20,000 crowd had been expected, only 5,000 hardy souls turned out in the wet. After a hectic opening half, Dundee went in at half-time leading 2-0 and it would take a combination of physical play (Alan Craig was said to be 'paying back in instalments' for fouls he had earlier sustained) and, at times, a seven-man attack to bring Well back into the reckoning with an eventual McFadyen double. Apart from his goals, Willie had been out of touch and it was left to McMenemy to run the show up front. Most fortunately for the Lanarkshire men, Rangers had slipped up in their home game against Old Firm spoilers Clyde, who had taken a point. Celtic meanwhile had fallen at Partick and so dropped down to fourth place, leaving what appeared to be a two-horse race. The reduced attendance at Dens had been bad news for Motherwell from a financial standpoint as it was followed by three home games, and that was not where the club made its money.

Since their tousy and bad-tempered meeting at Ayr back in August, the 'Honest Men' (Ayr's lovely nickname) had tumbled to the bottom of the League. Although it took 35 minutes for Well to break down their defence, it was one-way traffic afterwards and goalkeeper Hepburn put up a customary stout display to help keep the score down to an eventual six. John McMenemy's fine goal as he dribbled through the Ayr defence did not earn as big a cheer as the low pile-driver by Alan Craig from just outside the area. Goals by defenders or even wing half-backs were unusual enough at this time to warrant comment and special acclaim. Willie McFadyen's four meant that he was on course at least to equal the scoring record and the *Daily Record* pointed to the source of his rising total: 'He is getting every encouragement from his colleagues, for they are, without being slavish, liberal in their ministrations to him. As aiders and abettors, no centre-forward could hope for greater than McMenemy and Stevenson, while the extreme men [wingers] are also responsive.' The Well supporters had cheered the news at half-time that Rangers were a goal down at Greenock, but the Ibrox side came back to scrape a 2-1 win and so keep breathing down Motherwell's necks. Third Lanark crept up to third place as Celtic seemed to wave goodbye to their title hopes, going down to Hearts in Edinburgh.

A 2.20pm start for the local derby against Airdrie saw only around 6,000 inside Fir Park. Other clubs were also finding it hard going. Airdrie themselves and Hamilton were struggling; Clyde had only 3,000 at Shawfield for Aberdeen's visit, while even Celtic were affected, their vast Celtic Park hosting just over 7,000 for the visit of Leith. A benefit match at Tynecastle for Hearts' left-back Robert King had the attraction of Newcastle as opponents, but drew a mere 2,000. As Airdrie and Well mixed it in best derby tradition, referee Dougray let too much pass without taking firm action. Allan McClory put in a tremendous effort to prevent Airdrie from scoring.

Bobby Ferrier's two goals, thought the *Glasgow Herald*, came from shots that few other forwards would have attempted, never mind scored with. His first was a full-blooded volley hit low and hard on the drop that flashed past the goalkeeper into the far side of the net, despite the close attentions of the Airdrie defenders. Nine minutes later, Ferrier sent in a swerving 'special' that corkscrewed and curled away from the goalkeeper's despairing dive for his second. Although up against the best Airdrie defender – Scotland star Jimmy Crapnell – Ferrier's famous 'Cinquevalli' left foot had struck again. It had been Willie McFadyen who had opened for Well and the *Glasgow Herald* felt that his inside men were so intent on laying balls on for him to add to his vast tally that the Airdrie defenders knew only too well what to expect and so had him well policed. By the time Airdrie's McDonald had been sent off in the 65th minute, following a bad tackle on Ben Ellis, the game had been well won. Incidentally, sendings off were comparatively few at that time, as seen in the figures for the first five months of the following, 1932-33, season by which time there had been only five dismissals in the Scottish First Division and seven in the Second.

At least one transfer rumour proved to be more than paper-talk, as Willie Moffat made the short journey from Hamilton to Motherwell, spectating from the stand at the Airdrie game. By coincidence, Acas then signed John McMenemy's younger brother, Frank, to replace him. Moffat appeared at outside-right in Well's third successive home game, this time against St Mirren, a side that had made sufficient progress to sit now in fourth place in the First Division. Morning rain had left the Fir Park pitch sodden, while over at Douglas Park several hundred supporters had to be turned out and given their money back as Acas' match against Queen's Park suffered a late call-off. The result was that as the game at Fir Park progressed the crowd built up to over 9,000 – slowly augmented by football refugees from Hamilton. There was some controversy over the scorer of Well's opener, when Ferrier's shot had gone into a knot of players in front of goal and then found its way into the net. Bobby and his colleagues credited it to McFadyen, while most of the St Mirren players, as well as several newspapers, disagreed and thought it was Ferrier's. (The scorecard for 1931-32 that hung on the wall of the Fir Park office shows the pencilled name 'Ferrier' in the scorers' column has been changed to 'McFadyen'.) By this stage Willie was naturally becoming at least a little anxious regarding the expectations placed on him to break the magical figure of 49. Twice against St Mirren he was upended in the penalty box and twice his team-mates allowed him to take the spot kicks, and twice he missed! The *Sunday Mail* rather overstated matters: 'Indeed, take the driving force of Ferrier out of Motherwell's attack and there is little left.' The 4-1 win over St Mirren had four different forwards scoring. The two precious points lead over Rangers was maintained.

Celtic's proposal to revive the controversial unemployed gate was rejected by the footballing authorities, prompting the Greenock Supporters' Club to plan a demonstration in the local Town Hall. With top division sides such as Clyde and Airdrie suffering financially, it was felt that their only salvation would be to transfer some of their leading players. 'Scottish football is in a bad way generally,' wrote the *Motherwell Times* reporter: 'I can state with authority that Clyde and Airdrie are not the only clubs feeling the pinch. I had a talk with a Lanarkshire club director, and he told me quite frankly that his club were in a desperate position.' The industrial and employment scene continued to look bleak both nationally and even more so locally. Earlier in the year the Motherwell area's unemployed figures had reached 7,280 and then risen to over 10,100 during the summer holiday period.

A football spectator had to pay one shilling (5p) to watch a First Division game; a journey on a football special train to Hampden cost nine pence (about 4p) for a return ticket; a cinema seat could be had for ten pence, while a large commitment such as a house purchase was something from another world for the ordinary working person or family, never mind someone on the 'dole'. A bungalow in a 'good' area of Glasgow would set one back £675. 'Waverley' of the *Daily Record* considered seven pence (3p) a fair charge for an unemployed First Division gate but also recognised the ease with which such schemes could be abused, which was the main reason for the League ruling against it.

The second Saturday in December sent both Motherwell and Rangers away to face strong opposition and possible banana-skins in the race for points. Well were at Cathkin Park against Third Lanark, where only Kilmarnock had so far managed a win, and Rangers faced the long trip north to Aberdeen. Although lying in third place, the Dons were in something of a transition and several regulars had been dropped with the consequent introduction of new faces who were trying to fit in. Meanwhile, Motherwell's opponents from the south side of Glasgow had been going well until suffering a drubbing at the hands of Celtic the week before, when they had gone down 0-5 at Celtic Park. Thirds currently occupied fifth place. This was to be the first of three consecutive tussles with Glasgow clubs for Well, setting up further 'City v Provincial' contests against Queen's Park before the big one that football folk were already impatient for – against Rangers at Ibrox on Boxing Day.

Motherwell supporters packed three special trains and a host of buses to help swell the Cathkin crowd to 25,000. A goalless first half was the result of the contest between Thirds' 'young men in a hurry' and Well's more seasoned and studied side, thought the *Evening Times*. As the home supporters belted out their 'Hi, hi, hi!' chant it was the Steelmen who broke the deadlock when John McMenemy's lofted shot curled its way past defenders and goalkeeper alike. The pace of the game increased as both sides chased a goal, which eventually fell to McFadyen. As the ball squeezed between player-manger Russell Moreland's legs, Willie pounced to wheel around and give the goalie no chance and so seal the points. Well's half-back line had played exceptionally and snuffed out the threat posed by Thirds' centre Neil Dewar, said to be the subject of an £8,000 bid by Arsenal.

It appears that John Hunter was not at Cathkin to see his men pick up the points, but rather he had gone to take in the game between the local

Strathclyde Juniors and Bellshill Athletic, ever on the lookout for 'promising juniors'. Whenever he heard the final scores, the one from Aberdeen would have been as welcome as that from Cathkin: the Dons had held Rangers to a goalless draw.

When the amateurs of the Queen's Park club came calling at Fir Park it was a classic case of the bowler hats versus the 'bunnets', the headgear respectively of the supposedly middle-class Hampden men and the workers, or unemployed workers, who followed the Steelmen. In an all-action first period each of the Well forwards except Ferrier scored, while Queen's replied with a penalty: with no further scoring in the second half the match finished 4-1. The good news from Dens Park told the story that Dundee had gone one better than Aberdeen and had defeated Rangers by 2-1. The Steelmen had opened up a luxurious five-point gap between themselves and their main rivals. The scene was thus set for what many saw as the match of the season. Motherwell might well have been the more confident side: they had lost the fewest games of any senior side in Britain; their sole defeat was the only game in which they had failed to score; they were, in fact, the highest scoring British side, seven ahead of table-topping Everton in the English First Division; they also had the best goal average in all the Leagues.

Five London-Midland-Scottish 'special' trains ran from Motherwell to Ibrox on Boxing Day, the last of which was scheduled to arrive a mere ten bracing minutes prior to kick-off. When a black cat found its way onto one of the specials, which was stopped at Rutherglen station, the Motherwell supporters in the carriage interpreted it as a good omen and tried to grab hold of it, no doubt picturing themselves smuggling it through the Ibrox turnstiles; the poor creature was, however, hauled away by an unimaginative station porter. A stiff breeze and a sticky pitch did not make ideal conditions for exhibition football, but then only the most optimistic would have expected such. Before a 55,000 crowd, Meiklejohn, the Rangers captain, chose to kick with the wind and his side took full advantage of it to press Well. As the Lanarkshire men struggled to get to grips with the wind and to escape the shackles of the determined Ibrox defence, Sam English headed in to open after twenty minutes. Well's cause was not helped by Moffat twice missing glaring chances before the end of the half.

Most onlookers imagined that Motherwell would come out for the second period and take advantage of the wind behind them. The press photographers who had been gathered behind McClory's goal in the first half obviously thought similarly as they stayed where they were for the second. Well resumed disappointingly, still unable to pierce an iron-like

Rangers' defence: Stevie only once escaped Meiklejohn, and McMenemy never really got free from Brown, not helped either by the knock he had taken from an earlier collision with the Rangers' captain. Bobby Ferrier did contrive one piece of artistry. Escaping his markers he raced down the left wing and almost from the corner flag sent in an effort that spun its way into the goalmouth, where the ball deceived keeper Hamilton, only for the onrushing Moffat to slice it past an empty goal. At the close, Motherwell's lead had been reduced to three points, the Ibrox side still having that game in hand. The *Evening Times* wondered whether this might well initiate a period of 'staleness' for the challengers and perhaps hand the psychological advantage to the reigning champions. It wasn't the end of the world for the Well supporters or even of their championship hopes. It did mean, though, that the remaining fourteen games of the League programme would provide a serious test of nerve as well as of skill and stamina for the top two sides in Scotland.

Chapter 4

~ CHAMPIONS ~

(JANUARY–MAY 1932)

Motherwell began 1932 still smarting from what had been only their second defeat to date, at Rangers. Hamilton were to be their 'first foot' at Fir Park in the first of the traditional Ne'erday fixtures on Friday, 1 January. The holiday gave the local shopkeepers and merchants the chance to get along and actually see in the flesh the footballing personalities that they normally only got to read about. A healthy 13,000 crowd gathered despite a day of heavy rain and blustery wind, the heavy ground tending to be a leveller between footballing sides of differing quality, mitigating as it did against the type of 'carpet passes' favoured by many of the Motherwell side. In the end though, Well's 3-1 victory was achieved at a cost, John McMenemy taking some hefty challenges and ending up having to change places with Murdoch; in the days before the general use of substitutes, crocked players normally became 'passengers' out on the wing.

Next day, Scotland's second bout of holiday games took the Well to Falkirk, where the Bairns had claimed several League scalps, in contrast to their poor away form, where their sole victory had been away back last August. Even though both sides had come through tough games the day before – the Bairns had lost 1-2 at Airdrie – they now put up a fine display on a pitch adorned with 'ornamental little lakes'. Moffat stood in for the injured McMenemy and demonstrated that inside-right was more to his liking than being out wide on the wing. Stevie faced his brother John, who was one of Falkirk's better players on the day as Well, though easily the better side, edged through 3-2 with Willie McFadyen notching up his 41st League goal. The Old Firm derby at Celtic Park had been won by Rangers and it seemed to some that they now had an easier programme ahead of them than Well, who had to visit Partick, Aberdeen, Hearts, and Celtic. The Ibrox men's trickiest visits were felt to be those to St Mirren and Kilmarnock.

It was Killie who next visited Fir Park on a field swept by driving wind and rain that cut the crowd to 6,000 enthusiasts. Mastering the conditions better than the Ayrshire side, even with a weakened forward line – McFadyen and McMenemy were injured – Well played controlled football to storm through 4-0. Bob Ferrier's hat-trick included two penalties gained through Johnny Murdoch's strong running. Again Murdoch had been forced to move inside from the wing, this time to allow the limping Moffat to see out the rest of the game wide on the touchline.

League football took a back seat the following week as the Scottish Cup campaign kicked off, many Motherwell memories still raw from that final defeat of last season. Second Division Stenhousemuir were seen as easy meat at Fir Park and so it proved as Well ran up four goals in five minutes during the first period. Conditions were again atrocious, with wind and heavy driving rain and when Allan McClory fisted away a powerful drive from Muir's Sutton the ball, caught by the wind, flew over the bar, over the terracing and out into the street. McClory was renowned for his lengthy goal-kicks and, assisted by the wind, he could kick the whole length of the field. All of the Well forwards ended up scoring in the 7-2 rout that set them up for the visit north to Aberdeen on League duty.

The Dons had been the victims of the Cup's biggest upset when Second Division Arbroath eliminated them 2-1, and Well were prepared to face a side looking to restore its pride. The Aberdeen side ran out on to the field to a stonily quiet reception from the Pittodrie crowd, although it did warm somewhat as the game progressed, manager Pat Travers obviously having his men well motivated. A ding-dong battle ensued but without a goal by half-time. It was midway through the second period when Willie Telfer, having a tremendous game, set off on one of his runs from midfield and released to Murdoch on the right. Johnny's precise cross into the middle was headed in by Willie McFadyen, his 42nd goal equalling the old record of teammate Hugh Ferguson's from the 1920s. There was, however, some contention over the scorer of this, the game's only goal. Two national papers credited it to Telfer, but the *Motherwell Times* agreed with the *Daily Record*: 'Some doubt seemed to exist as to the scorer of the goal, but it is quite definite that it was McFadyen who headed through.'

The plum tie of the Cup's second round was the Steelmen's visit to Queen's Park's Hampden, both the Old Firm having been drawn away from the city. Around 58,000 gathered on the high Hampden slopes and some enthusiastic young supporters broke over the boundary wall to present their Well heroes with mascots before kick-off. Two soft first-half goals were enough to win what proved to be a disappointing match for the large crowd, Motherwell playing with only the odd 'touch of that rhythmic cultured football which has caused them to be respected the world o'er' (*Daily Record*).

With a trip out east to Leith's Marine Gardens in the Portobello district of Edinburgh, it was back to League business. The Motherwell squad had been 'recuperating and resting' out further east at Gullane with its sandy bay. Leith had been ensconced at the foot of the table since mid-December and as their support melted away their financial state became critical. Only the week before, some of their players had consented to a wage cut to help the club survive. Well again had to reshuffle their front rank as McMenemy still had not recovered from knocks he had taken and Stevenson had gone down with flu. Leith had a real go at the League leaders, belying their lowly position and off-field problems, but Well went two up before Leith's Allan fractured his arm in tackling Ferrier. Willie Dowall scored a hat-trick in the 5-0 win. Despite the earlier League view on unemployed gates, the Cup-tie at Shawfield saw more than half of the 10,000 crowd enter at a reduced charge and Partick's 16,000 attendance was around 50 per cent unemployed. The parlous state of one unnamed senior Scottish club was confirmed by the presence of a sheriff's officer during the first week of February at an away fixture. The officer had brought with him a warrant for almost £100 for taxes owing. Fortunately, the large attendance meant that the visiting club's share of the gate would cover the warrant.

Luckily Motherwell had no such concerns; the Queen's Cup gate had earned them around £1,100 and the third round promised further handsome return as Celtic were drawn at Fir Park. To take full advantage of the huge interest engendered by such an appetising contest, the club brought in squads of labourers to build up and terrace the south banking to its top which would 'enable spectators in that area to stand in a compact body, as in other parts of the ground'. The estimate was that the ground could now squeeze in over 40,000.

The gates opened at 1pm with kick-off now back at 3pm and admission ranging from the usual one shilling for the ground to five shillings (25p) for reserved stand seats. As early as 2 o'clock the ground had some areas quite filled but, conspicuously, near the Knowetop goal was an empty space. The reason became clear when rival flags were brandished by young supporters and then stones fired from catapults began to fly. The police escorted women spectators away to safety and young boys were helped over the stone wall that edged three sides of the park and on to the track. As hand-to-hand fighting broke out between rival fans, the Burgh Police, reinforced by Railway Police and Lanarkshire Constabulary, moved in with batons drawn and to general cheering nine youths were led away under arrest. It is unclear which team they supported.

There was some doubt as to whether the game would go ahead, but order had been restored and, as the teams appeared, swarms of young boys promptly ran on to regale their favourites with lucky mascots, Jimmy

McGrory attracting most of the attention. Celts' manager Willie Maley was risking the centre who had been out with a knee injury, while Well had McMenemy back after a fitness test, although George Stevenson had been unable to shake off the flu and sat in the stand, Moffat taking his place. The tie kicked-off before at least 36,000 spectators crammed in to establish a new Fir Park attendance record. Moffat had the ball in the net after fifteen minutes but the 'goal' was adjudged offside. Just five minutes later Johnny Murdoch nipped in to open the scoring.

Celtic's McGrory lasted only half an hour and had to be withdrawn after injuring his knee in a tackle. Down to ten men, Celtic fought back keenly and Napier – known as 'Happy Feet' among the Celtic supporters and now deputising at centre-forward – kept Motherwell's Alan Craig busy in defence. During the game it was sometimes difficult to follow play on the field as the crowd swayed dangerously, with many instances of crushing and fainting that kept the ambulance men on the move. A few crash barriers on the south terracing had given way and many spectators who had gone over the wall stayed on the track to watch the play. On the pitch, Ferrier was patently missing his partner, though he did manage to head in Well's second goal, ensuring a passage into the quarter-finals and salving at least a little those painful Cup memories. The other big tie had seen Rangers scrape past Hearts 1-0 at Tynecastle, where a record crowd had also resulted in crushing and spectators overflowing onto the track.

There was little time to savour this, Motherwell's first Cup win against Celtic in five attempts, as Wednesday brought Morton on a League visit. Among the crowd were many shopkeepers on their half-day holiday and they witnessed much finesse from the Well forwards in a side back to full strength, although a Murdoch headed goal was all they had to show by half-time. McFadyen improved after the break, adding two more to bring his personal total to 44 as Well ran out 4-2 winners. This, the only First Division game of the day, took Well five points ahead of Rangers, who now had two games to make up.

At Dundee United's Tannadice Park on the Saturday the Steelmen romped home 6-1, with Willie McFadyen's four goals pushing him to within one of McGrory's record. Rangers also registered the same score against Thirds at Ibrox, and then did the same again the following week when they disposed of Queen's Park at Hampden, while Well were in Edinburgh to meet Hearts. It had been back in February 1927 when Motherwell had last won at Tynecastle – Ferrier, Stevenson and McFadyen scoring to send Well to the top of the League. Now, despite the rival attraction of a rugby international, a 21,000 crowd turned up and were treated to a hard-fought contest won by a fine goal from Stevenson. Stevie had suffered a collision of heads with Hearts' King and both had retired for treatment. When he returned to the field Stevie received the ball and although he could have laid it off to McFadyen, he chose to squeeze it between goalkeeper Harkness and the post. Willie would have to wait a bit longer. Allan McClory had offered a defiant display in goal and when Hearts had pushed up and managed to get past the stalwart Alan Craig – not to mention the inside forwards, who also came back to bolster their defence – the Well goalie looked to be in international form.

The big games kept on coming: the quarter-final draw of the Scottish Cup brought out Rangers' name followed by Motherwell's. Opinion had it that the winner of this tie would win the Cup itself, and that it was a pity that one or the other would have to miss out on the final. Again there was talk about how huge the crowd might be and some considered that 100,000 was a possibility. Rangers had regulars Archibald and Marshall out through injury, but Well's two head-injury victims, Stevenson and Craig, were passed fit, as was McMenemy, after manager Hunter had denied rumours that he was a doubt.

Sweeping rain kept the crowd down to 88,000 but it was still a new record high for Ibrox. The Well defence and half-back line all played their part, Alan Craig looking inspirational in his close-fitting, leather 'protective helmet'. However, a goal in each half took Rangers through to a semi-final against Hamilton and thereafter to Hampden to meet Kilmarnock in the final. Well's biggest disappointment had lain with their forwards, McMenemy and Stevenson attracting special criticism for ineffectual displays which 'rather irritated some of the onlookers'.

After the match, Bailie J Buchanan of Rangers had naturally been upbeat, as the *Daily Record* recorded: 'And isn't that the sort of football, the sort of cup battle we wished to see? Let's have more of what we've just witnessed, and there will be less talk of football decadence, loss of interest in our great game, and, as a consequence, dwindling attendances.'

Sailor Hunter was philosophical, conceding that the better team on the day had won: 'Then, chortled Johnny, with that dry smile of his, "It's all in the game," and in a cheerier tone he added – "there's still the League Championship".' Rangers' victory meant that they would be piling up the postponed League games even further, while Well now had a clear run to complete their six remaining fixtures. One may speculate on what might have transpired in the League race if it had been Well who had knocked Rangers out of the Cup.

There wasn't much let up for Well, as Celtic at Parkhead was the next hurdle to be overcome. There would be no 'double' for the Steelmen but there was still much to prove after the Ibrox defeat and they set off at a tremendous pace with Murdoch opening in the fourteenth minute. McMenemy and Stevenson were going all out to make amends for their Cup disappointment and after Celts' Thomson had equalised, George met a Ferrier cross, rising to it 'like a bird' to head Well back in front. The team were now firmly in their stride, as the *Daily Record* saw it: 'that even-going, cool, calculating and rhythmic stride which has taken them to the top of the League ladder.' McFadyen played provider to set up the onrushing Murdoch to score his second.

McFadyen continued in this unselfish fashion until, on the hour, as he rushed between the hesitating McStay and McGonagle, he met yet another Ferrier cross to slip the ball into the net and put his side 4-1 up. It was also the record-equalling 49th strike, and although the Celtic fans must have groaned as it went in, the Well supporters' cheers were naturally full-throated. Celts reorganised and managed to grab another goal, the 31st that Well had conceded, and incidentally the last they were to lose this season. It was the same number that Rangers had lost, but the Steelmen had scored 108 while Rangers had only 99, their three most recent League games accounting for no fewer than seventeen of these. The League flag was looking a real possibility, provided Well could keep the momentum going. Even if Motherwell did slip up, Rangers had to win all their games in a programme that now appeared to be the tougher. Otherwise, the Ibrox championship run would be broken and Rangers would 'fail to make that winning sequence of six championships which they have set their hearts on' (*Daily Record*).

The *Motherwell Times* correspondent maintained that he was happy that McFadyen hadn't gone on to break the record at Celtic Park because Well had four home games from their final five fixtures and he preferred to see Willie do the business at Fir Park: 'Well, I am looking forward to the jubilant rejoicings when Willie breaks the record "before his ain folks". Which will be tomorrow, I hope.' That was not to be, as McFadyen had sustained a knee injury at Celtic Park and would miss the next two games, Moffat the first to take his place on Saturday, 19 March against Partick. The Firhill side were living up to their reputation for unpredictability but still had their sights set on a third-place finish, which would be their highest ever.

Almost from the 3.15pm kick-off at Fir Park, Well pressed and had 90 per cent of the possession but they couldn't get the better of an inspired Jackson in the Thistle goal until, with desperation setting in, captain Ferrier reorganised his front line with Stevenson coming into the centre. Only two minutes were left on the clock when Hugh Wales sent in a ball from the right touchline and, with Thistle centre-half Donnelly making a rare error, Stevenson slid in to prod the winner into the net. Meanwhile Rangers had won 3-0 against Killie, thus improving their goal average at a faster rate of knots than Motherwell: now 3.516 for Well as compared to 3.290 for Rangers. This, of course, would only come into contention if the Steelmen should drop a point and Rangers did not. The prospect for Well of a return visit to Partick in two weeks time gave some food for thought.

Motherwell's directors looked further ahead when arranging another overseas tour for the coming close season. A planned trip to Denmark and Sweden was abandoned in favour of a short tour of Belgium and France, with games fixed up in Antwerp, Liege and Paris.

Meanwhile, Willie McFadyen's knee injury prevented him from training, so he was able to demonstrate his other skill as a trained chiropodist all week at Lewis's (later Debenham's) in Glasgow's Argyle Street. Willie had come to Fir Park as far back as 1921 when, as a raw 17-year-old, he signed from the local Wishaw YMCA. It was in the outside-right position that he made his Motherwell debut in October 1923, after loan spells at Bo'ness and Second Division Clyde. His debut goal as a Steelman came in a 2-1 home win against Queen's Park in his seventh game. It was no easy task to break into a forward line which at that time boasted the prodigious talents of Hugh Ferguson, and which had Tennant, Banks and Cameron all vying for first-team places. One verdict on him in 1927 was grudging: '... always a 90 minute man; has not a football brain, but the knack of snapping a goal. A trier all the time.'

Willie was something of a utility forward when Sailor Hunter moved him to right-half for a time before returning him to the front rank in season 1929-30. McFadyen's first real flowering came the following season, when he netted nineteen goals in his final thirteen games. At 5ft 8½in and weighing around 11½st, he was a pacy and strong centre who was an ideal foil for the silky skills of McMenemy and Stevenson on his flanks. Of course, he positively blossomed out in South Africa, scoring 30 out of his side's 57 on the hard pitches there, before his zenith in 1931-32. Wearing his dark hair in a left parting, the stocky-framed player enjoyed socialising and, according to his son Ian, the house was rarely quiet when his dad was home. Willie's ties with the club took on a further dimension when he married the daughter of long-serving director James Crystal. Willie's brother, Ian, also signed for Motherwell and his son would play with the club in the 1950s.

The Scottish Cup semi-finals consumed most of the football interest on 26 March, with Lanarkshire well represented in Hamilton v Rangers and Airdrie v Kilmarnock. Well played host to Dundee in the League, and showed little mercy, despite the absence of McFadyen and McMenemy, who was being 'rested'. Three first-half goals in a twenty-minute spell put paid to the Taysiders and the final score of 4-0 helped improve the goal average.

By the Monday evening it appeared that there might be no need to resort to decimal calculations as Third Lanark went into an early lead against the defending champions at Cathkin. Although they were pegged back to 3-3, with nine minutes left, Thirds then scored again. The local *Times* got a little ahead of itself: 'Motherwell are already being congratulated as champions for 1931-32,' while the *Daily Record* struck a more cautious note: 'Congratulations to Motherwell are not quite in order yet.' On 2 April it was Well's turn to go to Firhill, for what was their last away game. A crowd of 32,000 attended and, as had already happened in front of a big expectant crowd, the match was a disappointment, lacking the excitement of the earlier tussle at Fir Park. Willie McFadyen had returned but the forward line had an off-day and it was the defence which took the plaudits in a goalless draw, with Dowall and Craig outstanding.

The Scotland selectors sprang a surprise for the big international against England, not so much in the inclusion of Alan Craig at centre-half, but rather in the relegation of George Stevenson to the travelling reserves. In the event, Stevie hurt his foot and ankle at Firhill and had to withdraw. Both Motherwell's and Rangers' games were put off on 9 April when the Scots went down 0-3 at Wembley, Alan Craig not showing up particularly well, failing to control Aston Villa's Waring, who scored one of the goals.

Prior to Well's penultimate game, against Cowdenbeath, on Cup final day, the *Daily Record* ran the headline: 'Motherwell All But Champions.' Following that dramatic 3-0 win over the Fifers, that included McFadyen's last-gasp record-breaker, the same newspaper declared: 'By defeating Cowdenbeath at Fir Park, Motherwell virtually won the Scottish League Championship, [although] not yet actually Scottish League Champions, but they look all right for the Flag.' As might be expected, the *Motherwell Times* went one better with: 'The Flag Won', ignoring the mathematics that said Rangers could still overtake Well on goal average if their backlog of matches were all won and the Fir Park men lost their last game, against Clyde.

To win the Cup would, of course, have been a tremendous feat, but, said the local paper: 'The winning of the League is a greater honour to Motherwell than even the winning of the Scottish Cup would have been.' Earlier, a Rangers director had admitted to the *Daily Record* that they would rather have lost in the Cup than relinquish the chance to equal Celtic's six League wins in a row.

Despite their desperate fight-back against Clyde at Shawfield on the Saturday, Rangers' eventual 1-1 draw meant that Motherwell were champions without any resort to goal averages. At the end of the Scotland v England Junior international that same day at Tynecastle, Well chairman Tom Ormiston could not content himself and left the boardroom to try to learn the outcome of the Shawfield game. 'It's all right,' Tom was reported to have chuckled on his return, 'Clyde have drawn with Rangers. We're League Champions.' Mr WCP Brown of Hearts proposed a toast among the several club representatives present. He reminded the assembled company that it had been he himself who had signed John Hunter for Hearts 22 years earlier in his own house. Tom Ormiston responded to the toast and Sailor modestly replied that they were a happy family at Fir Park and that his directors didn't stint him. In an interview in the *Daily Mail* the following week, the manager was a little more forthcoming on how the title was won: 'Give the players a square deal. Make them happy. Have harmony in the dressing room. As an old player, I am conversant with the ups and downs of the players. Make your ambitions theirs and get their confidence, exercise discipline reasonably, and the best that is in them will emerge spontaneously.'

So it was as League winners that Well sailed to Dublin on Monday to play a Leinster Select at Dalymount Park before 20,000 appreciative onlookers. As the Steelmen were winning 2-1 against the Irish side, back in Scotland, Rangers were collapsing 0-3 at Airdrie.

The last League Saturday, 30 April, was a pleasantly warm spring day. At Fir Park 7,000 came along to see the Scottish champions entertain Clyde, the side which had twice held Rangers to a draw, in a game that doubled as Alan Craig's benefit. Alan led his side as captain for the day and McFadyen and McMenemy opened the scoring in the first half. Clyde made a brave show in the second period and it was with only ten minutes remaining that McFadyen found himself well-placed as Bobby Ferrier's cross swung over. Willie coolly pushed the ball into the net for his 52nd League goal of the season and established a record that so far has endured for 71 years. Fittingly, it had been McFadyen who had scored Well's opening goal on the first League Saturday, and this was now Well's last. At the end of the game many of the crowd poured onto the field and, congregating in front of the stand they chanted 'We want the champions!' Unused to winning League championships, the players had gone into the bath, and from the stand Tom Ormiston made a 'series of little speeches' through a megaphone. Director Crystal then took over, and with some witty remarks persuaded the crowd to disperse. Congregating outside in Fir Park Street, the supporters mobbed and cheered John McMenemy as he emerged, followed by several other players who had to run the gauntlet of hand-shaking and back-slapping. A special reception was given to goal supremo McFadyen, and the crowd then waited on for the last two players to appear. Appropriately, Stevenson and Ferrier emerged together, to be smartly hoisted up onto shoulders and borne triumphantly into the street.

In the evening the directors held a commemoration dinner in the ballroom of The Grosvenor in Glasgow's Gordon Street, with about 200 guests present, each one greeted by Mr and Mrs Ormiston. Tom read apologies but also congratulations, including that from Lord Hamilton of Dalzell, long-time patron of the Club, and Mr Livingstone French, president of the South African FA. On behalf of the defeated champions, Rangers' Duncan Graham OBE JP retold a brief history of Motherwell FC but he touched on the key point: 'Where they had a body of directors, such as Motherwell had, who refused to sell their players, the result was success' (*Wishaw Press*). The chairman of Celtic, Tom White, made the speech of the evening and elicited laughter, confessing that he had been a Motherwell supporter this season, particularly since February, when Celtic had dropped out of contention. He didn't know whether he delighted more at Motherwell's success or at Rangers' failure and said that if Celtic were not to win the double next season, then he hoped that Motherwell would. Director William Duffy proposed a toast to the SFA, but went on to criticise the amount of international matches being played and suggested more midweek Scotland fixtures.

Bob Ferrier and Sailor Hunter then spoke, and the manager praised Bob, adding that he was looked up to by all of the players as their natural captain. Ferrier was certainly unused to public speaking and his unease showed as he replied in his turn. Special congratulations were extended to Willie McFadyen on his achievement. Provost McClurg of Motherwell hoped that prosperity would soon return to the area and that the club's gates would then improve too. The speeches over, the gathered company joined hands and sang Auld Lang Syne before retiring to another room, where the remainder of the evening was danced away.

Amidst the welter of praise and plaudits that came the way of the club, there remained the concrete facts and figures that testified to a special achievement. Apart from establishing a new individual goalscoring record, Motherwell's 119 total was also a new First Division high. They had ended five clear points ahead of Rangers and a whopping eighteen in front of Celtic in third. In all matches played, including friendlies and

Lanarkshire Cup ties, 151 goals had been scored for a loss of 44. Since 1922-23, when the Scottish League had settled on a twenty-club First Division, Well's 66-point total had been bettered only once, by Rangers' 67 points in 1928-29. Only Rangers had ever suffered fewer defeats, just one, in that same season. In Motherwell's storming last third of 1931-32, they had won thirteen of their final fourteen games, drawing the other. During that sequence, on only four occasions was their winning margin restricted to a single goal.

On Wednesday, 4 May, with the praises still fresh in their minds, fifteen players, the manager and directors Taggart and Cuthbertson, departed for Belgium. In the tourists' first game, against Beerschot in Antwerp, Well were at full strength, apart from Moffat standing in for Hugh Wales at right-half, and won 5-0, Willie Telfer scoring his first goal. In Brussels on the Sunday they met and defeated Standard Liege 4-2. A well-deserved week's holiday in Paris then ensued, when the party took in the sights of the city, going out to the races at Longchamps for a flutter. On Sunday 15th, Red Star Olympique were defeated 3-1 in Paris (Well had beaten them 5-0 at the end of their Spanish tour in 1927) and on the next day Motherwell met Racing Club. The weather deteriorated and, playing in steady rain and on rough grass, Racing went down 0-5 despite having three French internationalists in their ranks. The Paris side had recently lost to both Arsenal and Manchester City, but only 2-3 and 3-4 respectively. Although there was criticism in the French press for their own sides, there was also much praise for the Scottish visitors. 'L'Auto' of Paris wrote: 'It is no exaggeration to say that Motherwell, the champions of Scotland, demonstrated yesterday, at the Stade de Paris, that their team is one of the best formations that has yet played on French soil.'

Fir Park viewed from the south or 'Estate' end in the mid-1920s. In fact, the ground was never known as 'Motherwell Park'. Perhaps the caption is a printer's misprint of 'Motherwell's Park'.

Ben Ellis is the smartly dressed race-goer, here at Hamilton Park after the Second World War.

Having swapped his strip for a tweed jacket and the ball for a typewriter, George Stevenson took over as Motherwell manager in 1946.

Goalkeeper Allan McClory, centre, relaxes with the trainers in front of the stand at Fir Park in the early 1930s.

In season 1932-33 Ben Ellis won two Welsh caps: in a draw with England and in an easy win over Scotland.

A youthful Stevenson, left, and Ferrier in the late 1920s, their reputation already established.

AND MAIL, THURSDAY, APRIL 13, 1933 [illegible]

FOOTBALL MATCHES
On 14th, 15th and 17th April

SPECIAL TRAINS and CHEAP FARES

On FRIDAY, 14th APRIL

STONEHOUSE VIOLET v. KIRK-MUIRHILL JUNIORS.

At LESMAHAGOW.

		p.m.	p.m.	Ret. Fares. s.	d.
Stonehouse	leave	5.56	6.25	0	10
Blackwood	„	6. 7	6.35	0	4
Lesmahagow	arrive	6.12	6.40		

Returning from Lesmahagow at 8.45 p.m.

On SATURDAY, 15th APRIL

CELTIC v. MOTHERWELL.

At HAMPDEN.

An augmented Service of Trains will be run between Glasgow (Central) and Mount Florida between 1.30 p.m. and 2.45 p.m. A Train every few minutes.

Returning from Mount Florida immediately after the match.

The issue of all First and Third Class Ordinary and Cheap Tickets between Glasgow (Central) and King's Park and Stations on the Cathcart Circle Line will be suspended between the hours of 1.0 p.m. and 3.0 p.m. and only Third Class Tickets at a fare of 3d for the Single Journey and 6d for the Return Journey will be issued. The Issue of all First and Third Class Ordinary and Cheap Tickets from King's Park, Cathcart, Mount Florida, Crosshill, and Queen's Park to Glasgow and Stations on the Cathcart Circle Line will be suspended between the hours of 4.30 p.m. and 5.45 p.m., and only Tickets printed to "Any station on the Cathcart Circle Line" at a Single Fare of 3d will be issued during that period.

		p.m.
Bridgeton Cross (LMS)	leave	2. 0
Parkhead	„	2. 5
Tollcross	„	2. 8
Carmyle	„	2.15
King's Park	arrive	2.32

6d—RETURN FARE—6d.

Returning from King's Park immediately after the match.

		p.m.	Ret. Fares. s.	d.
Dalmuir	leave	1.20	0	9
Kilbowie	„	1.25	0	8
Clydebank	„	1.28	0	8
Yoker	„	1.30	0	7
Scotstoun (West)	„	1.35	0	7
Scotstoun	„	1.38	0	6
Partick (West)	„	1.40	0	6
Partick (Central)	„	1.45	0	6
King's Park	arrive	2.32		

Returning from King's Park immediately after the match or by any Evening Train via Glasgow.

		p.m.	p.m.	p.m.	p.m.	Ret. Fares.
Kirkhill	leave	1. 0	1.15	2. 5	2.20	4d
Burnside	„	—	—	2. 8	2.25	2d
King's Park	arrive	1.10	1.25	2.13	2.32	

Returning from King's Park immediately after the match, or by any Evening Train.

		p.m.	p.m.	p.m.	p.m.	p.m.	p.m.	p.m.	Ret. Fares, s.	d.
Bellshill	leave	12.45	—	—	—	1.45	—	2.15	0	8
Fallside	„	—	1. 0	—	—	—	—	—	0	6
Uddingston	„	—	1. 5	1.20	—	1.55	—	—	0	6
Newton	„	12.55	1.10	1.25	1.40	—	2.10	2.25	0	6
King's Park	arrive	1.10	1.24	1.38	1.55	2.13	2.25	2.38		

Returning from King's Park immediately after the match or by any Evening Train from Glasgow (Central).

		p.m.	p.m.	p.m.	p.m.	p.m.	p.m.	p.m.	p.m.	Ret. Fares, s.	d.
Lanark	leave	—	—	12.30	—	—	—	—	1.24	2	0
Cleghorn	„	—	—	12.35	—	—	—	—	1.30	1	10
Braidwood	„	—	—	12.45	—	—	—	—	1.40	1	5
Carluke	„	—	—	12.50	—	—	—	—	1.45	1	4
Law Junction	„	—	—	12.55	—	1. 5	—	—	1.50	1	2
Overtown	„	—	—	12.58	—	1.10	—	—	1.54	1	1
Wishaw (Cen.)	„	—	—	1. 3	—	1.15	—	1.45	2. 0	1	0
Flemington	„	—	—	1. 5	—	1.20	—	1.50	2. 5	0	9
Motherwell	„	12.55	1. 5	1.10	1.15	1.25	1.30	1.55	2.10	0	9
King's Park	arrive	1.25	1.30	1.38	1.45	1.53	2. 6	2.25	2.46		

Returning from King's Park immediately after the match or by any Evening Train from Glasgow (Central).

CHEAP EXCURSION TICKETS
Will also be issued to
GLASGOW (QUEEN ST.)
as under:—

From	Return Fares. By an train up to 12 noon. s.	d.	By any train at or after 12 noon s.	d.
Alloa	3	6	2	6
Alva	4	0	2	11
Cambus	3	6	2	9
Causewayhead	3	6	2	6
Dollar	4	0	3	2
Menstrie	4	0	2	11
Tillicoultry	3	6	2	10

Additional Train will leave Alloa at 12. p.m., due Glasgow (Queen Street) at 1. p.m., returning from Glasgow (Queen Stree at 7.17 p.m. for Alloa.

The Tickets will be valid for return by an Afternoon or Evening Train.

		p.m.	Ret. Fares s.	d.
Ayr	leave	1.15	3	6
Newton-on-Ayr	„	1.20	3	6
Prestwick	„	1.25	3	0
Troon	„	1.30	3	0
Irvine	„	1.40	2	6
Mount Florida	arrive	2.45		

Returning from Glasgow (St. Enoch) b any Evening Train.

		p.m.	Ret. Fares s.	d.
Uplawmoor	leave	1.40	0	11
Neilston (High)	„	1.45	0	8
Patterton	„	1.52	0	6
Whitecraigs	„	1.55	0	3
Williamwood	„	1.58	0	3
Muirend	„	2. 2	0	3
King's Park	arrive	2. 8		

Returning from King's Park immediatel after the Match, or from Cathcart at 5. p.m.

		a.m.	Ret. Fares s.	d.
Stranraer Pier	leave	6.45	8	6
Castle Kennedy	„	6.53	8	6
Dunragit	„	6.59	8	6
New Luce	„	7.12	8	0
Glenwhilly	„	7.25	8	0
Barrhill	„	7.39	7	6
Pinwherry	„	7.46	7	0
Pinmore	„	7.56	7	0
Glasgow (St. Enoch)	arrive	10. 7		

Returning from Glasgow (St. Enoch) 8 p.m.

Top: Special trains for the Scottish Cup final with Celtic.
Bottom: The tour party to South Africa in 1934 prepare for an excursion. Director Muirhead is in the dark suit, between Sailor Hunter and George Stevenson, kneeling.

Sailor Hunter and trainer Walker flank a group of black-tied players on board ship returning from the 1934 tour of South Africa.

Sailor Hunter, far right, looks in danger of being scooped up by an elephant's trunk during the club tour to South Africa in 1934.

THE Standard SCORING CARD

MOTHERWELL'S

FOOTBALL FIXTURES

1931-32

Club Stationery · Circulars · Tickets · Cards · Posters · Handbills · Booklets · Accounts · Visiting and Business Cards · Holiday Fund and Club Cards · Membership Cards

f. a. Last Season.		LEAGUE FIXTURES.		f.-Goals-a.	Pts.	GOAL-SCORERS.
3 - 1	Aug.	8—QUEEN'S PARK	Away	5 : [illegible]	2	
1 - 0	..	15—RANGERS	Home	[illegible]	[illegible]	
3 - 2	..	19—AYR UNITED	Away	3 : [illegible]	2	
4 - 1	..	22—KILMARNOCK	Away	[illegible]	[illegible]	
5 - 0	..	26—AIRDRIEONIANS	Away	2 : 2	1	Macfadyen, McMenemy
5 - 0	..	29—ABERDEEN	Home	3 : 0	2	Macfadyen 3
1 - 2	Sept.	1—ST. MIRREN	Away	1 : 0	2	Dowall
0 - 1	..	5—HAMILTON ACAS.	Away	2 : 2	1	Macfadyen, Ferrier
6 - 1	..	12—FALKIRK	Home	4 : 1	2	Douglas [illegible]
—	..	16—THIRD LANARK	Home	6 : [illegible]	[illegible]	[illegible]
6 - 0	..	19—CLYDE	Away	3 : 2	2	Wyllie, Douglas, Ferrier
4 - 1	..	26—LEITH ATHLETIC	Home	4 : 1	2	Macfadyen [illegible]
3 - 0	Oct.	3—MORTON	Away	[illegible] : 2	[illegible]	[illegible]
—	..	10—DUNDEE UNITED	Home	5 : 0	2	McFadyen (3) Douglas (2)
2 - 0	..	17—HEARTS	Home	2 : 0	2	Macfadyen, Ferrier
0 - 1	..	24—COWDENBEATH	Away	5 : 1	2	Macfadyen [illegible] Ferrier
3 - 3	..	31—CELTIC	Home	2 : 2	1	Douglas, Dowall
3 - 0	Nov.	7—PARTICK THISTLE	Away	0 : 0	1	
1 - 2	..	14—DUNDEE	Away	[illegible]	1	[illegible]
1 - 1	..	21—AYR UNITED	Home	6 : 0	2	Macfadyen (4) McMenemy Craig
4 - 0	..	28—AIRDRIEONIANS	Home	3 : 0	2	Macfadyen, Ferrier (2)
3 - 1	Dec.	5—ST. MIRREN	Home	4 : 1	2	Moffat [illegible] Stevenson
—	..	12—THIRD LANARK	Away	2 : 0	2	Macfadyen, McMenemy
2 - 1	..	19—QUEEN'S PARK	Home	4 : 1	2	McFadyen McMenemy Stevenson [illegible]
1 - 1	..	26—RANGERS	Away	0 : [illegible]	0	
3 - 0	Jan.	1—HAMILTON ACAS.	Home	3 : 1	2	Stevenson McFadyen Ferrier
1 - 0	..	2—FALKIRK	Away	3 : 2	2	Murdoch Moffat McFadyen
1 - 1	..	9—KILMARNOCK	Home	4 : 0	2	Ferrier 3 (P) Wyllie
4 - 2	..	23—ABERDEEN	Away	1 : 0	2	Macfadyen
4 - 4	..	30—CLYDE	Home	3 : 0	2	McFadyen (2) McMenemy 1
5 - 2	Feb.	6—LEITH ATHLETIC	Away	[illegible] : 0	2	Wyllie 2 Moffat (3)
3 - 0	..	13—MORTON	Home	4 : 2	2	Murdoch 2 Macfadyen 2
—	..	20—DUNDEE UNITED	Away	6 : 1	2	Murdoch 2 McFadyen (4)
1 - 5	..	27—HEARTS	Away	[illegible] : 0	2	Stevenson
3 - 1	Mar.	5—COWDENBEATH	Home	3 : 0	2	Macfadyen Ferrier McMenemy
1 - 4	..	12—CELTIC	Away	4 : 2	2	Murdoch 2 Stevenson Macfadyen
0 - 0	..	19—PARTICK THISTLE	Home	1 : 0	2	Stevenson
2 - 0	..	26—DUNDEE	Home	4 : 0	2	[illegible]
	League	Total	119 : 31 .. 66	119 : 31	66	[illegible] "Champs"

1930-31—Played, 38; Won, 24; Lost, 6; Drawn, 8; 56 Points. Goals Scored—For, 102; Against, 42

A POINT TO REMEMBER
WHEN PLACING ORDERS FOR PRINTING
We have a reputation — for Quality and Accuracy at moderate charges
"STANDARD" PRINTING OFFICE
133 Brandon Street, Motherwell 'Phone 102

THE Standard *TIME-TABLE*
PUBLISHED MONTHLY
PRICE - - TWOPENCE

MOTHERWELL
FOOTBALL HANDBOOK
Brighter and Better than ever
The best Pennyworth going

This fixture card for season 1931-32 was filled in by trainer Wull Walker in pencil. The final, understated, word is simply 'Champs'.

Back (left to right): McKenzie, Wales, Telfer, Mackrell, Ellis.
Middle: trainer Donaldson, Johnman, Dowall, McClory, Craig, Blair, trainer Walker.
Front: Murdoch, Moffat, McMenemy, Ferrier (capt), McFadyen, Stevenson.

THE MANAGER

Mr John Hunter

While many English clubs are credited with big offers for Motherwell players, it may not be generally known that star players are not the only attraction up Fir Park way. Many tempting offers have been made to lure Mr Hunter across the Border, but Motherwell's manager still remains loyal to his club—despite a recent very alluring proposition from one of England's leading sides. Mr Hunter's worth as a talent spotter and team builder is recognised all over England as well as Scotland and his opinion is frequently sought by football officials over the Border.

Left: The club handbook for 1932-33 highlights the reputation which Sailor Hunter had established for himself in British football. Right: in his last years as club secretary, Hunter was known as the Grand Old Man of Fir Park.

The classic Motherwell forward line that helped win the Championship:
Left to right: Murdoch, McMenemy, McFadyen, Ferrier, Stevenson.

Hugh Wales was just 19 years old when signed from Kilwinning Rangers in 1929.

Willie Telfer came from Blantyre Celtic, also in 1929. Wales and Telfer are wearing the vertical striped shirts of 1929-30.

Lef-half Willie Telfer later in his Motherwell career, when he was unfortunate with illness and injuries.

Leading by example, Ferrier was a fine captain and was never booked in over 700 first-class games for Motherwell.

FRIDAY, MAY 6, 1932.

MOTHERWELL MAKE MERRY

CELEBRATIONS IN THE "GROSVENOR"

CONGRATULATIONS FROM FAR AND NEAR

The season was brought to a triumphant close at Fir Park last Saturday when Motherwell defeated Clyde by 3-0 and brought their points total up to 66—5 ahead of the Rangers and 18 more than Celtic who occupy third place. It was a fitting wind-up to a season that will be specially noted in the history of the club.

The young players from Shawfield gave the new champions a good run, and had M'Clory not been in rampant form the home goal would not have escaped downfall.

A warm spring sun bathed the terracing in radiance, but in the shade of the stand it was found that the wind had still a bite in it. "See the conquering heroes come" played the band as the Motherwell players ran on to the field, and the cheer that greeted their appearance impressed one with the greatness of the occasion. After years of promise Motherwell at last had gained the League Championship — it was a great day for everybody at Fir Park.

And when play commenced it was early evident that the spectators were eager to see Macfadyen increase his record number of goals. The centre-forward did get two—the first and the third—but he might have got as many more. He finished the season with 52 goals to his credit, as against M'Grory's record number last year of 49.

At the end of the game the crowd congregated in front of the stand and chanted "We want the champions." It was rather unfortunate that the players were reclining in their baths at the time, and then there arose a shout for Mr John Hunter, the manager. A short speech by Mr Thomas Ormiston, C.B.E., M.P., struck a happy note, and the crowd broke up with the demand that Motherwell next season should gain the double—the Scottish Cup and the League Championship.

The crowd waited on and when the players emerged on to the street a number of them were carried shoulder high by enthusiastic followers of the club.

Scottish football. Bailie Graham concluded his speech by remarking that he sat down believing he had spoken the truth, the whole truth and nothing but the truth. (Applause.)

CELTIC CHAIRMAN'S HUMOUR

This toast was supported by Mr Tom White, chairman of Celtic F.C., whose jocular speech was fully enjoyed. In the first instance he thanked the chairman and the Motherwell directors for their kind invitation to come to this celebration dinner. "I am a supporter of Motherwell to-night," he said. "I have been a supporter of Motherwell since the beginning of February because at that date I knew the Celtic hadn't a chance of winning the championship. I don't know," he added, "whether I am more delighted at Motherwell winning the championship or Rangers losing it." (Laughter.) Motherwell, he said, had been knocking at the championship door for the last few years. This year they had opened the door and he thought they would all agree that they had deservedly won the honour. Apart from the Rangers supporters who wanted to see their club win, he thought that everybody else in Scotland wanted to see Motherwell win the championship this year and they had done it. "But," he jocularly remarked, "if I go on much further I will get into difficulties." It reminded him of the story of a Russian who got into a St. Patrick's Day demonstration in Broadway and the only comment the newspapers made was that he would have been forty years of age on his next birthday. (Laughter.) There was an old saying that a prophet had no honour in his own country, but when they found that Mr Tom Ormiston was the Parliamentary representative of the people among whom he lived and who knew him he thought there was a great deal of honour to Mr Ormiston. Mr Ormiston and Bailie Duncan Graham were the sort of men they wanted to be associated with football which was the people's game in this country and

The *Wishaw Press* of 6 May 1932 marks the Championship win with a review of the final League game and the subsequent celebrations in Glasgow's Grosvenor Hotel.

Motherwell's deadly left-wing duo in the late-1920s; between them, Stevenson (left) and Ferrier notched up over 470 League and Cup goals.

On 26 June 1934, some of the tour party to South Africa visited Yeoville Bowling Greens in Johannesburg. The short sleeves of certain players and officials suggest they participated in the bowling.

'Gentle John' McMenemy inherited many of the football skills of his father James, the 'Napoleon' of Celtic.

Like McMenemy, Ben Ellis, the 'Welsh Wizard', is shown in a change strip, with the claret and amber reversed.

Sprint training on the pitch at Fir Park in the mid-1930s. The specially extended flag-pole installed in 1932 can be seen at the far end of the stand.

The Scottish League team before the game with The Football League on 7 November 1931 at Celtic Park (not Hampden). Motherwell's John McMenemy is front, fourth left. Jimmy Crapnell, who joined Motherwell two years later, is second left, front row.

This silver dragon cigarette-lighter was presented to Ben Ellis as a member of Wales's Home International Championship winning squad for 1932-33. Wales repeated their success the following season.

Team-bonding carries over onto an Ayrshire golf course.
Left to right: Wales, Stevenson, McKenzie, Ellis, Crawley, Ogilvie.

The League flag is hoisted by Mrs Ormiston before the opening League fixture against Kilmarnock in August 1932. Chairman Tom Ormiston is to his wife's right; director J Taggart wears a bowler hat.

Manager Bobby Ancell's famous 'Babes' are linked to their illustrious predecessors by the presence of Sailor Hunter (far right) in his final season as club secretary.

The gold League Championship medals for 1931-32 were presented by the wife of Chairman Ormiston in Motherwell Town Hall.

Tom Ormiston, Chairman from 1929-37, was an entrepreneur in the British film industry as well as a qualified lawyer.

THE CHAIRMAN

Mr Thos. Ormiston, C.B.E., M.P.

During last season Mr Ormiston, chairman of the club, added other two letters to his name. In a picturesque and intriguing Parliamentary contest, fought out in true sporting style, Mr Ormiston successfully contested the Motherwell Division and has now a seat at St. Stephen's. During his stay in London, Mr Ormiston has had the opportunity of witnessing the leading English sides in action—yet he fancies his own club at its best to the finest of the English combines. His foreword, published on page 5 of this issue, will be read with interest by the followers of the club.

Mr Ormiston, whose three years' term of service as chairman of the club terminated last season, has been unanimously elected by his fellow-directors to another year's term of the chair.

WILLIAM YOUNGER & CO.'S ALES

can be obtained during permitted hours as under :—

	Monday to Friday		Saturday		Note
Aberdeen . .	10.30-2.30	5.30-9.30	10.30-2.30	5.30-9.30	
Airdrie . .	11-3	5-9	11-1	3-9	
Alloa . . .	11-2.30	5-9.30	11-2.30	5-9.30	Till expiry of Summer Time.
Do. . . .	11-3	5-9	11-3	5-9	Till beginning of Summer Time. 1932.
Arbroath . .	10-2	5-9	10-2.30	5.30-9.30	1st Sept. to 31st May.
Do. . .	10-2.30	5.30-9.30	10-2.30	5.30-9.30	June, July and August.
Armadale . .	11-3	5-9	11-3	5-9	
Ayr . . .	11-3	5-9	11-3	5-9	From October to May.
Do. . . .	11-2.30	5-9.30	11-2.30	5-9.30	From June to September.
Bathgate . .	11-3	5-9	11-3	5-9	Winter only.
Do. . .	11.30-3	5-9.30	11.30-3	5-9.30	Summer only.
Bo'ness . .	10-2	5-9	11-3	5-9	
Brechin . .	10-2	5-9.30	10-12	3-9.30	1st May to 30th September.
Do. . .	10-2	5-9	10-12	3-9	1st October to 30th April.
Do. . .	11-3	5-9			Winter. Tuesdays only.
Do. . .	11-3	5-9.30			Summer. Tuesdays only.
Clydebank .	10-2	5-9	10-12	3-9	
Coatbridge .	11-3	5-9	11-1	3-9	
Cowdenbeath .	11-3	5-9.30	11-3	5-9.30	From 29th Sept., 1932, to 13th November.
Do. .	11-3	5-9	11-2.30	4.30-9.30	From 14th November, 1932, to 13th February.
Do. .	11-3	5-9	11-3	5-9	From 14th February, 1932, to 27th May.
Dumbarton .	10-2	5-9	10-11.30	2.30-9	
Dunfermline .	11-2.30	5-9.30	11-2.30	5-9.30	From 28th May to 28th Sept.
Do. .	11-3	5-9	11-3	5-9	From 29th Sept. to 27th May.
Dumfries . .	11-3	5-9	11-3	5-9	June, July, Aug., Sept., 5-9.30.
Dundee . .	10-2	5-9	10-11.30	3-9.30	Winter only.
Do. . .	10.30-2	5-9.30	10-11.30	3-9.30	Summer only.
Edinburgh .	12-3	5-10	12-3	5-10	
Falkirk . .	11-3	5-9	10-12	3-9	
Forfar . . .	10-2	5-9	10-2	5.30-9.30	Winter only. Mondays 11-3; 5-9.
Do. . . .	10-2	5-9	10-2	5.30-9.30	Summer only. Mondays 11-3; 5.30-9.30.
Do. . . .	10.30-2	5-9.30	10.30-2	5-9.30	Tuesdays to Saturdays.
Glasgow . .	11.30-2.30	5-10	10-12	4-10	
Greenock . .	10-2	5-9	10-11.30	2.30-9	
Hamilton . .	11-3	5-9	11-1	3-9	Race Meeting, 11-2; 4-9.
Kilmarnock .	11-2.30	5-9.30	11-2.30	5-9.30	
Kirkcaldy .	10-2	5-9	10-2	5-9	
Lanark . .	11-3	5-9	11-3	5-9	
Leith . . .	12-3	5-10	12-3	5-10	
Montrose . .	10.30-2.30	5-9	10.30-2.30	5-9	June, July, August, 5-9.30 p.m.
Motherwell .	11-3	5-9	11-1	3-9	
Paisley . .	10.30-2.30	5-9	10-11.30	2.30-9	
Partick . .	11-3	5-9	10-12	3-9	
Perth . . .	11.30-2.30	4.30-9.30	11.30-2.30	4.30-9.30	
Stenhousemuir (Larbert) .	11-3	5-9	10-12	3-9	
Stirling . .	11-3	5-9	11-3	5-9	From 1st May to 30th Sept. closing hour is 9.30 p.m.

Scottish pub opening hours in 1932 left much less scope for celebrating Championship wins than modern licensing laws allow. In Motherwell, see above, pubs closed at 9pm.

Motherwell Football and Athletic Club, Limited 4

Ground and Registered Office:
FIR PARK

Motherwell 30th July 1935

Received from Bury Football Club Ltd
the Sum of One Hundred & Fifty --------- Pounds
------- Shillings and -------- Pence, being amount
due for Part payment for Transfer Fee agreed upon for Wm Dowall

£150: -: -

Motherwell Football and Athletic Club, Limited 42

Ground and Registered Office:
FIR PARK

Motherwell 5th September 1935

Received from Bury Football Club Co Ltd
the Sum of One Hundred -- --------------- Pounds
------- Shillings and -------- Pence, being amount
due for Balance for the transfer fee of William Dowall

£100 : - : -

With Thanks.

Utility-player Willie Dowall was transferred to Bury in 1935 for just £250. Secretary-manager Hunter has signed the receipts across the stamps.

A Motherwell squad from around 1935. The back of this photograph appears below.

Several tobacco companies promoted their cigarettes by printing football cards, which were avidly collected by young fans. The commercial association between football and cigarettes would be frowned on today, but in those days many players were smokers.

No. 104.

MOTHERWELL FOOTBALL CLUB.

Left to right, back row :—*H. Wales, J. Blair, A. McClory, B. Ellis (Capt.), P. McArthur, C. Johnston, T. McKenzie.* Front row :—*D. Ogilvie, T. Wylie, J. McMenemy, G. Stevenson, W. McFadyen, R. Ferrier, T. Crawley.*

Celebrating its Jubilee last year Motherwell, the famous First Division Scottish Team, is looked upon as an institution in Scottish Football. Nearly every football honour has been held by the club, and Motherwell players often appear in the Scottish International Team.

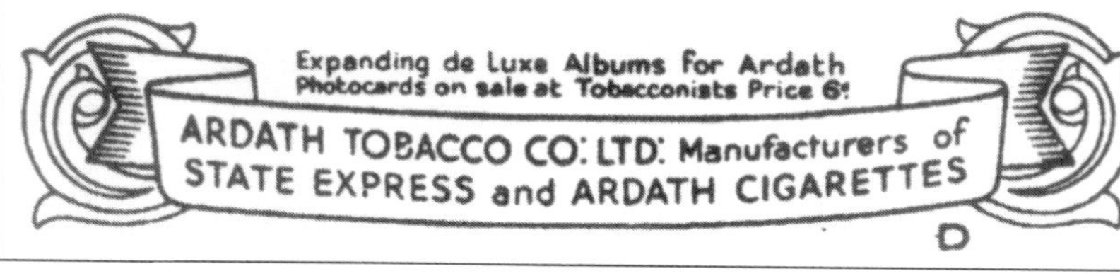

SEASON— —1935-6

CLAPTON ORIENT

FOOTBALL CLUB (1906) LTD.

Secretary : T. W. Halsey Team Manager : P. Proudfoot

Registered Office : 91 LEA BRIDGE ROAD, E.10 Telephone . LEYTONSTONE 1368

OFFICIAL PROGRAMME • 1D

THURSDAY, APRIL 30TH, 1936

FRIENDLY MATCH

versus MOTHERWELL

Kick-off 6.30 p.m.

Clapton Orient, now Leyton Orient, won this friendly 1-0. The east London side had also beaten Motherwell the year before. The first meeting between the two clubs, in 1934, was won 6-4 by Well before they sailed from Southampton to South Africa.

The Orient and Motherwell teams are listed in the programme in the traditional 2-3-5 formation of the time.

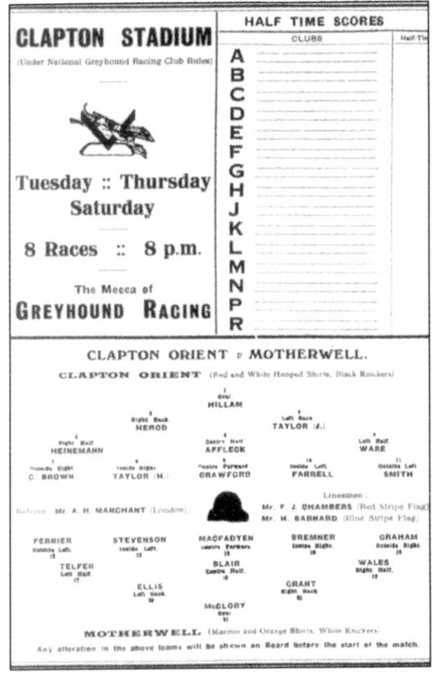

CLAPTON STADIUM

(Under National Greyhound Racing Club Rules)

Tuesday :: Thursday

Saturday

8 Races :: 8 p.m.

The Mecca of

GREYHOUND RACING

HALF TIME SCORES

CLUBS

A B C D E F G H J K L M N P R

CLAPTON ORIENT *v* MOTHERWELL.

CLAPTON ORIENT (Red and White Hooped Shirts, Black Knickers)

Goal HILLAM

Right Back HEROD — Left Back TAYLOR (J.)

Right Half HEINEMANN — Centre Half AFFLECK — Left Half WARE

Outside Right C. BROWN — Inside Right TAYLOR (H.) — Centre Forward CRAWFORD — Inside Left FARRELL — Outside Left SMITH

Referee : Mr. A. H. MARCHANT (London)

Linesmen : Mr. F. J. CHAMBERS (Red Stripe Flag) Mr. H. BARNARD (Blue Stripe Flag)

FERRIER Outside Left — STEVENSON Inside Left — MACFADYEN Centre Forward — BREMNER Inside Right — GRAHAM Outside Right

TELFER Left Half — BLAIR Centre Half — WALES Right Half

ELLIS Left Back — GRANT Right Back

McCLORY Goal

MOTHERWELL (Maroon and Orange Shirts, White Knickers)

Any alteration in the above teams will be shown on Board before the start of the match.

The smartly dressed Ellis family stroll down Motherwell's Brandon Street in the early 1930s.

This montage reflects the 2-3-5 format for listing team line-ups of the day. These eleven players first played together in a 6-0 win at Clyde in February 1931.

Close interplay in training for the benefit of the camera. Left to right: Wales, McKenzie, A Stewart, Ferrier. The Knowetop goal is in the background.

The squad which topped the Scottish League for much of the 1933-34 season. Sadly, it suffered injuries which tested the depth of the club's playing resources.

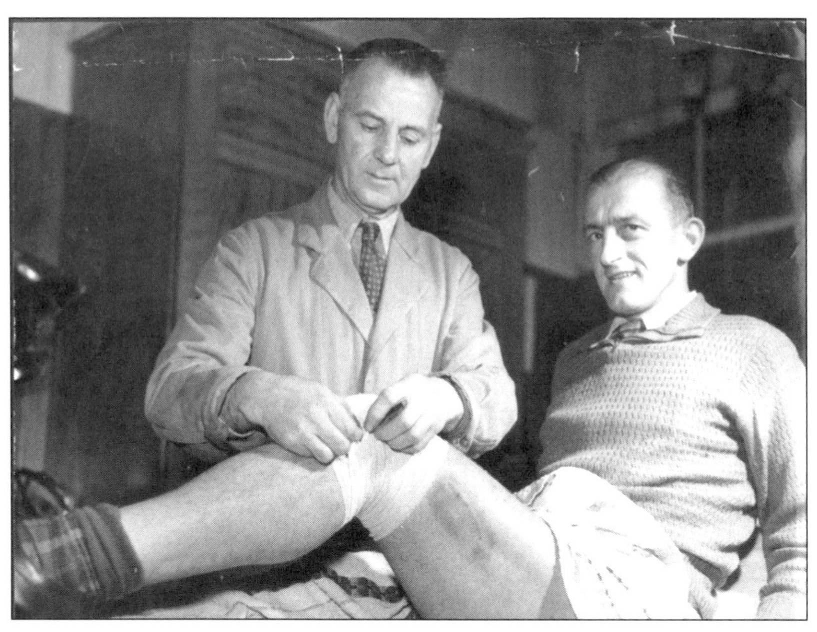

Tom McKenzie, Motherwell's right-half in the 1930s, became groundsman, trainer, and then physio. Here Tom tends Archie Shaw on the treatment table.

The sixteen tour players, with Sailor Hunter, director Muirhead and trainer Walker, dressed for dinner *en route* home from South Africa, 1934.

The Motherwell Cup final eleven beaten 0-1 by Celtic in April 1933: McClory; Crapnell, Ellis; Wales, Blair, McKenzie; Murdoch, McMenemy, McFadyen, Stevenson, Ferrier.

MOTHERWELL c.1937

Goalkeeper Peter McArthur

Right Back William Grant — Left Back Ben Ellis

Centre Half John Blair

Right Half Hugh Wales — Left Half Tom McK…

Centre Forward Alex Stewart

Inside Right Hutton Bremner — Inside Left G. Stevenson

Outside Right Duncan Ogilvie — Outside Left John McCulloch

Reserve

Score 2 : 1

Trainer

Team-sheet signed by the players for the League game against Rangers on 18 August 1937. McCulloch scored for Well in the 1-2 defeat.

Chapter 5

~ Hopes Raised High ~

(June 1932–February 1933)

When the club reached the final of the Scottish Cup in 1931, the Motherwell Town Council had agreed to mark the occasion, if the trophy had been won. Disappointed then, they now in June 1932 marked the historic Championship win with a Civic Reception in a Motherwell Town Hall that was bedecked in claret and amber. Chairman Ormiston thanked the Town Council, and Mrs Ormiston then presented the gold League medals to the players, despite the fact that Ellis, Stevenson and Ferrier were absentees. An enjoyable musical programme was followed by dancing (perhaps some waltzes and fox-trots) and whist (not merely a card-game, but a popular social pastime in those bygone days). Not everyone was happy, however, as many folk condemned the cost of such a function in the town at a time of 'such poverty and distress'. The No 1 Branch of the National Union of Railwaymen tabled a protest: why was it that no money could be found to aid 'the unfortunate unemployed in the way of food and clothing', while at the same time a fund could be used to fete football players?

The following week the club's AGM told a happy tale of £3,041 profit and a proposed dividend of 20 per cent to be paid to the shareholders. Despite the disappointing attendance at many home games, total income had actually risen compared to the season before, while income from away gates had fallen due to the quarter-final exit in the Cup. The club were carrying more fully-waged players than ever before and expenditure had increased by £1,800. Willie Telfer recalled top wages as being in the region of £7 or £8 per week, plus a £2 win bonus. This was felt to be good money and certainly enough to hold some of the best players at Fir Park.

All of the championship season's players had in fact been retained and a couple of 'promising juniors' taken on. Alan Craig was to be the new captain as Bob Ferrier felt that the honour should be shared around. Craig had been with Motherwell since 1924, signed from juniors Saltcoats Vics. The story went that Sailor Hunter had had his eye on Craig, but Rangers were also keen and Alan was actually due to appear in the Ibrox reserves for a try out. Sailor had met Craig several times before but could not get his name on the dotted line until, on one wet and windy day in Paisley, where Craig worked as a carter, Hunter confronted him. As the rain came down, Mr Hunter persisted and Alan grabbed the form and pen and, leaning on the horse's backside, signed on as a Motherwell player. Later in life he revealed his motivation: 'Well, it got rid o' him didn't it!' (*Motherwell Times*). Craig's role had been almost entirely a defensive one until midway through the championship season when he became more adventurous, bringing the ball upfield and combining with his wing-halfs. He had a powerful physique and used it in a spoiling fashion rather than constructively until that subtle change in 1931. He 'sticks to opposing centres closer than a brother', said one commentator.

Preparations were in hand for the opening fixture of the new season, when Kilmarnock would visit and the League flag be hoisted on a special flagpole about eight feet higher than the previous one. Twelve thousand turned up for the pre-season trial game at Fir Park, where Attack met Defence. The new faces from the juniors, Jimmy Johnston and Duncan Ogilvie, figured amongst the regulars. Erstwhile full-backs John Johnman and Sandy Hunter had departed from the club on free-transfers to English Third Division Stockport County and Scottish Second Division Bo'ness respectively.

On Saturday, 13 August, with the ground basking in sunshine, Tom Ormiston briefly addressed the 12,000 present before his wife, in silence, pulled the rope to unfurl the League flag. The Town Band played 'See The Conquering Hero Comes' (a popular melody by Handel) and, with the cheering continuing, the new season kicked off at a cracking pace. Motherwell were on the usual lines, apart from Tom McKenzie in at right-half for Hugh Wales, who had bruised toes. Killie didn't stand on ceremony and gave the champions a hard test in the 3-3 draw. Well's main challengers, Rangers, had an inconspicuous start, losing to St Mirren 0-2 at Paisley.

The Motherwell side was back to full strength for the visit to Pittodrie and another fast-paced encounter ended in another draw, this time 1-1, the retention of a point largely due to the international form displayed by Allan McClory. A Wednesday evening run up to Dundee, who had begun the season with two emphatic defeats, brought Willie McFadyen his first League goals in a 3-0 win. Already there were signs that this might be a more open League as Rangers dropped a home point to Clyde, Aberdeen hammered Killie 7-1, and Celtic went down at home 1-2 to Partick Thistle. The young Clyde team which had recently held Rangers then came to Fir Park and made the new champions work hard for their narrow win, clinched with a Ferrier penalty. Bob had put over a whole series of great crosses but to little avail, McFadyen scorning several good chances.

By the end of August the top of the table had taken on its old look, with Celtic and Rangers as joint leaders. They were not, however, among the only four sides in the First Division who still had not lost a game – Hamilton, Cowdenbeath, St Johnstone and Motherwell. It was another journey north next for Well as they tackled St Johnstone in Perth. Saints' manager, Tommy Muirhead, had assembled a fine blend of youth and experience and his side took a below par Motherwell side to the wire. But a Willie McFadyen strike won the match and inched Well further up the table, still headed by Rangers, while Celtic slipped after a surprise draw against second-bottom Falkirk. Both of the Glasgow big guns had played two games more than their nearest challengers, including Well, by fitting in midweek matches.

By now, Hamilton and Motherwell were the only unbeaten sides in the division and on 10 September the pair met at Fir Park on local derby day. The 4-1 home win rather flattered the Steelmen, whose defence and half-backs were flustered and harassed by the Acas' direct style of play. George Stevenson had been the man of the match and utilised all of his honed technical skills to set up three of the goals. There had been some fighting on the terracing behind the Knowetop (or Taggart's, after the car dealer's nearby premises) end as derby passions became inflamed. The result, of course, meant that Well were the solitary undefeated side now in the Scottish First Division and they climbed to second place, sandwiched by the Old Firm, who had cancelled each other out in a 1-1 draw at Parkhead. It had been this very week three years previously when Motherwell had last lost a League game at home.

	P	W	D	L	F	A	Pts
Celtic	9	5	3	1	25	10	13
Motherwell	7	5	2	0	16	6	12
Rangers	8	5	2	1	21	8	12

On the Wednesday evening, as Rangers took on Newcastle at Ibrox in a clash of the two Cup-winners in a challenge match (Rangers won 4-1), a small crowd saw Well work hard for the points against Ayr. It took all of the skill and guile possessed by Ferrier, McMenemy and Stevenson to carve out the chances to beat inspired goalkeeper Hepburn. Young John Blair had deputised most ably at centre-half for the rested Craig. Both Stevenson and Telfer were selected for Scotland against Ireland in Belfast on the following Saturday. Willie Telfer's first honour was surprising as

Rangers' Brown had successfully kept him out the previous season, whereas Stevenson was now winning his eighteenth cap. George played at inside-right and linked up well with his right-half and right-winger, while Telfer 'walked' through the game, largely untroubled in the 4-0 Scots' victory. Both internationalists were sorely missed in a reshuffled Motherwell eleven that faced a Falkirk side fresh from holding Celtic at Brockville the week before. In one of the most exciting contests seen at Falkirk's ground, said the *Sunday Mail*, John McMenemy scored a very late equaliser almost in slow motion to keep Well unbeaten but now down to third place.

A week later, with John Blair back in the heart of the defence but otherwise with all the regulars, Motherwell overran Morton at Fir Park by seven goals. The *Sunday Mail* thought Motherwell capable of beating any team in Scotland and that Bob Ferrier 'positively scintillated; he was another Cinquevalli, so perfect was his juggling with the ball.' The first goal of Bob's hat-trick had flown in from a typically acute angle and burst the net.

Well were now only one point behind leaders Rangers and had a game in hand, so that the meeting between the two at Ibrox the following weekend assumed the aspect of a crucial encounter. During the resultant 2-2 draw the Steelmen had gone ahead in a first half that they dominated, then Rangers had gone ahead in the second period before Well, bolstered by sterling defensive work from Craig and Ellis, who 'kicked like a mule and tackled like a terrier' (*Daily Record*), finally equalised. The *Sunday Mail* considered: 'Motherwell on this display, must be taken as likely to hang on to the League flag for another season, and up to now the only team whom I consider likely to take it from them is their opponents of yesterday.' With the status quo undisturbed, it was now a case of seeing who might hold their nerve and last the pace. Both contenders won their next game, Queen's Park bearing the brunt of Well's 'exhibition of carpet-weaving' and going down 2-7 at Fir Park.

	P	W	D	L	F	A	Pts
Rangers	12	8	3	1	32	12	19
Motherwell	11	7	4	0	34	12	18
Celtic	13	6	5	2	32	15	17

But now the world caved in. For the following few weeks the leadership of the League shifted around between Aberdeen and Celtic as both Rangers and Motherwell dropped points. A Tynecastle crowd of 36,000 saw Willie McCartney's Hearts upset the odds with a 2-0 win over Well, who dropped down to fourth, but only a point behind the joint leaders Aberdeen, Rangers and Celtic. Hearts' John White had done the damage to Motherwell in a keenly fought contest that brought an end to Well's 24-game unbeaten run.

October was to prove disastrous for Motherwell as, following the defeat by Hearts (who went on to beat Rangers 1-0 the following week), a hazardous trip to Celtic Park ended in a 1-4 loss. Missing was George Stevenson, who had hurt an ankle playing for the Scots against the Irish League on the Wednesday, when he had scored with only three minutes remaining in the 4-1 win. His teammates in the Scottish side also included McMenemy and Telfer, Willie also managing to get his name on the scoresheet two minutes after Stevenson. Stevie had been drafted into the League side to replace the injured Bob McPhail of Rangers and, along with John McMenemy, was content to pattern-weave against the Irish. 'They [the two Motherwell players] were never called on to play the superb football of which they are capable' (*Motherwell Times*). At Celtic Park, Motherwell found themselves outplayed as the Celts' right wing excelled in the fashion of Well's left wing, whenever all were present. As Celtic moved up to share top spot with Aberdeen, Well dropped to sixth.

It had been over three years since Motherwell had last suffered two consecutive defeats and the wind had certainly been taken from their sails. Willie Moffat had deputised for Stevenson against Celtic and he was listed again in that position for Partick Thistle's visit on 29 October. Moffat was one of the few senior players John Hunter had bought for his squad, 'a strong goer and a 90 minute man who never flinches,' according to the *Daily Record*, but Moffat couldn't match the effectiveness of the missing Stevenson. John Blair came in again for Craig at centre-half. A less familiar face was that of 21-year-old Duncan Ogilvie, signed from Alva Albion Rangers, who replaced Murdoch on the right wing. Unlike the waif-like Johnny Murdoch, Ogilvie weighed almost 12st at this time, but he could still show a fair burst of speed.

By half-time Partick were thankful that they had somehow kept Well at bay, with the game goalless, but Thistle started the second half in a more aggressive mood. Within twenty minutes of the restart they were two up and Well were forced to rely on the driving force provided by John Blair from midfield, but a 1-2 defeat was the demoralising result. Partick had achieved what no other League visitors had managed in almost 38 months, since 7 September 1929 – a win at Fir Park. Thistle had certainly not been favourites to take the points, sitting as they did in sixteenth place before the game. Celtic were beaten at Paisley, so allowing Aberdeen to take over the leader's mantle.

	P	W	D	L	F	A	Pts
Aberdeen	15	11	1	3	39	16	23
Rangers	14	9	3	2	34	13	21
Celtic	16	8	5	3	39	19	21
Hearts	15	9	2	4	28	16	20
Hamilton	14	8	2	4	46	23	18
Motherwell	14	7	4	3	36	20	18

Three games lost in a row could so easily have broken a side which was undergoing personnel changes. Indeed, the team chosen to face a hot and cold Dundee at Fir Park showed yet more reshuffling. The off-form Willie Dowall was replaced by reserve right-back Mackrell; Tom McKenzie came in at the last minute for a sick Telfer, and Willie Moffat swapped positions with John McMenemy. With five of the Flag-winning side therefore missing, Motherwell failed to take much advantage of injured Dundee goalkeeper Marsh in the first half. His right collar-bone fractured, Marsh did not reappear after the interval and Well banged in five to finish 6-1 winners. The oft-repeated boast of the previous season that the Steelmen had adequate cover for all positions was now well tested. Elsewhere, although Rangers continued on a seemingly relentless winning march, Celtic were again defeated, this time by Well's recent conquerors, Partick.

Apart from the return of Willie Telfer, the same reshuffled side travelled to the west coast to take on an Ayr team which had slipped from its previous mid-table perch to the bottom quarter of the table. Well's 6-2 win over the 'Honest Men' from Ayrshire had the Lanarkshire side looking as if championship form had been regained at last as they clawed their way back up the table to fourth place, now three points behind the new but familiar leaders, Rangers. These two handsome wins boosted Well's confidence and appeared to have resuscitated their League challenge, and with a visit to Lanarkshire neighbours Airdrie next on the cards, the future looked brighter.

The economic climate, however, continued in a depressing vein. It was estimated that out of every ten people in Motherwell and neighbouring Wishaw, six were being supported on the rates by the other four. Practically half of the working population of Lanarkshire was out of a job but many folk held on to their pride and tried to avoid the degradation of applying for rate-relief. Still, over the past year in Lanarkshire there had been an increase of 183 per cent Poor Relief, which had now reached £25,292. Even those who were fortunate enough to be in work often found their hours or their wages cut; the railway workers were moved to protest when their rates of pay were threatened. In the football business, Airdrie FC was certainly suffering and the 6,000 at their local derby with Motherwell, which might otherwise have been felt a poor turnout, was thought a fair one in the circumstances. On the field, despite a blank first half, the Steelmen won comfortably enough by 4-1. Bob Ferrier played the part of wounded hero, coming on after receiving treatment, his leg bandaged, and proceeding to score a double. The downside was that Bob's injury meant that he would miss the next game, against St Mirren at Love Street. On the previous Wednesday Ben Ellis had played at left-back for Wales against England in a 0-0 draw, the first time since 1927 that that the English hadn't won the fixture.

Against St Mirren, in place of the injured Ferrier, Dowall resumed at his own old position and Mackrell filled in at right-back. McMenemy continued at inside-left as Stevenson hadn't regained his fitness. St Mirren in sixth place were 'hot' at this time and the form of their international centre-half George Walker had apparently enticed representatives north from Everton. They saw Motherwell, without their usual left-wing pair – the more frequent transfer targets –- overcome a determined Saints' side 5-2, with stand-in captain McFadyen contributing a hat-trick.

As November slipped into December, Motherwell and Hearts sat a point behind second-placed Celtic, with Rangers a further two points ahead. During the previous season Third Lanark had received a six-goal thrashing, when McFadyen had bagged five goals, and now, on their 3 December visit to Motherwell, they again lost six and Willie again scored five. The difference was that this time Well conceded three. Bob Ferrier had made a welcome return and on the next Saturday he was rejoined by his left-wing partner, now back from injury at last after seven weeks out, to face East Stirling. The promoted outfit from Falkirk were accounted for by 4-1, so that since they had sacrificed their unbeaten home record, Well had now won all six League games and scored 31 times. Having been held at Hampden to a goalless draw, Rangers' lead over Celtic was cut to a single point. The following week they were level on 33 points although Celtic had played two games more. Hamilton had done both Celtic and Motherwell a favour by taking a point from Rangers at Ibrox. Despite being under strength, the Douglas Park men had come back from 0-3 down to finish at 4-4. In third place sat Motherwell, who had beaten Cowdenbeath 2-0 in a Fir Park gale; they now had only a single point less than Rangers from the same number of games. But Well supporters were wondering just when they would be seeing Stevenson again at Fir Park because, after his one game comeback from injury, he had now caught the flu and so missed the Cowdenbeath fixture.

George was sufficiently recovered to rejoin the squad for the testing visit to Kilmarnock on Christmas Eve. A fierce contest ensued and Duncan Ogilvie netted his sixth goal for Motherwell to open the scoring; then, in the second half, it was his cross which was nodded in by McFadyen to complete a hard-earned 3-1 win. With this, their 22nd game, Motherwell had now scored 72 goals – by far the highest in the First Division – but they had also conceded 31, the same total as for the whole of their championship season, and that might prove costly.

The New Year holiday period saw a series of three League fixtures, Motherwell's first being at Fir Park against Aberdeen on Hogmanay. After an hour of play Well found themselves three goals down, the Dons' Irish centre-forward Paddy Moore inflicting most of the damage and scoring twice. The Steelmen's fight-back was spirited but too little, too late and, as the match was ending at 2-3, Ben Ellis damaged his ribs in a clash with inside-forward Adam and had to be carried off. Rangers, meanwhile, had dropped another point, this time at Ayr, while Celtic went crashing at home 0-3 to Hamilton, who were Well's next opponents. A 16,700 crowd at Douglas Park defied the strong winds and rain on Monday, 2 January as Well 'first-footed', and they were rewarded with a full-blooded derby spectacle. Well's three goals in as many minutes were all long-range efforts aided by the wind and they were enough to deny Acas in the 3-2 win. The Old Firm derby at Ibrox finished goalless as Celts held the leaders, who were now only one point ahead of Motherwell, closing fast in second place. The next day brought Falkirk to Fir Park as the third of the traditional holiday fixtures kicked off at 2.15pm. Well's only change was at centre-half, where Alan Craig now reappeared from the reserves for what would be his last game with the Steelmen.

The solidly built Craig was known as the 'life and soul' of the squad and would be missed by his team-mates. Alan did well to hold Falkirk's opportunist Bartram, but Mackrell was the best defender on view, playing against his former side as Well came through 2-0. With Rangers once again drawing, 0-0 at Partick, Motherwell went joint top. They were behind on goal average, but would have been leaders at this point if today's regulations were in place; although their goal difference was the same, they had scored more: Well's goals record read 79-36, and Rangers' 66-23.

Chelsea now paid £4,000 for Alan Craig, who had relinquished the captaincy of the side earlier in the season. It had reverted to Ferrier again. With John Blair back at centre-half, Motherwell had to weather a gutsy Clyde performance on a gluey Shawfield surface. The dog-racing which helped the Rutherglen club survive financially also brought the benefit of covered terracing as well as 'canned music' with popular favourites such as 'You Are My Heart's Delight' blaring out. Duncan Ogilvie delighted the Well supporters with his late winner but the side's 3-2 win wasn't a patch on Rangers' 5-1 drubbing of Airdrie. The status quo held good the following week as St Johnstone were beaten 1-0 at Fir Park while Rangers narrowly won at East Stirling. For Well, McFadyen's goal had rounded off a sterling display that led the *Daily Record* to describe him as 'a vastly improved player from a year ago', and to nominate him as the best forward afield. Willie was now on the 28-goal mark, but at this point in the championship season he had amassed 41.

For their first round Scottish Cup-tie across the River Clyde at Hamilton, Well would field their new right-back, the experienced 29-year-old Jimmy Crapnell, bought from cash-strapped Airdrie for £2,000. It appeared that Motherwell would indeed let players go if it had to, as in the case of Craig, but that at least some of the money received was used to reinforce the side. Crapnell was an internationalist with nine Scotland caps and five League ones to his credit. He cut a compact figure, standing only 5ft 6in, but tipping the scales at 12st. The local *Times* thought that the tie could break Douglas Park's attendance record of 21,000 and that the largest movement of people between the neighbouring towns on a single day might materialise, as over 10,000 were expected to cross the river, either by the new Clyde Bridge or by rail. The weather on 21 January was cold and frosty and 70 tons of sand had to be carpeted on the pitch. The 16,500 attendance was a mite disappointing, but the game itself was a rousing contest with end to end action fought out at a rattling pace. Each side squandered a penalty but Well's two first-half goals were enough to clinch it.

Against Morton in the League at Greenock the next Saturday, another frozen pitch made controlled play almost impossible, as McMenemy returned to the side after a seven-week absence and Moffat was missing due to an injury picked up in the Cup-tie. An unusual sight was witnessed when almost the entire Motherwell team, at 2-1 up, fell back to successfully defend their lead. The side was still keeping pace with Rangers but it would require a further slip-up by the Glasgow giants to take Well into a clear lead at the top. Hearts and Celtic were five points off the pace, and in any case they had played more games than the top two. The ideal time for a Rangers' slip would be their next game – against Well at Fir Park. Before that, the Scottish Cup's second round brought Second Division strugglers Montrose to Motherwell.

Expecting little in the way of a contest, only around three thousand spectators turned up. The *Glasgow Herald* thought the 7-1 win was little short of farcical and that the League champions had deliberately eased off in the last twenty minutes, after the visitors had lost their left-back. Such sporting instincts were not unusual, but magnanimity was easy from a comfortable winning position. The forthcoming Rangers' game would put sporting feelings to the test.

Ellis, Ogilvie, Wales and goalkeeper McClory went along to Hampden to watch Rangers' midweek Cup replay and saw Queen's Park again hold them to 1-1. 'Big Allan' McClory – he was, at 6ft, taller than any team-mate – had been a miner in his native Armadale in the West Lothian coal-field when he had signed as Motherwell's new goalkeeper in 1924. The directors had in fact decided to go for McSwick of local juniors Shieldmuir Celtic, but as soon as that had fallen through, Sailor Hunter snapped up McClory from Shotts United. Allan's career had begun at juvenile side Harthill Bluebell, but he had found getting to games from his mining job difficult. His club were loath to drop him and on occasion he had to rush onto the field not having had time to tie his boot laces. At Shotts he had attracted the attention of senior clubs. Sailor had had him watched and was well aware of his potential. His tousled hair crowning his long, thin features, Allan was a bit of a country lad, not having ventured further west than Coatbridge in Lanarkshire. On his way to Motherwell for his first game he had felt it prudent to stop off for a shave and a spruce up to impress his new club. Prior to playing his first game for Motherwell, Allan had only ever seen three senior matches. But in his first nine seasons at Fir Park so far, he had missed only six games, two of these being for internationals. To date he had kept goal against Wales and Ireland, as well as in a couple of Inter-League games against the same opponents.

By 1933 it seemed as if Dawson of Rangers and Harkness of Hearts had put paid to McClory's international career, despite his seventeen championship clean-sheets and continuing good form. It would be 1934 before he gained his next, and final, cap for Scotland. Allan's bony frame and squared-off shoulders made him look awkward physically, but his aerial command and long reach were superb and his goal-kicks prodigious in length. He was always, according to the local *Times*, 'ready to pounce out at the feet of an indarting forward, or to jump to a high cross. [He was] particularly good at the high stuff.' In his personality he was seen as modest and even retiring, 'a very reticent and unassuming gentleman,' and this was reflected in his playing style, which was never showy.

Now, to face Rangers in the table-topping clash, Tom Wyllie took the place of the injured Ogilvie on the right wing in an otherwise full-strength Well side. Meanwhile, out-of-favour Johnny Murdoch was still turning out for the reserves. With over 30,000 jammed into Fir Park, the top two League sides fairly set about each other without much in the way of skilful football on view. As Blair and Crapnell got in a fankle, Fleming pounced to open for Rangers. Well came more into the play and Bob Ferrier's penalty brought them level. Although Rangers' right-back Gray failed to reappear after the interval, the ten Ibrox men were still much on the offensive in the scrappy and bad-tempered encounter. Centre-forward Sam English used his weight and several times had barged McClory. As Allan punched one effort clear, he was 'somewhat unnecessarily charged by English', said the *Glasgow Herald*. McClory saw red and clicked the heels of the centre as he went past, English going 'to earth' and wriggling in apparent agony. Alerted to the plight of the prone Ranger by his teammates and the vociferous Rangers' supporters in the crowd, referee Hudson consulted with both of his linesmen. McClory was sent off – the first Motherwell player expelled since Davie Thackeray in 1927 and the first Well goalkeeper ever to be dismissed – and a penalty awarded to Rangers. Bob Ferrier went in goal but was beaten by the spot-kick. Five minutes later Ferrier came out and Ben Ellis took over, saving well from inside-left Smith. Sam English had sufficiently recovered to prove a constant source of danger up front. As feelings on and off the field became further strained, Main's pass to Fleming resulted in the winger's second and Well finished 1-3 down and thus two points now adrift.

Dundee were drawn at Motherwell in the third round of the Cup and on a glorious February afternoon 8,000 (no doubt the size of the crowd suffered because of Rangers' win) saw Well cruise through 5-0. The game turned on the dismissal of Symon, who had 'thrown himself' at Ellis. As Ferrier had missed an earlier award, Ben took the penalty-kick himself and fairly thumped it in. Unfortunately, Willie Telfer had picked up an ankle injury that would keep him out of the next League game – at Hampden against Queen's Park, unbeaten since Hogmanay.

Sleet and rain made the day raw for players and fans alike and attendances all over the country were affected. Only 7,000 were spread around Hampden's bowl. Queen's looked lively and dangerous from the start, whereas Well seemed content to play a 'tip-tapping' game that left Ferrier idle for long spells. Ogilvie was back on the other wing and, along with Stevenson, missed some great chances during a period of ascendancy. Two goals from Dodds, added to an early Queen's strike, left Well in the unfamiliar position of being three down at the break! Crawford then beat three Well men to score the 'pluckiest goal' of his career to date and the *Daily Record* was incredulous: 'Mighty Motherwell four goals down! Go, think of it!'

Having now ditched the 'tip-tapping', the Steelmen took the game to the amateurs and forced several corners before McFadyen got one back and Blair sent home a 35-yarder. It wasn't enough of a fightback and, with only eight games now left to play, the defeat left them four points behind Rangers, who had seen off Dundee by 6-4. Willie Telfer's ankle injury was diagnosed as serious enough to prevent his reappearance for the remainder of the season, and although his deputy, Tom McKenzie, was a cultured and constructive player, he lacked the experience of Telfer, who would be missed.

	P	W	D	L	F	A	Pts
Rangers	30	20	8	2	87	32	48
Motherwell	30	20	4	6	88	46	44
Hearts	31	18	5	8	68	36	41

Chapter 6

~ Almost There ~

(March-May 1933)

It might have been hoped that the quarter-finals of the Scottish Cup would bring some much-needed relief, following two bad League defeats, but when it was learned who Well's opponents would be there was a hint of anxiety expressed. Kilmarnock at their own Rugby Park were a formidable proposition; they had just eliminated the Cup holders, Rangers. Motherwell had last been paired with Killie in the Cup away back in January 1897 when, after a 3-3 draw at Fir Park, the Ayrshire side had taken the replay 5-2.

Johnny Murdoch was brought out of the reserves and the championship forward line was thus renewed. The right-winger quickly imposed himself on the game of 4 March, no doubt keen to remind club officials of what he was capable. He sent over a corner for McFadyen to score in the third minute and proceeded to carve out the next two goals for Motherwell too. Killie tenaciously stuck in and equalised three times for history to repeat itself, dangerous winger 'Bud' Maxwell grabbing two of his side's goals.

The Rugby Park attendance of over 20,000 was bettered in the replay at Motherwell on the Wednesday, when 23,846 turned out, a higher attendance, too, than that at Celtic Park on the same day for Celts' replay against Albion Rovers. At Fir Park the sides were unchanged from the Saturday, but by half-time the Steelmen had gone three goals up. In a second-half goal-feast, Killie scored three times but, with McFadyen on top form and John Murdoch again proving the wisdom of his selection, Well finished the tie as 8-3 victors. The win and its emphatic margin now had Well installed as favourites to lift the trophy for the first time.

Further good news came with the verdict of the Referees' Committee: Allan McClory had merely been mildly censured for the sending-off incident against Rangers. Scot Symon, the Dundee right-half (and future Rangers' manager) who had been sent off in the Cup-tie against Well, was severely censured and also fined £3, equal to around half a week's wages. With regard to McClory's dismissal, the Committee had interrogated referee Hudson, whose written report had given only the bare facts of the case. The *Sunday Mail* wondered whether the referee hadn't been too harsh in his sending off of McClory, judging by the verdict handed out. If it was a case of being misinformed by his linesmen, then they too should have been called before the Committee. Motherwell had indeed written to request an inquiry into the incident, but the letter had been passed, unread by the SFA Council, on to the Referee's Committee and so the matter rested.

As the second weekend of March approached, with Celtic due to visit Motherwell, there was still some lingering optimism at Fir Park that they could get back into the running for the title race. Rangers after all, had some tough nuts to crack in their remaining programme: Aberdeen, St Johnstone, Cup conquerors Kilmarnock away, and Hamilton.

On 11 March the top four sides took on each other, Hearts visiting Ibrox as Well went into their match with Celtic in determined fashion. Watching from the stand were Scots entertainer Sir Harry Lauder and left-wing politicians including Jimmy Maxton, the Independent Labour Party MP, and John McGovern, one of the 'Red Clydesiders'. For the first fifteen minutes Celtic were unable to break out of their own half, McMenemy spraying fine passes to Murdoch behind the opposition half-backs and McFadyen constantly harrying the defence. All of the Well forwards, and even Ben Ellis, had good attempts but then retaliation by Tom McKenzie brought Celtic a penalty. Allan McClory, who had been pretty idle, dived to smother the kick. Inspired by the save, the Steelmen went two goals up through a McFadyen double. Frank O'Donnell replied for Celtic almost immediately and although Jimmy McGrory headed in with ten minutes left, it was sandwiched by two further McFadyen counters, which took Well to a thrilling 4-2 victory. Noted the *Glasgow Herald*: 'In these days of jaded palates, a clean, clever and well-contested game such as that at Fir Park on Saturday is a welcome tonic.'

As the Well were beating Celtic, Rangers were dropping a point in their 4-4 draw with third-placed Hearts so that flicker of optimism now seemed justified. Further League business for Motherwell, though, had to wait as they prepared themselves for the Scottish Cup semi-final, with Clyde as their opponents. Since losing in the League to Well in January, Clyde had won their succeeding three home League games, the most recent a 7-2 rout of Hamilton. The tie took place at Ibrox, whereas that involving Celtic and Hearts went ahead at Hampden. Despite the kind weather, the crowd which turned up at Ibrox numbered a disappointing 25,000. A bright opening fifteen-minute spell flattered to deceive and excitement faded out of the game after that, with the Motherwell defence and Ben Ellis in particular taking most of the plaudits. Some interest was generated, just as Clyde were about to take a free-kick, by Allan McClory's protests over a 'bent goal-line'. A couple of groundsmen came on, the offending curve was quickly repainted and play resumed. Willie McFadyen had been strong and speedy up front and the vital opener fell to him late on, followed by an easy one for Bob Ferrier to clinch the outcome and send his side into the Cup final. Folk remembered that two years earlier a similar semi-final at Ibrox had eased Well past St Mirren and they had gone on to meet Celtic in a heartbreak final. A similar scenario had now unfolded and the April showpiece of Scottish football at Hampden Park would again feature the same two adversaries.

The Motherwell directors allowed Hunter to take his squad to the Ayrshire coast at Turnberry with its well-known golf course, for training and the advantages that sea air had over the smokier kind that hung over the industrial parts of Lanarkshire. Just at this time, the Scottish poet and novelist Edwin Muir set off on an odyssey by motor-car around Scotland. His experiences were published two years later as *Scottish Journey*. For Muir, industrial Lanarkshire (he neglects the unspoiled rural parts) and parts of Glasgow provided a stark contrast to the Highlands and Islands, especially at this time of dark depression: 'The open shops had an unconvincing and yet illicit look, and the few black-dusted miners whom I saw trudging home seemed hardly to believe in their own existence. The scene actually evoked a sense of peace: the groups quietly talking at the street corners or walking among the pit-dumps, the shafts rising smokeless, and the neglected roads.'

Being merely a passer-by, Muir's impressions of industrial towns such as Motherwell were one-sided and unrelentingly bleak: 'Airdrie and Motherwell are the most improbable places imaginable in which to be left with nothing to do; for only rough work could reconcile anyone to living in them. Yet a large population lives there in idleness; for there is nowhere else to go, and little prospect that Monday will dawn for a long time' (Edwin Muir: *Scottish Journey*, Mainstream, reprinted 1999).

Still, this was how an outsider saw the area and it is a reflection of just how desperate conditions were for many people at this period. Ironically, and unknown to Muir or most folk in Motherwell, a recovery had actually begun and the unemployment figures would gradually decrease year by year until the Second World War began. It is important to put football into this real-life context: going to watch a colourful game of football must have been a welcome diversion to those who could afford it; one commentator quipped that Motherwell FC was the town's only thriving industry.

Airdrie and Motherwell, the two Lanarkshire towns of Muir's focus, met on the football field when the Diamonds (from Airdrie's red diamond on a white shirt) came to Fir Park. On a day of blissful weather the poor 4,000 crowd was due as much to a lack of interest in seeing second top versus third bottom as to the prevailing economic conditions. The top of the League table also showed that, even if Well were to win all of their games in hand, they would still be three points behind the leaders. The *Glasgow Herald* commented after the game that the Well forwards had great difficulty in controlling the 'light ball'. The shock opener from Diamonds' centre-forward Connor was wiped out in fine style by two John McMenemy drives, aided and abetted by McKenzie and Stevenson. In the second half Bob Ferrier headed against the post and Hugh Wales sent in the rebound, but somehow goalkeeper Morrison had acrobatically twisted to save it. When Morrison got to his feet, Ferrier sportingly shook his hand. Motherwell's 4-1 win kept them in touch and set them up for a Wednesday meeting with third-placed Hearts, the side who presumably would offer their stiffest test in the closing weeks of the League programme.

It had been back on 18 December 1917, in the latter stages of The Great War, when manager Hunter reported to his board of directors that he had successfully signed up one Robert Ferrier from Glasgow junior outfit Petershill. Bobby's debut for the first team did not come until the first League game of the next season, 1918-19, against Kilmarnock at Fir Park, but he was only one of six different left-wingers used in that campaign. The regular occupant was Billy Morgan, who had been with Birmingham but had been lured north by work in the local munitions industry during the War. In the following season, with Morgan gone back south, Bobby Ferrier quickly made the left-wing berth his own. His subsequent long tenancy was due to his unarguable skill and his high level of fitness, so that, by the time of the 4-1 win over Airdrie, Bob had played 532 League games for Motherwell. Ferrier's reputation as a classy outside-left, whose ball skills had inspired that 'Cinquevalli' tag from the *Daily Record* – which was afterwards borrowed by most other papers – was sufficient to gain him international recognition.

There was tragedy for Scotland in the football sense, however, in the fact that Ferrier had been born in Sheffield. Despite having a Scottish father, himself once a Sheffield Wednesday half-back, and having been brought up, educated and played his football in Scotland, Bobby Ferrier was barred by the rules of the day from playing for his country. He had, though, been capped seven times for the Scottish League between 1922 and 1930, five times against the Irish, and twice against the Football League, scoring five goals in total. Even his selection for the League had been fraught with initial difficulty. In 1921 he was picked for the Scots' side against the Irish League but was then dropped when it was realised that he had been born in England. This led to a hasty alteration in the rules so that any player of Scottish parentage was eligible to represent the Scottish League, irrespective of place of birth. Bob's first honour, against the Irish at Celtic Park in 1922, saw a win made in Motherwell, as Bob scored on his debut and his Fir Park teammate Hugh Ferguson got the other two in the 3-0 victory. Much debate had been generated in the press and among supporters over Bob's international dilemma, but the swell of support for his inclusion in the Scotland side redoubled as his left-wing partnership with George Stevenson flowered from the mid-1920s onward. Unfortunately, the renowned pairing would never be allowed to appear together for Scotland, although they did so for the Scottish League on three occasions. Bobby Ferrier was also unfortunate in having Alan Morton as his main rival for the League's left-wing slot. The renowned Rangers' and Scotland winger was known as the 'Wee Blue Devil' and was one of the Wembley Wizards who had beaten the Auld Enemy 5-1 at the London stadium in 1928.

Ferrier had grown into maturity over the course of the sixteen years he had spent at Fir Park. His hair was wavy and his face and frame had filled out a little. At 5ft 8in, and weighing 11st 4lbs, Bob was never the speediest of wingers but he more than made up for a lack of pace with intelligence on the ball and a supreme ability to send in pinpoint crosses that contributed so much to the goalscoring tallies established by Willie McFadyen. Bob's own goal exploits fairly soared in the late 1920s, and in 1929-30 he had scored those 30 goals to establish a record for a top division winger. His seemingly uncanny facility of being able to send in a swerving rocket shot, often from almost on the by-line, had many a top goalkeeper fooled as the ball veered round him. It was not unknown for a goalie beaten in such a way to go round to his side-netting to check for tears! Ferrier had been appointed captain in 1927 and he held the honour until it had gone briefly to Alan Craig, when Bob had advocated sharing the responsibilities around. A lot of the team spirit that helped the side play and stay together was due to the influence of Ferrier as captain.

The Hearts game had been put back until 29 March because of Well's Cup quarter-final involvement and the attendance suffered as a consequence, only around 5,000 being present. The first half was all Well's, with Stevenson's form reviving calls for further international recognition – eight of the present line-up had appeared either for the League side or for the full Scotland team. Fittingly it was Stevie who opened the scoring with a spectacular volley from the edge of the box that had Hearts' and Scotland goalie Harkness beaten all ends up. Murdoch and Ferrier added powerful drives to build a convincing half-time lead. Although Well eased up somewhat in the second half, allowing Murray in to pull a goal back, McFadyen's two counters in the last ten minutes helped to earn a handsome 5-1 victory.

Although the Hearts' challenge had been brushed aside, it was remembered how awkward Partick, their next opponents, could be, especially at their Firhill ground. Thistle had ex-Well man George Watson at inside-left, an ex-soldier who had been stationed at Hamilton Barracks when signed by Well from Motherwell Juniors in 1928. Nicknamed 'Sodger', Watson had been a prolific scorer in the Fir Park reserves, running up a 55-goal total in 1930-31. In an early first-team appearance he had scored six in Well's 7-0 win at Falkirk. And yet, George was never to command a regular first-team place and now, on Monday, 3 April, he was out to impress his former club, putting up a fine display in the process. A 20,000 Easter holiday crowd saw a game that was far from a classic but full of incident and excitement, won for Well by a solitary McFadyen goal. Tom McKenzie had been taking the eye with his deft footwork and bursts of speed and he had begun the move, holding the ball up just over the halfway line. Running on, he swung over a long crossfield pass to Murdoch on the right. Johnny took it in his stride, carried on and centred fast and low for McFadyen, who flicked it into the corner of the net with the side of his foot. With Rangers idle (Scotland had defeated England 2-1 at Hampden on the Saturday), the two top sides had now played 34 games. Well would need to overhaul the leaders' three-point advantage if they were to retain the championship.

Only four League games now remained for Well to do so. They had St Mirren and East Stirling at home, followed by visits to Third Lanark and Cowdenbeath; Rangers would entertain Falkirk and Queen's Park, with Aberdeen and Hamilton away. There was still scope for the Ibrox machine to come unstuck, provided Well kept on winning.

A week before the Cup final, mid-table St Mirren came calling. Ferrier and Stevenson each had a goal to enliven the first-half showing, but after the break the game fizzled out as a contest, the Lanarkshire men winning 3-0 but obviously with an eye on the forthcoming final with Celtic. The *Glasgow Herald* correspondent complained that a fine afternoon had been wasted, 'being grilled under a corrugated-iron roof.' Rangers disappointed the Well fans by cantering past Falkirk 5-1 at Ibrox.

The Motherwell directors settled on the same eleven for the Cup final as had done duty for the previous eight games, winning the last seven. To counterbalance the lingering painful memories of the final defeat of two seasons past, there was at least the knowledge that Motherwell had at last beaten Celtic in a Cup-tie – the 2-0 win of last season. To reach this year's final on 15 April, Celtic had begun with a 7-1 win at Dunfermline, then beaten Falkirk and Partick, before stumbling at Coatbridge in a 1-1 draw with Albion Rovers. Winning 3-1 in the replay, Celtic had drawn 0-0 in the semi-final with Hearts before 90,000 spectators at Hampden. The replay had been easier for Celtic than the 2-1 result might suggest, and so they looked forward to what would be their third game at Hampden in their current Cup campaign.

As the teams appeared, Motherwell in their amber shirts with a wide claret band – colours first seen in 1913 when the claret shirt had amber neck and cuffs – and Celtic in their green and white hoops, which they had worn since 1903, the 102,399 inside Hampden erupted in cheering. Men, boys and mere infants came over the perimeter wall and onto the field to hand over good-luck tokens to their favourites. Celts' captain Jimmy McStay chose to kick with the slight wind but it was Motherwell who went on to show themselves the more impressive side in the first half. However, a combination of stubborn goalkeeping by Kennaway and lacklustre forward play, that often left McFadyen unsupported, kept the scoresheet blank. Inside men McMenemy and Stevenson struggled to match the pace of the game, while Murdoch and Ferrier out on the wings were not able to shine as they could.

Both Stevenson and McFadyen mustered good efforts touched away by Kennaway, and Allan McClory had to look lively to fist clear from Jimmy McGrory. Barely three minutes after the second half had begun, a defensive comedy of errors was Well's undoing. Bert Thomson passed inside from the right but, instead of clearing it, Tom McKenzie turned it back. Ben Ellis then attempted to clear the ball but only succeeded in thumping it against McKenzie, and when Ellis tried it once more, again it bounced off McKenzie. At this, McGrory nipped in smartly to touch the ball home. Although Well had chances to level – Stevenson had only the goalkeeper to beat but shot straight into his hands – they faded out of the now scrappy contest and Celtic had again bettered them in the Cup final. The Parkhead chairman, Tom White, accepted the trophy and maintained that he would like to see Motherwell win it, as long as it wasn't at the expense of his club.

After the anti-climax of Hampden, a crumb of comfort was snatched with the news from Aberdeen that the Dons had held Rangers to a 1-1 draw. The title now depended on whether Motherwell could win their last three games and Rangers only gain a maximum of one point from their meetings with middle of the table Queen's Park and Hamilton; Rangers' superior goal average meant that two points would be enough for the title. When East Stirling came to Fir Park as the division's bottom side, they had already conceded 108 goals whereas Motherwell had scored 105. Duncan Ogilvie was named on the right wing, Johnny Murdoch having played his last game for the club in the Hampden Cup final, and Ogilvie scored twice in a mediocre game that was watched by a mere couple of thousand spectators. The judgment of the *Glasgow Herald* was that Rangers' win over Queen's Park at Ibrox, by dint of a single Bob McPhail goal, was enough to reinstall them as champions: Well could possibly match them on points but their goal average was vastly inferior at 2.096 compared to 2.658 for Rangers.

The visit to Cathkin Park to play Thirds was therefore academic and again only two thousand turned up. Allan McClory sustained facial injuries and a groin strain and had to be taken off after only seventeen minutes. After being checked by the Thirds doctor, he did not reappear. Willie Dowall had been brought into the side for the injured Ben Ellis and he now had to demonstrate the extent of his versatility by going into goal. Well's new inside-forward, Jimmy Johnston, and Hugh Wales dropped back into defence but it was Thirds who scored first. A 30-yard Stevenson rocket followed a minute later and the match ended all square. Despite the circumstances, both sides had contributed to a competitive game. There was now no need to perform any miracles in goalscoring – Motherwell had been deposed as Champions of Scotland.

The last Saturday of the season, 29 April, took the same Well side out to Cowdenbeath. Although the game was tight in the first half, with the score at 1-1, a McFadyen hat-trick and a late Ferrier curler made it 4-1 to close Well's League campaign. At Douglas Park, Acas had found the new champions too strong and they went down by 2-4. So, despite Well scoring 114 League goals to Rangers' 113 (only English champions Arsenal with 118 had more in Britain) and winning more games than anyone else in the First Division, three points separated the two top sides. Although all losses of points over the course of a season are cumulative, it hadn't so much been the draw with Thirds, or even the February losses which had broken Well's challenge, but rather the disastrous run at the turn of the year when Hearts, Celtic and Partick had done the worst damage. That had coincided with a time of personnel change and perhaps the vaunted strength in depth had been overstated. Only nineteen players had been utilised in the League all season, the same as in the championship year. Coincidentally, it had been during that rough mid-season period that George Stevenson had been missing through injury picked up on international duty. The side's proud unbeaten home record of over three years had of course gone but, rather more quietly this time, Willie McFadyen had again topped the scoring lists. His 45 League goals was the highest in Scotland, Jimmy Smith of Rangers a long way back in the First Division with 33. When Scottish Cup goals were added on, McFadyen's total of 60 goals was actually higher than in his record season. The two-horse League race between Well and Rangers, coupled with the Celtic Cup final victory, meant that the Steelmen were the nearly men, twice over.

The number of goals conceded had risen dramatically from just 31 in the championship season to 53 in 1932-33. The biggest factor had been the goals lost at home – 24 – bettered by six other teams in the division. Although Alan Craig had been transferred, John Blair had at least been his equal in the centre-half slot. The right-back position had again gone through an unsettled period when Dowall lost form, Mackrell had been brought in, followed then by Crapnell, before Dowall was restored.

A short tour of France had been proposed for the close season, Thomas Cook offering to organise it for £16 16s per head. Two games in Paris were agreed on for a £600 guarantee but, in the event, the club cancelled the whole tour. It had been an exhausting season and the club had little need of the money. Motherwell's share of the Cup final gate was £1,936. Although their final appearance of two seasons earlier had also netted income from the replay, this season the quarter and semi-finals against Kilmarnock and Clyde had brought in over £1,500. The AGM in June would announce a healthy profit of £4,388 over the season. In order to maintain its hold on its sought-after stars, the club had to spend considerably: the outlay on players' wages and bonuses had risen from under £7,000 – still a high sum – for a couple of years past, to £8,305 now.

Several clubs were running greyhound racing at their grounds in order to supplement their income. Second Division Armadale from West Lothian took in more from the dogs than they did from their football. When the Scottish League therefore ordered them to discontinue the racing because it was infringing onto their playing field, the club soon afterwards went to the wall. They were quickly joined by Bo'ness, another West Lothian side, and neither of them was replaced in the Second Division.

Dog racing was obviously a life-line for some clubs, but the Scottish League saw it as sullying the 'purity' of football. Certainly there were visual distractions in the strings of wiring and paraphernalia connected with greyhound or other animal racing (apparently cheetahs had also been used), but the main objection of the League was in the taint of betting that racing brought to football stadia. Motherwell thankfully did not have to bring in the dogs and it is a moot point whether they would have, even if they had been strapped for cash. For a start, their track was not big enough, and the pitch, widened as recently as 1929, might have had to be encroached upon. In late 1929 the club had been approached with offers of advertising, which would have been painted on to the cement wall around the track. The club did not want or need it, as the minutes of a board meeting recorded: 'Resolved not to allow advertising inside Fir Park.'

While he was at a meeting of Edina FC in Edinburgh, John Hunter expressed regret that the SFA had not been able to help out Armadale or Bo'ness. The truth was, however, that there were too many clubs competing in Scotland at a time when the support was never guaranteed, many waged people being forced to pick and choose the games where they would hand over their shilling admission. Even Rangers had played at least a half dozen games at Ibrox before crowds numbering under 10,000 during the past season. Sailor also took the opportunity to question the wisdom of a recent ban on representative matches being played by clubs while on tour; the Association's thinking was that too many defeats of Scottish club sides could bring its national game into disrepute. Motherwell had had the distinction of having played three official Test Matches against South Africa, as well as games against the Argentine FA and Brazil. Yet, said Sailor, the national team had been beaten abroad in recent years by both Austria and Italy. It appeared that English clubs were now stepping in and playing representative games while the Scots held back.

Although the club stayed at home this summer, they had received an invitation from the Roseberry Charity Cup committee to participate in a tournament in May. Normally only Edinburgh and district teams were allowed to compete for the trophy, which had been instituted by Lord Roseberry, Honorary President of the SFA, but as this was the Jubilee year of the Cup, it was felt that something special should be done to mark it. In truth, one of the Glasgow giants would have been first choice as guests, but both of them were staging their own charity matches in the city. So, as runners-up, Motherwell were asked and accepted without hesitation. They met Hibs in the semi-final and a Stevenson goal was enough to put them into the final against Hearts at Tynecastle on 13 May. Hearts had won the first Roseberry Cup in 1883 and were keen to add it to their trophy cabinet in its 50th year too. They did so, winning by 3-1 with the son of the late Lord Roseberry presenting the Cup in a Tynecastle stand adorned in his colours of primrose and pink, worn occasionally by Scotland sides. So, with Well's last late football of the season, the committee was happy to announce that the revenue raised for the charity had been a third higher than the previous year.

Chapter 7

~ Clear Leaders ~

(June–December 1933)

The whole of Britain sizzled under a scorcher of a heatwave that summer, and at weekends a million people would leave the sticky and dirty confines of London for the coast and the countryside. From all over Britain there were the thousands who went in the opposite direction and converged on the cities. They were taking part in the 'Hunger Marches', protesting against unemployment and the policies of an unsympathetic government. Often numbering twenty or thirty thousand, with large Scottish contingents, they were soon to be threatened with withdrawal of their unemployment benefits if they continued to march. On short marches – to Edinburgh from the West for example – they relied perhaps on their own corned beef sandwiches on the way; on longer marches – many went to London – sympathetic donations of food or perhaps organised 'field kitchens' kept them going, and often they had to doss down wherever they could at night. Many from Lanarkshire joined in and several marches came through the area.

There had been little major transfer activity over the close season in Scotland, apart from the buys by Dundee, who had also made changes at managerial and directorial levels. Motherwell's pre-season trial game was watched by 8,000 at Fir Park and many must have echoed the thoughts the press had about the squad for the season: McClory, Crapnell and Ellis were all certs in defence, as was Blair, who had looked good enough for a cap; the two other half-backs would come from Wales, Telfer and McKenzie; Stevenson had gone through a lean spell and hadn't always looked 100 per cent fit; McFadyen had shown much improvement in his control and distribution; McMenemy had had his off moments but he still showed plenty of subtlety; Dowall's versatility had worked against him establishing his own position – he'd filled all five forward spots, full-back and done well in goals. Young Jimmy Johnston looked as if he had a future and Ferrier seemed to go on for ever.

A free transfer had been given to Johnny Murdoch at the end of the 1932-33 season with the hope that Duncan Ogilvie would be a capable replacement. Murdoch had been fast and had great positional awareness, being in the right place to receive Ferrier's long crosses and scoring most of his goals from close range, so earning his nickname of 'the poacher'. Davie Colquhoun of Clyde and later Spurs had once quipped that if the police were ever on the lookout for Johnny Murdoch, all they had to do was dust any goalposts in Scotland for his fingerprints! New manager Willie McCandless of Dundee snapped up the winger, who would revisit Fir Park with his new side in the third game of the season. Initially, Willie Dowall filled in at outside-right until Ogilvie became the regular right-winger. Ogilvie was a strong and well-built young player, but he lacked Murdoch's craft and positional sense.

It was still oppressively warm when the League kicked off on 12 August 1933 with Well at Clyde's Shawfield. Dowall started at outside-right to add some 'punch' but when Jimmy Crapnell was hurt in the course of the game, man-of-any-position Willie dropped back into defence. Crapnell had been pretty robust in the tackle and when he had received his injury the home supporters cheered, which, said an indignant *Motherwell Times*, 'was not called for'. A Ferrier first-timer was enough to secure the opening points while, back in Motherwell, the reserves had begun their Alliance League campaign with a 10-0 romp over Ayrshire side Galston. Each of the scorers was to figure in the first team at some point during the coming months; Tom Wyllie with five and Jimmy Johnstone with three goals had already had some experience there. The shock of the opening day was Celtic's defeat by newly promoted Queen of the South down at Dumfries.

Two home games brought teams from the east as visitors, first up being ex-Ranger Tommy Muirhead's St Johnstone, who had been a success story last season after their promotion, finishing fifth, while fellow newcomers East Stirling had slipped down again to the Second Division. Home supporters had to be content with another 1-0 win, and that score was in fact repeated when, along with their new right-winger Johnny Murdoch, Dundee took the field on the Wednesday evening. After three games Well's goal record read: For 3, Against 0. Rangers' was: For 14, Against 2 and this had included a 0-0 draw with Hibs. Pre-season predictions of another two-horse race seemed to be correct but there was even talk of some other side perhaps being able to break their monopoly. No other 'provincial' team had looked like producing a sustained challenge so far and Celtic's start had been decidedly shaky.

George Stevenson had met Celt Bert Thomson at Glasgow's Central Station and wished him well as Thomson headed south to Blackpool, transferred for £2,000 after being disciplined for breaking training rules. It had of course been Bert's cross which led to Alan Craig putting into his own net in the Cup final of 1931; he had then scored two in the 4-2 replay win, and also provided the cross that led to the winner in the 1933 final. It wouldn't be the last the two forwards would see of each other.

Only three sides remained unbeaten in the First Division: leaders Rangers, who had played a game more, Queen's Park and Motherwell who now made the trek south to face Celtic's conquerors, Queen of the South. There was some unease over Well's meagre goal tally compared to Rangers' twenty; even Queen's Park had scored eight. The tail-end of the heatwave made Palmerston Park a broiling arena for the 10,500 crowd but on the field none was hotter than Willie McFadyen who had two goals before the break and another three after it to silence the critics. Well eased into second place as the three unbeaten sides all won, the Steelmen having the added distinction of being the only side not to have conceded a goal. This would be severely tested when Rangers descended on Fir Park on 2 September.

Meanwhile, things on the employment front seemed to be taking a turn for the better. There was good news that local production was to be increased at Dalzell Steel Works in Motherwell, at Clydesdale in Mossend, and at Smith & McLean's in Gartcosh. Some local labour was also involved in building work at the town's Watsonville district, where substandard single-story housing was at last being replaced.

The first half of the Rangers' game was goalless, but the pace was fast, the best football being seen in that opening period. Wales and Blair shone in the Steelmen's defence, while Rangers' centre-half McDonald held his lines firm. The breakthrough came with McFadyen fairly charging goalkeeper Dawson, as he caught a ball on the line from Wales's free-kick. Such goals were not unusual at this time, as goalie and ball went over the line. Two McPhail efforts were chalked off, one for offside and the other for handball, before the little Northern Irishman, Stevenson, equalised – the first time McClory had been beaten legally this season. Motherwell's lead was restored when Ferrier and Stevenson tip-tapped the ball near the corner flag. Having drawn out the defence, Stevie then released to McFadyen in a prime position to net the winner. With a better goal average (10.00) than anyone else in Scotland, Well went top on the same ten-point mark as Queen's Park and a point ahead of Rangers. The *Glasgow Herald* was moved to write: 'Motherwell FC's achievements in recent years have broadened and brightened the Scottish League competition to an extent that can scarcely be overestimated, and there is excellent prospect that the Lanarkshire club are again to take a leading part in making the current season's competition interesting.'

The next week at Hamilton, Well won the local derby and looked as if they had more in reserve, despite having Jimmy Johnston on in place of

Stevenson. Jimmy Crapnell had been the best back on the field but Ellis had been rather 'brusque' in a game of keen challenges that kept referee Hudson on his toes. First Division referees received £2 2s fee per game and linesmen half that, plus third class rail fares. Well's bonus came in the form of an Old Firm draw at Ibrox, followed by Queen's Park dropping a point to Hearts at Hampden on Wednesday. Motherwell, meanwhile, weren't at their best against Hibs, promoted back into the top division, but Stevenson was back and on top form, claiming one of the two headed goals that helped settle Well into a one-point lead at the top.

Aberdeen had unloaded some top players over the previous couple of seasons and much of their support was disillusioned. They were now even more unhappy when young inside-forward Beattie was transferred to Wolves. At Fir Park the Dons faced a Well side without Telfer, off with the Scotland team that was to lose 1-2 to Ireland at Celtic Park in what would be Telfer's last cap. A second-half push brought a 4-1 win over Aberdeen and, as Queen's Park went down to a Johnny Murdoch goal at Dundee, Motherwell were left as the sole undefeated side in Scotland; three sides in the English League kept them company.

Queen's Park's powers of resilience were tested the following week when it was the Steelmen's turn to visit Hampden Park. The amateur side had enjoyed one of their best ever League starts and they went ahead first, through Dodds, but were unimpressed by some heavy challenges from a determined Well. As the Lanarkshire men gained the upper hand, McFadyen and Ogilvie grabbed a couple of goals each, then Bob Ferrier casually 'dummied' full-back Campbell before sending in a fierce low drive from twenty yards, near the goal-line, to make it 5-1. Glowed the local *Times*: 'By such play League flags are won.'

The fixture card quickly reunited Well with Aberdeen. The squad went up north to spend the weekend at nearby Stonehaven prior to the game on the Monday, a local holiday, at 11am. By 11.25 Well had gone a goal up through Stevenson, but the Dons' centre-forward Moore headed in an equaliser with twenty minutes left. It was a tribute to Well's centre-half John Blair that this goal, only the fifth conceded so far, was the first scored by an opposing centre-forward. It was also the first point dropped by Well. Worryingly, Allan McClory had hurt himself in the first half and Ellis had gone into goal before Allan returned, but it was obvious that he still wasn't right. He wouldn't be 'right' for some time, in fact, so breaking an attendance run that stretched back 152 League games to August 1929. As McClory limped from Pittodrie, it was feared his knee ligaments had been badly torn. The top three sides – Well, Rangers and Kilmarnock – had now played ten games each, the Steelmen three points clear.

Unusually for an Inter-League match, it was a Saturday, 30 September, when the Scots and Irish representative sides met at Windsor Park, Belfast. It meant that John McMenemy missed the League game at home to Falkirk, where Motherwell were made to fight all the way for their 2-1 win, Jock Robertson making his Well debut in goal. The highlight for the home fans was the good display by Stevenson, trumped by his spectacularly taken goal as he first-timed a dropping ball for the winner. Over in Belfast, the League side had gone down 0-3 in a sorry display against the Irish, but McMenemy was still selected to join the full Scotland team to play Wales in Cardiff on the Wednesday.

In Cardiff, John Blair's fine club form had been recognised as he lined up for his country alongside teammates McMenemy and McFadyen. Stevenson was absent because his 'back leg muscles' were giving him problems. With Ben Ellis at left-back, the fighting Welsh side went 3-0 up before the Scots rallied to pull two goals back through Duncan of Derby County and Willie McFadyen. Blair improved somewhat as the game progressed, but he still couldn't reproduce his usual club standard and, in common with McMenemy, he wouldn't figure for the full Scotland side again. Taking the Motherwell presence at the game up to seven were Crapnell, the travelling reserve, and directors James Taggart and Harry Thomson. Sailor Hunter, too busy back home, hadn't travelled and so had missed a disappointing night for the Scots and for his club.

Against a backdrop that increasingly featured news and images of the rising German Nazi party and its leader Adolf Hitler, football continued to provide a means of distraction for thousands: whether they attended in person, used it as a topic of conversation, or bet on it through the Pools coupons. The best football attraction in Scotland the next Saturday was at Kilmarnock, where the day's biggest crowd, 20,000, watched Killie and Well serve up a tight contest. The Steelmen eventually won through 3-1 – due in no small measure to McFadyen's varied play and clever distribution – so keeping them three points out in front of Rangers.

A series of fixtures against sides in the lower half of the table, including struggling Celtic, filled the coming card for late October and into November. Beforehand, however, third spot Hearts journeyed to Fir Park. The Edinburgh side had previously suffered only a single defeat and now they contributed to a game that was 'an absolute thriller for 90 minutes, … a feast of high grade football, … [an] engrossingly attractive contest, packed full of incident,' according to the *Glasgow Herald*. Bobby Johnstone on the right wing gave Ben Ellis a hard time and it was he who opened the scoring for Hearts, but a left-foot drive from Ferrier made it all square at half-time. In a further pulsating 45 minutes that only added to the tradition of fine play and exciting contests provided by these two teams, Stevenson was fortunate to pick up a rebound off referee Peter Craigmyle to net a wonderful winning goal.

The *Daily Record* was as much taken by the crowd as by the game: 'A pleasing feature of this Fir Park match was the attendance. Does this 12,000 crowd mean that at long last, at their own place, Johnny Hunter's clever combine are to be given the patronage they deserve – the patronage they are entitled to?' The local paper welcomed the competitiveness that challenging sides brought to Fir Park: 'even the ardent Fir Park man will welcome the change, particularly at his own doorstep, where too often for the good of the game, and incidentally the gates, Motherwell win in a common canter.' Having beaten rivals Kilmarnock and Hearts on successive Saturdays, the *Glasgow Herald* considered 'Motherwell's prospects of regaining the Championship are appreciably brightened'.

Celtic continued to stutter, losing 0-3 at Aberdeen two weeks previously and languishing now in thirteenth position. Nevertheless, a large crowd was expected at Fir Park as Celts faced the only unbeaten side in Britain. After the gates had opened at 1.45pm, the Motherwell and Wishaw Town Band entertained spectators until the 3pm kick-off. Disappointingly, only around 18,000 were present when the football began, Well putting the Glasgow side – without regulars McGrory and Napier – under considerable pressure. Until centre-forward Crum scored in the second period, Celts had mustered only six shots to Well's thirteen. Three minutes only remained as Bob Ferrier, previously lamed with a thigh knock, lured out the keeper and lobbed in for McFadyen to head the equaliser. During the game McMenemy had shown beautifully crafted passing movements but Stevenson had had an off day, due largely to the recurrent leg muscle problem that left him with a 'crampy' feeling after a game which only wore off during the week. Despite their poor form, Celtic had come closest yet to toppling the leaders, as the *Herald* admitted: 'Motherwell, the unbeaten leaders, are having the experience common to clubs in that position, and each week finds them faced with opponents keyed up to special endeavour.'

A specially commissioned feature in the local *Times* compared the current Motherwell side favourably with Everton and Arsenal, both of whom the writer had seen in action. This was an uncommon claim in those days when most Scots' only experience of such sides might be the brief clips included in British Pathe newsreels shown as part of the programme at the cinema. Twenty thousand at Firhill was Scotland's largest crowd of the day, as bottom placed Partick Thistle failed to interrupt the march of the leaders, who won 4-1 on a wet and windy Saturday. A reporter on his way back to Glasgow met Bob Ferrier *en route* after the game and Bob told him how well Thistle had started off against them; typically, he modestly omitted that he had played a large part in the win, creating two of Well's goals.

Prior to heading north to Dundee on 4 November, the present Well side was praised as the best ever by the *Daily Record*. The half-backs and forwards were still considered top class, while the defence had undergone some changes. Nevertheless, Robertson seemed a capable deputy for the injured McClory, Blair was at least the equal of Alan Craig, and Ellis had developed a good understanding with Crapnell at the back.

A special train from Motherwell, for a five shilling (25p) return fare, helped the Dens Park crowd touch the 20,000 mark. The game was made dramatic by a generous Well side who nearly gave away the points to a side they had dominated for almost the full 90 minutes. New Dundee boy Norman Kirby from England twice set up centre Robertson to score. Well won the two points as McFadyen and Ogilvie countered, Duncan's second header clinching it with only three minutes to spare. But Jimmy Crapnell had hurt his arm and would miss the following game.

Scotland's next international was scheduled for late November against the visiting Austrians. As good outside-rights were at a premium, many felt that Ogilvie might get his chance; apart from new goalie Robertson, Duncan was now the only uncapped player in the Well side. It was also felt that Motherwell's most capped player, Stevenson, was again displaying international form, and the fact that two of the selectors would be at Motherwell's next game at Fir Park seemed a happy coincidence.

Hibs had taken Moffat, Well's utility forward, from Fir Park earlier in the season and he now returned with an ambitious club anxious to retain its regained top division status – they had vainly tried to sign Neil Dewar, ex-Thirds, from Manchester United. However, it was Hibs' present centre-forward, Flucker who, against the run of play and set up by Moffat, opened the scoring. The superiority shown by the Steelmen did not translate into goals until, in a five-minute second-half spell, McFadyen and Ferrier strikes won the points. Now it was Ellis's turn to take a knock, his leg injury meant that he would miss out on Wales's meeting with England at Newcastle.

As the Austrian game approached there was renewed debate around Bob Ferrier's eligibility to play for Scotland. The *Sunday Mail* condemned the ruling that kept him out as being outmoded, having been drawn up in an era when, in the world, only the four home nations played international football. If Celtic's Kennaway, born in Canada, and Hodgson in England, born in South Africa, could play for their countries then why not Ferrier, whose quality Scotland needed – 'What would Scottish football be like just now without Motherwell?' the newspaper asked. The answer to the controversy lay in the ruling that a player born in one of Great Britain's widespread dominions or colonies could take his father's nationality. Thus, Kennaway's father hailed from Dundee and Hodgson's father was English. Despite his parents belonging to Dumbartonshire, and his growing up in Scotland, the fact that Ferrier was born while his parents were in Sheffield technically made Bob 'an Englishman'.

Two further home games followed for Well and provided an opportunity to consolidate their lead at the top. Airdrie arrived on a raw day that cut the crowd to only 6,000. A heavy pitch made controlled play difficult but, although Well were in command, Moore made a mazy run to open for the visitors. Ogilvie bravely launched himself at a Ferrier cross to equalise and McFadyen followed with a scoring drive. Although Willie added another fifteen minutes later, the *Sunday Mail* considered that McMenemy, Stevenson and McFadyen 'should have had about 10 goals between them'. The Old Firm endured a bad day; Rangers lost 1-3 to St Johnstone in Perth while Celtic were beaten by the same score at Ayr. It meant that, although Rangers had a game in hand, Well were now six points in front. The momentum was maintained against St Mirren when a 1-0 win took both points in a dour struggle. Given a share of good fortune, Well looked to be on track for a serious title challenge.

Duncan Ogilvie's continuing good form was recognised with a call up by the international selectors for the Austria game. McFadyen was also included, his goal-tally for his club standing at 22. George Stevenson was ruled out of contention as his 'muscle knock' was still troubling him. Some of the press in England seemed dubious about an incapacity that kept him from the Scotland team but not from his club's. Sailor retorted: 'The Trainer has to take the utmost care of him. George requires almost constant attention to keep him fit for one match a week' (*Daily Record*). Alex James, Arsenal's legendary diminutive inside-left from Mossend, had faced criticism in April when he had withdrawn from the Scotland side but then turned out for the Highbury club on the Saturday.

In Vienna two years earlier, the Austrians had shaken Scottish football with a 5-0 humiliation of the visitors, so there was an element of pride at stake. The two Motherwell men certainly shirked nothing and gave their all in the eventual 2-2 draw. An own-goal by the Austrians had been followed by a McFadyen strike after Ogilvie's header had come off the bar. Duncan again came close when his shot hit the side-netting. Despite this plucky show by both players, neither would again feature in the full Scotland line up.

On the first Saturday of December, Rangers faced a tricky visit to third-placed Aberdeen, while Well had a comparatively easy task at Third Lanark, entrenched in relegation trouble in third bottom. The Steelmen opened the scoring through Ogilvie, after he had exchanged cross-field passes with Ferrier. Just after the break McMenemy shot in a second and everything looked rosy. The turning point came when McFadyen missed a sitter and Thirds came back with two goals in half a dozen minutes to share the points. If Thirds had played that way every week they wouldn't have been relegation candidates. For Well it seemed as if the very fact of still being the nation's only unbeaten side was too much of a burden, intensifying as each game came up. 'Brigadier' commented in the *Daily Record*: 'I wonder if a defeat would do Motherwell good by taking off some of the strain, because if it would do that it would be worth it.' There was bad news in Rangers' 2-1 win at Pittodrie that clawed back Well's lead to five points with a game more played. More worrying was the fact that McFadyen and Crapnell had suffered head knocks, the full-back requiring stitches.

Alex Gibson's Ayr United were themselves on an unbeaten run of eleven weeks, and although they were eleven points behind Well they had supplanted Aberdeen in third place. The Ayrshire club were reported to be trying to emulate the successful Motherwell set-up: building on strong wing play, using a speedy and strong centre, refusing to part with their best players, etc. All of the game's seven goals came in an action-packed second period when the Steelmen were 4-0 up by the 65th minute. The 'Honest Men' didn't give up and grabbed two late goals after McGibbon had hit his penalty against a post. McMenemy, the most accomplished forward on the park, scored the last from a narrow angle at his second attempt for a 5-2 victory. Amazingly, though perhaps in a way that was indicative of his commitment, Ben Ellis had played on with a fractured collar-bone for much of the game. He had been hurt when sandwiched between the goalkeeper and centre-forward McGibbon. Unfortunately for club and player, it was expected that Ellis would be out for at least six weeks.

Ben Ellis had been born in Aberbargoed in Mid Glamorgan and played for local sides Bargoed Town and Tredegar before going over to Northern Ireland and Bangor FC. It was from there that word reached Motherwell of promising full-back Ellis, prompting John Hunter and director Taggart to go over and see for themselves. According to Ben's daughter, Nita, it was actually her uncle Bill, the Bangor right-back, they had gone to look at, but were more impressed by his brother Ben on the left. Learning that Ben was available for £800, a second visit, this time with director Cuthbertson to lend weight, was duly arranged, but Motherwell were only prepared to go as high as £500.

In the event, Ben came to Fir Park for a mere £350 plus a further £50 after he had played twelve first-team games. Ben would go on to play many more than the required dozen. Variously described as 'a dashing young Welshman', 'breezy and stylish', he cut a trim figure at 5ft 9in tall with a comparatively light build, his top weight being 10st 10lbs. With his sandy blond hair swept back against his head, even in repose Ellis gave the impression of speed; the *Motherwell Times* described him thus: 'Ben is the type of player who goes all out all the time and his spectacular punting was a source of delight to the Fir Park habituees.' At left-back Ellis replaced Sandy Hunter who had shifted between there and the right side, and he quickly established himself as a strong and wholehearted defender. He had quickly gained international recognition at Fir Park and had turned out three times so far for Wales. Many years later, Ben's wife Laura and daughter Nita spoke of him as being 'a happy soul and was always smiling'. His son-in-law added, 'You could not have met a more peaceable man' (*Motherwell Times*). Needless to say, this was not the way some opposition fans would have viewed the never-say-die, two-footed defender who went into the tackle with a lion-hearted commitment.

Nita still speaks of her father as a mild-mannered person, but recalls how, before a game against Celtic, he hoped that the speedy and dangerous outside-right Jimmy Delaney would know within the first five minutes that Ben was around! On the other side of the Old Firm, Nita was once introduced to Rangers' Willie Thornton as Ben's daughter, only for Thornton to remark that yes, he knew her father, 'and I've still got the bruises to prove it!'

Ellis was usually among the first to turn up for training, not just because he lived nearby in Edward Street (the site of the present Fir Park club), but also because of his dedicated and professional attitude. Sailor Hunter had all his men turn up for training in smart dress: suit, shirt, tie, and hat, too, for some. Ben wore a bowler, then a trilby later.

Ellis's committed attitude apparently carried over into family holidays. The Ellis family were close to Willie Dowall's, going on holiday together to Blackpool, where the hotel was hand-picked by Ben, situated as it was near to a handy ground he and his teammate could use for training. One day, as the group strolled along the Pleasure Beach, a 'Beat the Goalie' set-up proved too much of a temptation for the two Motherwell men to pass by. With prizes of jars of sweets and toys on offer, Ben and Willie took turns to blast the shots in. After several successful 'goals' the owner asked Ben if he would like to move along. The two players apologetically explained their professional status and left the man in peace, but Nita went away with her arms full of sweets and dolls.

Ellis would be missed while his collar-bone healed. There had been anxious moments for the Well support with several narrow wins, sometimes secured only with a late winner, but the 5-2 win over Ayr had helped allay concerns. Rumour had it that the Austrian agent – or 'impresario' – Herr Meisl, had asked the club to visit his country but Hunter denied this. More concrete was the expected and welcome invitation from the South African FA to return in the coming close season. The successful tour of 1931 brought back fond memories for those who had participated, particularly as it had been the precursor to winning the championship. A telegram was sent off accepting the offer, subject to approval by the SFA. The hard financial facts were that Motherwell would receive £1,200 'plus other allowances as 1931'.

There was renewed speculation that Scotland centre Hughie Gallacher might arrive at Fir Park as he was 'fed up' at Stamford Bridge, but others were expressing interest in him too, among them Sunderland, Everton, who needed to replace the injured Dixie Dean, Manchester United, as well as continental sides such as Nimes. Motherwell's present centre, McFadyen, on 22 goals, was seven behind leader Jamie Smith of Rangers. Of greater concern was the fact that Willie had not scored for a month, but there might be an opportunity to redeem that at Cowdenbeath.

The fog that blanketed parts of the central belt put paid to four First Division fixtures, including Hamilton's meeting with Rangers, but out in Fife the air was clear enough, although Cowdenbeath's field was bone hard. Jimmy Crapnell was shifted over to left-back in order to allow Willie Dowall to cover for Ellis, and although Ferrier had undergone a dental operation a couple of days before, he was fit to play. Bob's and Willie McFadyen's goals gave Well a half-time lead that the eager Fifers were unlucky not to claw back in the second half. McFadyen then added two more with hard-driven shots for his hat-trick, his best tally since he'd taken all five goals at Dumfries back in late August's heatwave. And now, although they had two games to make up, Rangers had fallen seven points behind Motherwell – the widest gap the Steelmen had ever opened up over their rivals:

	P	W	D	L	F	A	Pts
Motherwell	22	19	3	0	56	18	41
Rangers	20	16	2	2	64	20	34
Ayr	22	10	7	5	55	59	27
Aberdeen	21	11	4	6	52	30	26

Unfortunately, the serious injuries that had taken out two of Well's international players were merely a precursor to a horrendous spate of knocks and hurts that were now visited upon the Steelmen. A run-of-the-mill home game against Clyde saw enforced changes due to Crapnell dropping out with a 'sprung muscle' and Bob Ferrier suffering from a knock behind his knee, their places being taken by two youngsters signed earlier from the junior ranks – Andrew Sinclair and Charlie Johnstone respectively. The Well half-backs, perhaps overly conscious of the two reserves behind them, were nervous throughout. The unfamiliar line-up pressed forward early on, but Clyde went ahead against the run of play when a shot deflected in off young Sinclair. John Blair's penalty before the break brought some hope but Clyde had gained the upper hand and, with the Well forwards making poor defenders, Carroll's 55th-minute goal was enough to win the game. With this, the first League defeat since February, Well's run of 31 unbeaten games was thus surrendered tamely. Perhaps, with that record now broken, the pressure might be released as some commentators had felt. But as the three-game holiday period approached, the injuries came thick and fast. The schedule read: away to St Johnstone on Saturday, home to neighbours Hamilton on Monday for the New Year derby, and away to Falkirk on the next day. Rangers had two home games, the other being at Celtic Park.

Play-anywhere Dowall was moved up front to stand in for Ferrier against St Johnstone, Hugh Wales was shifted to right-back, and Tom McKenzie came in for him at right-half. Crapnell had failed a fitness test and young Sinclair, having made his debut the previous week, was out with a bad dose of the flu. A quick shopping trip to Hamilton brought back Willie 'Puggy' Allan, a sturdy little right-back whom Well had tried to buy for £1,600 a couple of years earlier, when the position had been posing problems. George Stevenson captained the depleted side as a goalless 45 minutes was fought out at Perth, but a goal apiece came soon after the restart. Well keeper Robertson joined the growing list of injured when he cut his hand badly; in those days goalkeepers either had no gloves or wore a woolly type that offered little protection. Who else but Dowall stood in for him in the last half-hour and put up a brave display, making a fine save from Fulton, Saints' earlier scorer. Five minutes remained when captain Stevenson rose to nod a dramatic winner. The *Sunday Mail* was moved to ask: 'Who said Motherwell weren't a fighting team?' They would certainly need to be in the coming days and weeks.

Chapter 8

~ WALKING WOUNDED ~

(JANUARY–APRIL 1934)

New Year's Day, 1934, in Lanarkshire dawned on a dismally overcast Monday. As Motherwell prepared to field their third goalkeeper of the season, against derby day opponents Hamilton, comments made back in November by Celtic manager Willie Maley now seemed prophetic: 'Motherwell ... with a luck which seems proverbial with them, have sailed along in full strength to their well-deserved position on the table today. They are worthy leaders, but I would advise them to get ready for that turn of injuries which they cannot always escape. ... Motherwell's freedom from real injuries cannot last, and Rangers with their powerful team of seasoned reserves may yet pull in the Lanarkshire lads, although, to be quite candid, I think another flag for Motherwell would be more popular than another one for Ibrox' (*Evening Times*). 'Seasoned reserves' were something in which the Fir Park club was beginning to be found wanting. Twenty-year-old Bobby Walker would now be Well's last man in defence, while the rest of the rather makeshift side that had fought back so bravely in Perth kept their places against the Acas.

The 12,000 crowd had hardly settled when Hamilton right-winger Park opened in the second minute. As the game progressed it took on an ever more desperate character for the Steelmen, starting with McFadyen having to be carried off with a head knock that resulted in an eye injury. Willie Dowall's run up the left wing ended with his fifteen-yard drive levelling the scores, to the relief of the Motherwell supporters present. There would have been mixed emotions as Willie McFadyen reappeared after the break, but out on the left wing, as Dowall now filled the centre's berth. Further knocks were taken by Ogilvie and Dowall, but the wounded McFadyen proved to be Well's saviour with a match-winning header, even though there were still 30 minutes left. With the numbers of injured growing, it had been a costly two points earned.

Celtic Park witnessed another Old Firm draw that helped edge Motherwell six points in front, but that good news was outweighed by that of the walking – albeit limping – wounded around Fir Park. The casualties invited much concern on the part of everyone, from the trainers Wull Walker and Andy Donaldson, to Chairman Tom Ormiston.

Duncan Ogilvie's ankle ligaments were damaged, Dowall had hurt his shoulder, McFadyen's right eye had required four stitches, while both McMenemy and McKenzie had finished the game at Douglas Park hirpling off the field.

There was, literally, no time for feeling sorry for themselves as a trip to Falkirk was on the card for the following day, the third of the holiday fixtures. The latest reserve to be drafted in was Hugh Murray, signed from junior outfit Cambuslang Rangers at the start of the season, and Murray now found himself pitchforked in at right-half in a side showing four further changes from yesterday's makeshift line-up. At least 20,000 crammed into Falkirk's reconstructed Brockville ground, many finding unconventional vantage points from which to view the impending action: some sat on the boundary wall, others were perched atop the numbers board used for the dog-racing, while, most dangerously, a large group squeezed onto the roof of the enclosure. Their weight made the roof begin to sag, but when warned by the police, they merely inched away from the sagging middle.

Before the game, Chairman Tom Ormiston had optimistically 'talked up' the reserves who had come into the side. They certainly put on a fighting display and despite the Bairns opening in a breakaway, goals from Charlie Johnstone, who was set up by McFadyen, and then from McFadyen himself, set up in his turn by Johnstone, were quickly followed by one from Tom Wyllie. After the 3-1 victory a relieved Mr Ormiston was perhaps more frank when he admitted to the *Daily Record*: 'If we have any more serious injuries, we are done. ... We have taken our chance with reserves. Our policy has paid. We don't believe in releasing players and that policy has been justified. We hope to go on and win the League and Cup in order to encourage provincial football.' As the players' bus prepared to leave Falkirk, news came that sent hearty cheers ringing around the coach: Partick had held Rangers to a 2-2 draw at Ibrox, meaning that Motherwell had now restored that huge seven-point lead at the top of the table, with just twelve games to play.

	P	W	D	L	F	A	Pts
Motherwell	26	22	3	1	64	23	47
Rangers	24	18	4	2	81	26	40
Aberdeen	25	14	5	6	64	32	33

'Puggy' Allan had been forced to play at left-back since his signing from Hamilton in December, but with Jimmy Crapnell passing his latest fitness test, Allan was fielded in his more accustomed right side. The only section of the team left intact for the visit of Queen of the South was the half-back line of Wales, Blair and Telfer. Queens had earned a great deal of respect with their wins at Hearts, Celtic and Ayr, but on 6 January it was Well who shot in front after only seven minutes through stand-in centre Wyllie. This bright opening wasn't followed up, and that was to prove fatal. Queens were gifted an equaliser inadvertently set up by Crapnell who later broke down, his injury obviously not yet fully cleared up. The Dumfries side's winner was down to some bad fortune when the ball bounced off referee Hudson for Cumming to drive it past an edgy Walker in Motherwell's goal. In a desperate attempt to grab the equaliser McFadyen, his head wound heavily plastered, switched to the centre, but it was to no avail and both points were gone.

Inevitably, the press billed the Steelmen's visit to Ibrox as a possible championship decider, but as Well's injury list looked to be shortening, their supporters must have felt hopeful. Goalkeeper Robertson, Ben Ellis, Tom McKenzie and Willie Dowall all were set to return for duty and, encouragingly, Allan McClory had at least been able to look in on training at Fir Park. He had finished attending the Glasgow Nursing Home where he had been receiving treatment and would now have massage at the club. These dark days of so many injured players meant that, unusually for Motherwell, the team sheets were not given out until the last minute.

A healthy Well following was helped on its way to Glasgow's Govan district by football 'special' trains from Motherwell to Ibrox station for a shilling (5p), as well as by many buses and motor cars. (In January 1933 there were only 615 cars registered in Motherwell and Wishaw, while Greenock had 594 and the whole of Glasgow a little over 12,000.) The crowd of 70,000 saw Bob McPhail's sixth-minute opener sting Well, who then attempted to hold the Ibrox men with an offside trap, the shout of 'All out, boys!' erupting from the defenders. It didn't work fourteen minutes after the turnaround: Main looked offside as he gathered McPhail's pass, then hit the woodwork before McPhail latched onto the rebound to double Rangers' lead amid the protesting Well players.

Ellis looked decidedly unfit by now but the Ibrox crowd had shown little affection for 'the hard-going, devil-may-care Ben' (*Sunday Mail*). When he 'accidentally' caught centre-forward Fleming's head with a high boot he was roundly barracked each time he got a touch thereafter. (The story was told that Ben's wife and daughter were at Ibrox that day, when a man behind them in the stand cast doubts on the stop-at-nothing Ellis's parentage. Able to stand these insults no longer, Mrs Ellis turned and laid into the offender with her umbrella. Later, at one of the many snooker exhibitions in which Ben participated, one of the officials was introduced to Mrs Ellis. She was mortified when he revealed that he had been that man in the stand.)

A recent directive had laid down that players should stop badgering the referee over his decisions. At Ibrox, while Well were protesting over offside controversies, the Rangers players, according to the *Glasgow Herald*, continually complained and appealed against referee Holborn's decisions; Meiklejohn seemed the worst offender, gesticulating and arguing, and the rule appeared to have gone by the board. Four goals in a sixteen-minute spell saw Stevenson snatch one back before Fleming added two more for the home side. Stevie then completed the scoring with a late 25-yard drive to finish it at 2-4. Where they had been 'red hot favourites' only a few weeks earlier, the two sides were now the *Daily Record*'s joint favourites for the title; Rangers lay only three points behind Well but with the advantage of having two games in hand.

The Scottish Cup's first round brought non-League Gala Fairydean from the south of Scotland to Fir Park. Well's 4-0 win was distinguished by the recall of Bob Ferrier. The *Motherwell Times* light-heartedly commented on the visiting supporters' familiarity with the Gala players, calling out their *first names*: 'which shows the tremendous change in football. Among the higher classes of soccer the spectator would have had almost to send a registered letter to the Board of Directors asking their leave to do such a thing.'

On the last Saturday of January it was back to the struggle to keep Motherwell's noses out in front in the League. As the side began to resemble its old familiar shape again, Queen's Park were seen off more easily than the 3-0 score suggests. Ogilvie had made a fine return to the right wing and Ferrier proved to be a constant danger, roving up and down on the left.

So it was with lighter hearts that Sailor Hunter's side took on Partick Thistle at Firhill in the Scottish Cup second round before the day's biggest crowd of 33,000. Thistle had been struggling around the bottom quarter of the First Division for some time and it wasn't a great surprise when Well went three goals up in 35 minutes. There was surprise in the fact that, after McMenemy had scored a couple, the third came from Ellis's boot; Ben had gathered just over the halfway line, run forward, given a couple of jumps, then from 30 yards out 'biffed' a low, spinning shot past the goalkeeper. At this point, totally in command, the Steelmen had their half-backs joining the forward line in sweeping eight-man attacks but had then complacently lost a goal a minute later. Motherwell lacked sufficient urgency in the second period and Thistle were able to stage a brave fightback to level the scores with six minutes left on the clock.

Wednesday's replay brought out the local shopkeepers and their assistants on their half-holiday and they were treated to a second-minute Ferrier corner-kick headed in by Stevenson. Tom McKenzie was tried out on the right wing in the place of the injured Ogilvie but he couldn't get the ball over decisively enough. Each side added a scrappy goal apiece and the 2-1 win would take Well through to a third round pairing with East Stirling of the Second Division.

On the Saturday beforehand, George Stevenson appeared in his less favoured inside-right position for the Scottish League in their 2-2 draw with the Football League at Ibrox Park. Neither Rangers nor Motherwell had a League game scheduled for that Saturday, so the clubs took the opportunity to replay their drawn Scottish Second XI Cup first round game at Fir Park. Well had Robertson, Telfer, McMenemy and McFadyen in their line-up, while Rangers fielded internationalists Hamilton, McDonald, Craig, Archibald, Marshall and Venters. The strength of the squad at Ibrox was further demonstrated by the fact that they also provided six men for the Scottish League side that day. Thus it was that the two star-studded 'reserve' sides confronted each other before an 8,000 crowd, with Well winning through 2-1.

Perhaps hoping for an historic Cup victory over the League leaders, East Stirlingshire were photographed before the kick-off at Fir Park; the Larbert club hadn't progressed past the first round since 1929. It took only 30 minutes to shatter any lofty dreams as Well had gone four goals up by then, the last of which was a thundering volley first-timed from just inside the box by Ferrier. The Shire men won a penalty but missed the kick before a Stevenson drive completed the rout; any Cup shock would have to wait.

Returning to League matters, an easier than expected 2-0 home win against Kilmarnock maintained the points differential at the top. While Killie had suffered without their centre 'Bud' Maxwell, a pleasing aspect for Motherwell had been the fact that they were at almost full strength, missing only Crapnell and McClory.

The Cup's quarter-finals paired Well with Lanarkshire neighbours Albion Rovers, the sole Second Division side left in the competition. As was also the case at Clyde, Falkirk and Partick, Rovers' Cliftonhill ground doubled as a greyhound racing venue. The *Motherwell Times* smugly noted how it made the ground look 'unsightly' and gave a false atmosphere, unconducive to a football match, but it also had to concede that: 'had Motherwell been the home club much of the appeal about the tie would be lost.' As it was, over 16,000 were on the Cliftonhill slopes, attracted by the prospect of seeing the top side in Scotland taking on an Albion team going well in their division – they would go on to win it. Albion had scored ten goals so far in the competition and taken the scalp of Kilmarnock in the second round.

Motherwell goalie Jock Robertson was called into agile action early on as he bravely dived at the feet of centre Renwick, but most of the pressure came from a Well side finding it hard to finish off their forward moves. When Ben Ellis petulantly kicked the ball away after conceding a foul, referee Watson immediately made the full-back retrieve the ball and replace it for Rovers' free-kick. Further Motherwell pressure after the turnaround led to a series of corners and, at last, as Ogilvie swung the ball into the middle, McFadyen gathered and shot smartly home. The lead was short-lived as seven minutes later, also from a corner, McPhee nodded in Rovers' equaliser.

At the Wednesday replay a wintry sun slanted over Fir Park's ash and earth terracing, covered now with a dusting of snow. Well made up for their previous poor finishing by running up a four-goal lead, including a McFadyen hat-trick, by half-time. Anxious eyes must have been cast skywards as swirling snow and sleet fell in semi-darkness before the sun reappeared as the second half began. Hugh Wales took advantage when Rovers' goalkeeper Crosskey was off the field receiving treatment to drive in the fifth. The *Daily Record* thought that the six Scotland selectors in the stand would have departed unimpressed by Ogilvie's lacklustre display. He had missed several excellent chances, although he did manage to net the sixth five minutes before the end.

A vital League trip was next made to Celtic Park with the Steelmen lacking only McClory from their full strength line-up. Celtic were still stuck in mid-table but with, in some cases, five games fewer played than sides around them. There was little to choose between the sides at Celtic Park but when Crum began to master Ellis, the tenor of the game swung in the home side's favour and the O'Donnell brothers, Hugh and Frank, grabbed a goal each before the interval. John Blair had fouled Crum in the box and Frank O'Donnell's penalty was stopped by Robertson, only for Frank to follow up and crash the ball in. In the midst of their second-half fightback, Well had the wind taken out of their sails when, in a breakaway, Hugh O'Donnell put in the third. It was the first time that Motherwell had failed to score in any match since the Cup final against Celtic the previous April; the last League occasion had been against Hearts away back in October 1932. The local *Times* thought the roof had fallen in and the League title hopes were 'decently, soberly, interred at

Parkhead. Rangers, meanwhile, had edged out a strong Hearts' challenge 2-1 in Edinburgh and were now just a single point behind Well. Worse though, was still to come.

The signs were ominous: last season's collapse had come, almost at the same time of year, with a defeat by the other half of the Old Firm followed by a run-of-the-mill fixture against Queen's Park which had relinquished two more points. Now, on the heels of the Celtic defeat, run-of-the-mill Partick came calling. For the second time, Motherwell rewarded their sporting and talented winger Bobby Ferrier by nominating this game as his benefit; the first had been against Celtic in 1926. Again injuries enforced changes to the side: Tom Crawley from Hamilton Acas replaced McFadyen at centre, while 'Puggy' Allan came in at right-back for Crapnell. Despite a rainy day and a poor 6,000 crowd, Well's bright start gave them a 2-0 lead by the interval, courtesy of goals from Stevenson and new boy Crawley. Thistle's goalkeeper, Johnstone, prevented further scoring and after he had stopped a powerful Stevie header, the game suddenly turned. With Ellis again losing his grip on the right-winger, three Thistle goals within nine minutes left Well reeling. With the game fizzling out, and Ellis receiving treatment on the field, it is debatable whether many of the Fir Park spectators appreciated Thistle left-winger Bains' efforts to entertain them by doing handstands! Elsewhere, a draw for Rangers against Killie was of little comfort for the Motherwell fans. Their side, leaders since 2 September, now lay in second place, and with an extra game played. Even though Well still had six matches to play, there was little doubt in the headline of the *Motherwell Times*: 'Exit The Flag'.

Both of the top sides now faced midweek games, Well on the Tuesday at St Mirren – who were also their next opponents in the Cup – and Rangers at home to Thirds on the Wednesday. Perhaps fearing that the quality of their reserve pool was inadequate for the rigours of fierce League competition, Motherwell recruited two new forwards from Manchester United to help fill the gaps caused by injuries, although, in Bob Ferrier's case, he was being 'rested'. Willie Stewart was a small – 5ft 5in – left-winger, skilled in dribbling and of such promise that he would be viewed as a possible eventual replacement for Ferrier. As a linotype operator in a printing firm, he had 'set up' his own transfer story when moving from Cowdenbeath to Old Trafford. His teammate, Charlie McGillivray, was a stockily built, perhaps less skilled but brave forward who would be played on the right wing.

Although Saints opened the scoring through Knox, the two recruits each notched their debut goals to give a half-time lead. The portents for

Motherwell's Cup semi-final were looking promising as McFadyen added a third and McMenemy and Stevenson delighted with their skilful ball control and fine passing movements. Saints, despite their League placing of seventeenth, could play much better, as those who had seen them eliminate Celtic 2-0 in the quarter-final knew well.

The latest newcomer to Fir Park, in the shape of Hugh Carlyle from local juniors Shieldmuir Celtic, lined up at centre-half in place of Blair in the League fixture at Airdrie. Although Carlyle had interested both Hearts and Aberdeen, where he'd had a trial, he did not show up particularly well and this would be his only League appearance. Hat-tricks for Stewart and McFadyen at a sunny Broomfield were enough to take the points in a 6-3 goal-feast. Running short of cover, the club brought Carlyle back again at the last moment for Blair in the Cup semi-final. As McKenzie had to replace the injured Telfer, the half-back line assumed an unusual look, with only Hugh Wales in his accustomed place. In practice, of course, the centre-half played between his full-backs, his main task being to nullify the threat posed by the opposing centre-forward, while the backs attended primarily to the opposition wing men.

Motherwell's star-studded forward line meant that their half-backs were often neglected when plaudits were handed out, but that section of the team was as important as any, and it was said that if the half-backs were on form then so was the team. Hugh Wales at right-half had been signed as a nineteen-year-old from Ayrshire juniors Kilwinning Rangers in 1929. Photographs show him as keen-looking and apparently always smiling, even when training, his thick dark hair combed back without a parting. Hugh had sturdy, muscular legs – once described as like billiard table legs, but perhaps that was only in comparison to Ellis's thin limbs – ideal for the decisive tackling and dead-ball striking that Wales was renowned for.

Willie Telfer, his partner at left-half, was facially similar to Wales when he arrived as a twenty-year-old Lanarkshire coal miner working in the mines at Shotts. Telfer also came from a junior side, Blantyre Celtic, in 1929 and he quickly established himself in the left-half position. Willie was also a strong tackler, which he combined with a two-footed ability to direct telling passes over the field. His skill in being able to receive a ball, control it and then pass it, as if all in one movement, made him a fans' favourite.

As Telfer linked productively with the left-wing partnership of Stevenson and Ferrier in front of him, he was often instrumental in initiating the sweeping forward moves that led to many of Well's goals. The *Motherwell Times* reminisced with Telfer 50 years later, noting wistfully:

'And these were indeed great days for the man from Shotts, playing behind the most celebrated left wing partnership in the game in Scotland. There were no preconceived plans about how each match ought to be played. Motherwell's style of play in the late 20s up to the the mid 30s followed a natural progression.'

Both Motherwell and St Mirren were unhappy at having to travel out to Edinburgh's Tynecastle for the 'other' semi-final, while Rangers and St Johnstone were at Hampden Park. Rangers and Well were favourites to contest the final, Motherwells' odds for their tie being 4-9 on. No less strange than the SFA's ruling to stage the tie at Tynecastle was the Motherwell board's (and possibly manager's) decision to stick with Stewart on the left wing. Although Stewart had done well so far, and was the latest in a line of candidates speculated upon as an eventual replacement for Ferrier, few expected Stewart to figure ahead of captain Bob. The *Sunday Mail* reported Ferrier's reaction: 'I never got a bigger surprise than when Mr Hunter informed me on Tuesday that I would not be playing. I understood I was only being rested and would be brought back for the Semi-Final, so you can imagine my feelings, especially as I did not think my form had fallen off.' The *Sunday Mail* calculated that Ferrier had played 562 League games for the club and scored 232 goals to date. There had in fact been a story circulating that he was going to stay on in South Africa after the tour to take up a coaching job, but he denied this: 'I want to make it clear, that I have no notion of giving up football, and fully intend resuming next season. I feel I have a few good years in me yet.' Ferrier then wished Stewart the best of luck.

The red hot favourites seemed to playing up to their form in the opening minutes of the semi-final but Saints weathered the storm and began to take control. Carlyle was looking suspect under pressure, lacking the commanding presence of Blair. The first goal arrived when Carlyle fouled centre McGregor and right-winger Jimmy Knox fired in the free-kick. Well looked disjointed but still managed to come back at Saints. Disaster struck, however, when Carlyle pulled his man down and Knox converted the penalty. That man Knox popped up again just four minutes later, driving in low for the third. It was scant consolation when McFadyen hit in a partial clearance with barely two minutes left on the clock. Perhaps the news placards offered headlines similar to the wordplay once employed when Saints had beaten Rangers with a Knox hat-trick: 'Paisley knocks for Rangers!' Well took around £700 from the game but little else: McMenemy had been cautioned for dissent and Jimmy Crapnell's poor display seemed to have blown his chances of a cap against England.

Hopes of the double had been dashed again; only the League championship was left to chase. Third Lanark were struggling to avoid the second relegation place – Cowdenbeath were already doomed – but now found themselves facing the League's two top sides in successive games. Rangers scraped home at Cathkin on Monday, 2 April to leave matters looking bleak for Thirds, who travelled to Motherwell on the Saturday. Well's outlook seemed equally bleak: out of the Cup and four points behind Rangers. Sleet and snow returned to make a mockery of recent sunny weather as Bobby Ferrier was reinstated to the side. Telfer was asked to fill in for the still-injured Blair, and Telfer's disorientation must have been apparent as he failed to cover his man to let Thirds open the scoring in only ten minutes. The old guard came to Well's rescue as Stevenson equalised and Ferrier put them into the lead; with eight minutes left, however, Thirds levelled – a classic tale of Well squandering their chances while Thirds took all of theirs.

There was still the outside mathematical possibility that Motherwell could overtake Rangers' lead of five points, with three games remaining in which to do so, but not many supporters saw it that way and only 1,500 turned up on the Wednesday for Fir Park's final League fixture, against relegated Cowdenbeath. Allan McClory made a welcome return and, despite fielding four reserves and McFadyen displaying his versatility at centre-half, Motherwell ran out 6-1 winners. It was highly improbable, but if Rangers lost their last three fixtures the title was still mathematically possible.

John McMenemy had played at outside-left in place of Stevenson, who later bumped into a *Daily Record* man at Central Station in Glasgow. George had a small brown case with his boots, 'stockings' and other kit and was on his way to Fir Park to find out his train arrangements for going to London. He had received a surprise call-up to the Scotland side to play at Wembley on the coming Saturday and, as Bob McPhail was off form, Stevie would fill the inside-left slot. He hoped to get some training in while at Motherwell. In the international, despite putting up a brave show, Scotland would go down 0-3 to their old foes.

Motherwell had two games left: at Hearts and Ayr; Rangers had a Cup final against St Mirren, away fixtures at Falkirk and Queen's Park, and Hamilton at home. The timing meant that Well would have completed their fixtures on 21 April, before Rangers had played any of theirs. Their final game was not until the 30th.

At Tynecastle many of the crowd arrived late, coming from the horse racing out at Musselburgh, for Motherwell's penultimate League game. The kick-off was at 6pm on a sunny Edinburgh holiday Monday. Hearts'

League challenge had faltered but an entertaining contest was still anticipated, as Well had to win to keep their title chance alive. Although Ellis was out, injured, John Blair returned to the side and Motherwell played some good football, but only in fits and starts with a hard-driven Stevenson grounder giving a half-time lead. A moment of madness saw Crapnell foul inside-left Coutts, but the referee waved away penalty claims, whereupon a youth jumped on to the field and made for the Well full-back. Allan McClory intervened and, playing policeman, assisted the interloper back over the perimeter wall. Coutts did muster a goal for Hearts but it came between two of McFadyen's that maintained Well's challenge, one point behind but with two more games played.

The *Daily Record* felt that the Glasgow side would have no difficulty in extracting at least a single point from their three games, but added a warning to remember 1931-32. The difference was, of course, that the Ibrox side was out in front before even kicking a ball. Cup final day still saw seven First Division fixtures, and Motherwell completed their programme at Ayr, where Ayr Races offered a counter-attraction. 'Puggy' Allan had now joined Ellis on the injured list and Sinclair deputised at left-back, while Crapnell moved over to his favoured right side. The match was a tight affair with end-to-end play, but Well's bit of extra class told. McFadyen levelled Moir's early goal before half-time then, after McMenemy had first-timed in a Ferrier cross, Willie took the ball from the halfway line, outstripped the Ayr defence and shot home from fifteen yards. Rodger pulled one back soon afterwards, but the 3-2 win brought Well's points total to 62. Motherwell were back on top of the League, one point ahead of Rangers – easy 5-0 Cup winners on the same day.

It was not a case of sitting back wondering if Rangers would overtake them, but more a resigned acceptance that the title which had seemed within their firm grasp had slipped away irretrievably. As the train carrying the tour party for South Africa steamed south towards the Scottish border, Rangers kicked off their game against Falkirk, winning 3-1. That was followed with a 4-2 win over Hamilton on Saturday, 28 August – by which time the Steelmen were aboard the liner 'Kenilworth Castle'. Rangers finished their campaign with a 1-1 draw against Queen's Park, before only 8,000 at Hampden.

Motherwell had failed to reach three figures in their League goals tally for the first time since 1929; Willie McFadyen on 38 was the second highest in Scotland behind Jamie Smith of Rangers on 41, although Willie's Cup goals took his total to five more than Smith's. From being clear favourites to take the title, Britain's only undefeated side for so long, the horrendous crop of injuries that might have been absorbed over the course of a season, hit the team in a way that Willie Maley had prophetically foreseen. That concentrated accumulation of knocks had left Motherwell desperately trying to claw their way back. Losses to the Old Firm were easier to take than the six home League points dropped to vastly inferior opposition.

Chapter 9

~ How the Mighty Fell ~

(From 1934)

The second visit to South Africa was again highly successful, both in financial terms and in an ambassadorial sense. On the hard playing surfaces the Steelmen performed even more convincingly than in 1931, their tour record comprising sixteen games, all won, with 81 goals scored for the loss of twelve. Three 'Test Matches' against the South African side were now classed as unofficial by the SFA, but they still drew crowds of 25,000. The seven-week marathon was more extensive than the first tour had been, taking in two games in Southern Rhodesia (Zimbabwe) and involved 8,000 miles of criss-crossing an enormous land. Twenty-one nights were spent on board trains, with facilities so basic that Bob Ferrier thought the rail system a throwback in time. To get from East London to Port Elizabeth along the east coast it had taken from 9.30am on Thursday to 4pm the next day, normally only seven leisurely hours by motor car. Such a gruelling schedule naturally took more of a toll on the older players but it was hoped that some of the youngsters would benefit from the experience.

Back home in July, filled with memories of the warm welcome afforded them by the various South African Caledonian Societies, the returning tourists were given a week's rest before training began. Ferrier agreed that the captaincy of the side should not be his exclusively and it was handed to George Stevenson for season 1934-35. The League programme threw up an early test of character with Rangers in wait at Ibrox on 18 August, followed only four days later by Celtic's visit to Fir Park, and made all the more difficult without Ferrier, injured at the opening trial match. While a Meiklejohn goal denied Well the points at Ibrox, the same line-up nosed in front of Celtic, courtesy of a goal by John McMenemy. By mid-September, Well had reached fourth place in the table but a poor spell with defeats at St Johnstone, Hearts, Airdrie and St Mirren saw them plummet to an unaccustomed ninth position by November. Tom McKenzie had filled the left-half slot since the Rangers' game, as Willie Telfer was out with tonsil trouble. Telfer required a stay in an Edinburgh nursing home, where he had them removed, as well as all of his teeth! Telfer wouldn't resume till the middle of November.

Included in the Scottish League XI which defeated the Irish League on Wednesday, 3 October were John Blair, Tom McKenzie and Willie McFadyen, who scored a double in the 3-2 victory. Meanwhile, George Stevenson was included in the Scotland side that fell 1-2 in Belfast; it was his last international call-up.

While Motherwell's home results included some high-scoring wins, such as a 9-3 rout of Dunfermline, the away form was frustratingly weak with several narrow losses. When Duncan Ogilvie was sidelined in early December, the club fixed up its old tormentor from the 1931 and 1933 Scottish Cup finals in the shape of ex-Celt Bertie Thomson, bought for £550 from Blackpool. Thomson's first game was against his old side at Celtic Park, when Well were beaten 2-3. On the last Saturday of the year a 2-2 home draw with Rangers prolonged Well's unbeaten home record. With little Jimmy Crapnell now retired and trying his hand at a career in insurance, injuries to Dowall and Allan meant that Hugh Wales was played at right-back. Jimmy Crapnell returned to the reserve side after the turn of the year, before retiring once again. He eventually took up football management, beginning at Alloa.

The New Year derby at Hamilton's Douglas Park degenerated into a rough-house and a humiliation for Motherwell. Ben Ellis back-chatted referee Watson and was ordered off. The red mist then descended over Hugh Wales, too, and he received his marching orders for over-physical play. With two other players off injured, Well found themselves for a time only seven-strong on the field. It was half-suggested from the sidelines that the team should leave the field in protest, but it was feared that rioting might be provoked. In the event, Motherwell finished at the wrong end of a 1-6 humiliation, dropping to eighth place. The debacle hadn't quite finished, however, as the referee also reported Chairman Tom Ormiston, director William Duffy, and manager Hunter for entering his dressing room after the match.

Still, Motherwell remained the division's only unbeaten home side until Aberdeen broke the run at Fir Park on 12 January 1935. In the Scottish Cup, a quarter-final home tie with Rangers ended with a 1-4 reverse, before a crowd of 30,000.

Although Blair, Ellis and McFadyen finished with perfect appearance records in League and Cup games in that 1934-35 season, no fewer than 25 different players had been used in the League campaign, in which Motherwell finished a distant seventh. It must have felt strange to have so many meaningless League games to play, as well as a great disappointment for a side that hadn't been out of the top five for the past nine years. A loss of £118 was declared for the season but the club maintained that finances were sound. Chairman Ormiston expressed disappointment that some of the new players 'did not fit into the Fir Park machine'. One of its useful cogs, Willie Dowall, joined English Second Division Bury during the close season, having already been loaned to St Mirren. Dowall's move seems to have been prompted by the age-old wish to improve one's earnings but the fact that he could never call any one position his own might have contributed. Winger Bertie Thomson retired from the game and sadly died only two years later.

John Blair was appointed captain at the start of 1935-36 while unlucky Willie Telfer underwent surgery for an ulcer and would as a consequence miss the first half of the season. Telfer's contract didn't allow for wages while out through illness but the club gave him £3 weekly until he was able to train again. (Telfer would receive a benefit this season, in common with Hugh Wales and George Stevenson – the second for Stevie.) As for McMenemy and McFadyen, they would now languish in the reserves for long spells. An indifferent start to the League campaign was compounded by defeats at the hands of the Old Firm, the first time Celtic had managed a win at Fir Park since 1926. Following a 0-2 home collapse against Queen of the South, the *Motherwell Times* wrote frustratingly of the sight of 'hundreds' aiding and abetting the Celtic-Rangers dominance by leaving the town to follow the Glasgow giants, so that the home-town team did not receive the support it deserved. This state of affairs has, of course, unfortunately continued down the years.

An indication of modern technological developments was seen when BBC radio broadcast its first commentaries from Fir Park. Sportswriter Alan Breck of the *Daily Express* did the commentary at the Clyde game on 11 January 1936. At Molineux, the irrepressible Ben Ellis, gaining his fifth Welsh cap, starred in a 2-1 win over England. More disappointment awaited Motherwell in the Scottish Cup, when struggling Clyde won a quarter-final 3-2 before 25,000 at Shawfield.

It seemed that the old policy of not selling top men was finally extinguished when Duncan Ogilvie was sold to Huddersfield for £2,900 in March 1936. Before long, Celtic thrashed Motherwell 5-0, but the eventual champions were the only side to take maximum points from Well, who finished fourth. Ferrier proved that he still had the old Cinquevalli left foot by ending up the club's top scorer, but with a mere fourteen goals. The season's total of 77 was the lowest for ten years and could be traced directly to Ogilvie's departure and to just 22 games for McFadyen – Willie had been the reserves' top scorer with eighteen.

The 1936-37 season saw an early six-game unbeaten run under the captaincy of Ben Ellis. McFadyen again figured at centre-forward but

Ferrier made only nine first-team outings and John McMenemy played his final game for the club on a quiet Monday evening in a Lanarkshire Cup-tie at Fir Park, when Albion Rovers were beaten 6-1; he moved to Partick Thistle for £1,000 – only £100 less than what he'd cost the club eight years before.

Following a 2-3 defeat at Ibrox, Allan McClory was dropped to the reserves. Well's veteran goalie would leave in 1937 to spend three years at Albion Rovers before returning to Fir Park during the Second World War. 'Big Allan' would give several years' more service to his first senior side, but not always as the first-choice goalkeeper. Centre-half John Blair's form, however, was such that he was chosen for the Scottish League and he played in the 5-2 victory over the Irish League at Ibrox, and Ellis again figured in a winning Welsh side when they defeated Scotland 2-1.

It seemed safe now to let McFadyen leave but, by the time he joined Huddersfield in December 1936, he had still managed thirteen goals. He was exchanged for the recently departed Ogilvie, who returned to his out-side-right berth without missing a game until the end of the season. Motherwell capitalised on the connection with Huddersfield, playing them twice – at Leeds Road in a charity game for Huddersfield Infirmary (3-1) and then in April for Ellis's benefit at Fir Park (2-2) when McFadyen returned, scoring both of his new side's goals. Willie Telfer's bad luck continued, damaging his ribs in a motor car accident.

In January 1937, after a month-long illness, chairman Tom Ormiston died. The ebullient head of the club, often pictured wearing his bow-tie and a well-tailored jacket, had been a flamboyant personality. However, things hadn't gone well for him latterly. When Ormiston had stood again for Parliament in the General Election of 1935, the Labour candidate had retaken the seat, and while the club were enjoying their South African summer tour in 1934, Ormiston had faced trial for reckless driving. It was obviously a blow for himself and his family when he was found guilty and fined. At his funeral hundreds stood along Motherwell's Clyde Street (Hamilton Road) and Merry Street as the procession made its way from the 'Moorings' to Dalziel High Church and thence to Glasgow's Western Necropolis. The players wore black armbands at the Rangers game on 16 January at Fir Park and the Town band played the hymn 'Abide With Me'.

A Scottish Cup quarter-final replay with Celtic established a new Fir Park attendance record of 36,500, but Celtic came from behind to win. They went on to take the Cup, beating Aberdeen in front of an all-time record Hampden attendance of 147,000. A few days later Motherwell crushed Celtic 8-0 in the League at Fir Park, to this day Celtic's heaviest ever defeat. Motherwell's storming finish in 1936-37 carried them to fourth place, on the back of 96 goals, but the days of challenging for the championship were far now behind them.

A blend of youth and experience gave grounds for optimism for the 1937-38 season, and Well lost only twice in their first twenty games. They went top of the League on 23 October and they held pole position until the wheels came off in December, when Celtic avenged that 0-8 white-wash by scraping a 2-1 win at Fir Park. John Blair was out injured for five matches and during his absence thirteen goals were conceded and three games lost.

In the Cup, wins over Clyde, Stenhousemuir and Hamilton earned Motherwell an easy-looking quarter-final tie with Second Division St Bernard's in Edinburgh. Saints seemed to be trying to milk their meeting with the big boys by doubling the terracing charge to two shillings (10p) although it was ostensibly to keep the crowd at manageable proportions. A partial boycott by both sets of supporters did the trick, keeping the crowd down and only 3,600 were in at kick-off. On the wet and windy afternoon it was 1-1 at half-time, with the crowd building to over 5,000 through the unattended turnstiles. Saints then proceeded to put two more past a complacent Motherwell to record a shock of major proportions. That result remained one of St Bernard's landmarks until their demise during the Second World War. Motherwell never really recovered and a fifth place finish concluded a disappointing season, in which the club recorded a loss of £3,000.

After twenty years at Fir Park, Bob Ferrier now decided to call it a day. He had made a total of 697 Cup and League appearances for Motherwell, scoring around 270 times. (There are conflicting figures given for his goals total.) His deadly left foot hadn't only provided much of the ammunition for McFadyen, but had also made Bob himself one of the highest scoring wingers in British top division football. In May 1938 Ferrier was appointed the club's first assistant manager, with responsibility for coaching, scouting and supervising training; it was also specified that he assist Sailor Hunter in various administrative tasks. Ferrier's wages were set at £4 per week. Meanwhile, his old left-wing partner, George Stevenson, had missed only seven games during the season.

Against a happier backdrop of falling unemployment (Scotland's 28 per cent unemployment in 1932 had dropped to 16 per cent in 1938) the strident tones of approaching war became louder. Football again proved to be a welcome diversion and, as the employment situation improved, the crowds increased.

John Blair was appointed team captain for the 1938-39 season, which opened in a blaze of goals with an 8-5 win over Queen of the South, an indication of the quality of their attack and defence. Motherwell slid ever lower down the League, eventually finishing twelfth, conceding 86 goals, their lowest position since 1924-25.

Results went better in the Cup. Victories over Huntly (8-1), Dundee United (5-1), St Mirren (4-2) carried Motherwell into a home quarter-final against Celtic, in what was Fir Park's first all-ticket match. On match day the sight of mounted policemen in the ground to help control the 31,000 crowd was also a first but, as before, certain areas were susceptible to crushing and hundreds jumped over the wall onto the track. Playing with a T-panel ball from local suppliers McKendrick's, Motherwell won 3-1.

After an absence of five years the semi-finals of the Cup beckoned at last. Opponents Aberdeen lay in third place in the League, seven places above Well. As claret and amber were deemed to clash with the Dons' black and gold, both sides had to change strips and both hoped to wear white. The toss of a coin was guessed correctly by Motherwell and they turned out, as the *Motherwell Times* put it, 'in Corinthian garb' of white shirts and black shorts, reminiscent of the old amateur side. The game, at Ibrox, finished 1-1, but Motherwell came from behind the take the replay, also at Ibrox, 3-1.

A final without either of the Old Firm was not unique but it was unusual. Clyde had knocked Rangers out at Ibrox by 4-1, but, like Well, they had already made two unsuccessful previous appearances in the final. Media interest now, of course, included radio broadcasting and on the Friday evening before the final of 22 April 1939 a special programme featured John Hunter and Pat Travers, managers of the two clubs. On the day, against the run of play, Clyde scored first, with Motherwell's intricate displays of ball control making little headway. Well had been using their old tactic of springing the offside trap, but it backfired to present Clyde with a second. Two more goals were conceded in the closing minutes to leave Motherwell on the wrong end of a 0-4 defeat. Sailor Hunter's team were bridesmaids once again. Little consolation would be had from the tag of being the best side never to have won the Cup.

During Motherwell's years as champions and challengers, there had been stories of English club's hopes of enticing Hunter south. Now the rumours were of his possible retirement, perhaps fuelled by the news that assistant manager Ferrier was to move from Dumbarton into a house in the town's Braedale Avenue to be closer to his work.

The Cup final had seen an appeal for volunteers for the Services and in May 1939, apparently on the advice of Hunter, several Motherwell players joined the Territorial Army so that they could complete their service while having time to train and play football. When war did eventually break out, however, they were among the first to be called up into the regular Army. Meanwhile, Ben Ellis was included in the SFA summer tour to the USA and Canada, enhancing his already fearsome reputation when he burst the net with a penalty during a game in British Columbia.

In one of the last representative games before the German army invaded Poland, Ellis played for the Scottish League against their Irish counterparts in a 3-2 win in Belfast on Wednesday, 30 August 1939. Ben's daughter Nita recalls that, with the ferry to Ireland in mid-channel, all the ship's lights were switched off as a precaution against rumours of enemy submarines. Four days later, Britain declared war on Germany. The new football season was only five games old and the Scottish League was suspended. From the team of Motherwell's 1931-32 champions, Ben Ellis, Hugh Wales, John Blair, Willie Telfer and Tom McKenzie were all still first-team men at Fir Park.

George Stevenson had made his final appearance a week before war was declared; his glorious Motherwell career had spanned 510 League games and another 63 in the Scottish Cup, with twelve full international caps for Scotland and a further nine for the Scottish League. Along with assistant manager Bob Ferrier, Sailor Hunter continued to guide the side he had once moulded into champions. He would hand over the managerial reins to Stevenson after the war's conclusion, but found it hard to leave the club he had served since 1911. Hunter would stay on as club secretary until his retiral at the grand old age of 80.

A glance down the list of Scottish League winners through the years throws up the name of Motherwell as a lonely beacon in the midst of the repeated 'Celtic' and 'Rangers' in what was otherwise an Old Firm stranglehold. Not until 1947-48 would another club repeat Motherwell's achievement of winning the Scottish League Championship against the tide of the Rangers-Celtic dominance, when Hibernian finally took the title. The Second World War changed people, families and indeed society itself. The hard times of the Depression would quickly assume the quality of a lost age. It wasn't a golden age by any means, but one in which a provincial club like Motherwell could be Champions of Scotland.

Epilogue: The War and After

The war played havoc with many aspects of daily life, including the established football world. In the resurrected Scottish regional leagues, clubs had to operate within the strictures imposed by shortages of various materials and, of course, personnel. It was during the course of the conflict that several of the championship side bowed out of the game.

When war came, Johnny Murdoch, the quick-thinking 'poacher', had already retired and set up in business in Corby. Many Lanarkshire folk had gone to the burgeoning Northamptonshire steel town when manufacture had been switched there from Scotland. Murdoch had migrated south in 1936 after hanging up his boots and built up a newsagent's business in the town. It was in Corby that he passed away in September 1964, aged 63.

Willie Telfer had guested for Airdrie at the outbreak of war before turning out on three occasions for Dumbarton, who were in the same regional League as Motherwell. However, the inconvenience and cost of getting from Lanarkshire – Willie stayed in Shotts – to Dumbarton for a wage of only £2, hastened his departure from the game. His former teammate at centre-half, John Blair, served in the auxiliary police force; his duties meant he had to miss a game on occasion. Blair played on at Fir Park until he retired in 1944. A short street of new housing next to Fir Park was named 'Blair Path' in his honour in 1990, his nephew doing the honours at the ceremony.

John McMenemy, or 'Gentle John' as Alan Craig christened him, had moved from Partick Thistle to St Mirren in 1937-38. He turned out at his old familiar inside-right position or sometimes on the left for the Paisley club, but by 1940 he had retired. In later years he took up writing on football in the Glasgow press and continued to lead a quiet life. Ever the 'natty dresser', McMenemy had, along with Hunter, set the sartorial standard for the Motherwell players off the field. He died in Glasgow Royal Infirmary in February 1983 and was buried in Linn Cemetery, a couple of miles from Hampden Park.

Both Allan McClory and Hugh Wales left Fir Park after the war. 'Big Allan' returned to Motherwell in 1940 after his three-year stint at Albion Rovers and, after hostilities had ceased, he was given a free transfer in 1946. McClory spent time in Ireland with Brideville, a new Dublin side, before returning to his native Armadale where he kept working until he was 70. His comment on the era of the champions at Fir Park was simple: 'Wonderful, we were all as one – a team, and we were all good friends.'

Switched to left-half in 1939, Hugh Wales confessed to quite liking it there. He joined the Royal Artillery and played for an Army XI against Scotland in 1940 and in 1941. Late in the war he guested for Charlton, then Chelsea and Luton. His last game after returning to Motherwell was in 1946 before he too was given a free transfer. Emigrating to Canada in 1947, he worked as a mill-wright and even made a go of turning out for the Winnipeg Scottish side over a couple of seasons.

Writing in the *Motherwell Times*, John Taylor recalled seeing Willie McFadyen play for Huddersfield against Sunderland; thinking Willie was 'still lean and fit as a fiddle'. McFadyen appeared for Huddersfield when they were beaten finalists in 1938's FA Cup final, losing 0-1 in extra-time to Preston. It seemed that his new side's luck in Cup competition was no better from his old one's. Clapton Orient, whom Motherwell had visited several times for friendlies, was McFadyen's last playing venue before war came. Willie was in the RAF as a PT Instructor and played for the RAF, along with the legendary Stanley Matthews. On his return to Scotland, McFadyen became manager of Second Division Dundee United and guided the Tannadice side for several years. Both his brother Ian and his son, also Ian, played for Motherwell. Willie died aged 68 in Birmingham in 1972.

An injury sustained in 1943 while he was working at a local engineering concern put paid to Ben Ellis's career on the field. He found it hard to leave Fir Park, however, and first took on the role of groundsman before becoming assistant trainer in 1947 and then coach in 1949. After 25 years' connection with the club, he finally left in May 1955 and set up as a masseur in nearby Manse Road. Years later his wife told the *Motherwell Times* how, out in the evening for a walk, somehow they would invariably end up at Fir Park. Ellis suffered for years with arthritis, perhaps brought on, thought his daughter Nita, by being so often soaked on the wet and muddy field without having the luxury of a change strip. He passed away at his home aged just 61 after he had taken unwell at his work. Next to 'Blair Path', mentioned above, is 'Ellis Way' – a street opened by Ben's daughter in 1990, and just a stone's throw from Fir Park.

When resigning as assistant manager in May 1940 Bob Ferrier felt that he was being underused and that his long playing experience could have been better harnessed. Ferrier had moved his family from Dumbarton, thinking his services would more often be called on, but this hadn't transpired. He had been barred from board meetings and 'never took part in team selection'. Leaving Motherwell, Ferrier did war work in the Food Control Office before taking up the managership of Airdrie on a part-time basis in 1943. He took up the full-time manager's post at Ayr United near the war's end, and met up with his old left-wing partner, Stevenson, when Ayr met Motherwell in a friendly in April 1947. Sadly, they would also meet at the funeral services of old colleagues as the championship men slowly passed from the scene. Ferrier himself died in Dumbarton in April 1971, aged 71. He had been a consummate sportsman and in a career spanning over twenty years he had never been booked or sent off. His son Bob became a noted sports journalist and author.

Hunter had recommended to the board in May 1946 that George Stevenson take over as manager when he himself found the dual role of secretary-manager too onerous. With Sailor as a constant font of advice, George steered the club to Cup glory, firstly the League Cup, which was won in 1950-51. The blue riband of the Scottish Cup was secured a year later. Stevenson then oversaw the club's first relegation, although twelve months later they were back. He took charge of Scotland's Under-23s against their English counterparts in 1955, but later that year tendered his resignation. George insisted: 'I have been very happy here with Motherwell and I shall part with the club on a friendly basis.' George often returned to visit Fir Park and his son-in-law, Jim Forrest, played for the club in the 1950s. Well's most capped player for 60 years, Stevenson died in 1990 aged 85, in a residential home in Strathpeffer.

The Grand Old Man of Fir Park, John Sailor Hunter, was 67 when George Stevenson took over in 1946. Hunter's eyesight had been causing problems and he had undergone treatment in Glasgow Eye Infirmary in 1944. When he finally resigned as Secretary in 1959, aged 80, he was the longest serving Scottish football official. In April 1952, the Scottish Cup was specially brought from Hampden to Fir Park so that he could see it – bedecked in claret and amber – before it was taken on its tour around the burgh. On his retirement, Sailor was given a weekly pension by the club he had served for 48 years. Aged 87, he died in hospital in January 1966. The funeral was held at Daldowie Crematorium and his remains were interred in Airbles Cemetery, Motherwell. The mourners included Scot Symon, manager of Rangers, Celtic's chairman Robert Kelly, manager Jock Stein and old centre-forward Jimmy McGrory. It was appropriate that representatives from the Old Firm were present, recalling the feat that Sailor Hunter's championship side had once achieved.

In 1984 Hugh Wales came to Scotland to visit a relation in Irvine and the *Motherwell Times* took the opportunity to arrange a reunion of the four surviving championship men. In the Fir Park boardroom, Hugh met his left-half partner Willie Telfer, George Stevenson, and Tom McKenzie; Tom had served the club in various capacities for 53 years by then. All looked remarkably fit and well, despite Hugh Wales's once black hair now being as white as that of his old teammates. Hugh summed up the feelings of all: 'Those days at Fir Park were wonderful. They were a great bunch of guys to play with. You could not help being a good player alongside them. I was a very lucky lad to get into that team in 1931 when I was only twenty. It was so easy to play with them in the same team. We always played with the joy of playing. With the genius of manager John Hunter behind us, I suppose we just could not miss.'

GUIDE TO SEASONAL SUMMARIES

Col 1: Match number (for league fixtures); Round (for cup-ties).
e.g. 4R means 'Fourth round replay.'

Col 2: Date of the fixture and whether Home (H), Away (A), or Neutral (N).

Col 3: Opposition.

Col 4: Attendances. Home gates appear in roman; Away gates in *italics*.
Figures in **bold** indicate the largest and smallest gates, at home and away.
Average home and away attendances appear after the final league match.

Col 5: Respective league positions of Motherwell and opponents after the game.
Motherwell's position appears on the top line in roman.
Their opponents' position appears on the second line in *italics*.
For cup-ties, the division and position of opponents is provided.
e.g. 2:12 means the opposition are twelfth in Division 2.

Col 6: The top line shows the result: W(in), D(raw), or L(ose).
The second line shows Motherwell's cumulative points total.

Col 7: The match score, Motherwell's given first.
Scores in **bold** show Motherwell's biggest league win and heaviest defeat.

Col 8: The half-time score, Motherwell's given first.

Col 9: The top line shows Motherwell's scorers and times of goals in roman.
The second line shows opponents' scorers and times of goals in *italics*.
A 'p' after the time of a goal denotes a penalty; 'og' an own-goal.
The third line gives the name of the match referee.

Team line-ups: Motherwell line-ups appear on top line, irrespective of whether they are home or away. Opposition teams are on the second line in *italics*.
Players of either side who are sent off are marked !
Motherwell players making their league debuts are displayed in **bold**.

N.B. For clarity, all information appearing in *italics* relates to opposing teams.

No	Date		Att	Pos	Pt	F-A	H-T	Scorers, Times, and Referees	1	2	3	4	5	6	7	8	9	10	11
1	A	QUEEN'S PARK			W	5-1	2-1	McFadyen 34, 39, 60, 87, Murdoch 65	McClory	Johnman	Ellis	Wales	Craig	Telfer	Murdoch	McMenemy	McFadyen	Stevenson	Ferrier
	8/8		*10,000*		2			*McKenzie 29*	*Peden*	*Campbell*	*Walker*	*Hosie*	*Gillespie*	*Grant*	*Crawford*	*Bremner*	*McLelland*	*Fitzgerald*	*McKenzie*
								Ref: M Hutton (Glasgow)	With a swirling Hampden wind and Queen's reputation for unpredictability it's no surprise when the Amateurs open the scoring. However, Willie McFadyen proves himself a forceful but nippy leader with his goals. He turns provider, laying-on for Johnny Murdoch to blast home.										
2	H	RANGERS		1	W	4-2	1-1	Murdoch 40, 80, Dowall 65, Steve' 66	McClory	Johnman	Ellis	Wales	Craig	Telfer	Murdoch	McMenemy	McFadyen	Stevenson	Dowall
	15/8		**25,000**	*6*	4			*Fleming 26, Smith 71*	*Dawson*	*Gray*	*McAulay*	*McDonald*	*Meiklejohn*	*Craig*	*Fleming*	*Brown*	*Smith*	*McPhail*	*Nicholson*
								Ref: J Hudson (Glasgow)	Bill Struth's League champs open with a Fleming drive. Deputising for injured captain Bob Ferrier, Willie Dowall makes Murdoch's leveller. 'Stevie' goes on a dribble and scores a 20-yarder. Murdoch's late second earns top spot in table. It is six years since Gers last conceded four.										
3	A	AYR UNITED		1	W	3-1	1-1	McFadyen 10, Robertson 70 (og),	McClory	Johnman	Ellis	Wales	Craig	Telfer	Murdoch	McMenemy	McFadyen	Stevenson	Dowall
	19/8		*8,000*	*16*	6			*Brae 43* [Dowall 83]	*Hepburn*	*Robertson*	*Fleming*	*Turnbull*	*McLeod*	*McCall !*	*Armory*	*McGillivray*	*Merrie*	*Taylor*	*Brae*
								Ref: W Webb (Glasgow)	A bad-tempered midweek battle. With the game evenly balanced, Ayr's McCall is sent off after persistent fouling. Under pressure, Robertson heads into own net as trouble breaks out on the terraces. Willie Dowall again proves a fitting replacement for Ferrier and nets to seal the win.										
4	A	KILMARNOCK		5	L	**0-1**	0-1		McClory	Johnman	Ellis	Wales	Craig	Telfer	Murdoch	McMenemy	McFadyen	Stevenson	Ferrier
	22/8		*12,500*	*4*	6			*Maxwell 44*	*Clemie*	*Leslie*	*Nibloe*	*Morton*	*Smith*	*McEwan*	*Connel*	*Muir*	*Maxwell*	*Napier*	*Aitken*
								Ref: A McLean (Rutherglen)	Bob Ferrier returns for Well, and Killie have international left-back Nibloe restored. Well allow themselves to be rattled by a side able to mix it better than they. Aitken swings over a perfect cross for Maxwell to head home before break. After a strenuous struggle, Well tumble to fifth.										
5	A	AIRDRIE		6	D	2-2	1-2	McFadyen 20, McMenemy 60	McClory	**Blair**	Ellis	Wales	Craig	Telfer	Murdoch	McMenemy	McFadyen	Stevenson	Ferrier
	26/8		*12,000*	*19*	7			*Robertson 5, Armstrong 39*	*Wilson*	*Crapnell*	*McQueen*	*Preston*	*Blake*	*Sharp*	*Paterson*	*Robertson*	*Armstrong*	*McDonald*	*Bertram*
								Ref: P Craigmyle (Aberdeen)	The Diamonds go into this derby after five defeats. Alan McClory makes two early errors and is beaten by Robertson's 18-yarder. Murdoch hits the post before McFadyen nets with an oblique shot. Ferrier hits bar but Armstrong puts Airdrie ahead. McMenemy's swerver ties game.										
6	H	ABERDEEN		4	W	3-0	3-0	McFadyen 11, 30, 37	McClory	Johnman	Ellis	Wales	Blair	Telfer	Dowall	McMenemy	McFadyen	Stevenson	Ferrier
	29/8		7,000	*7*	9				*Smith*	*Cooper*	*Jackson*	*Black*	*McLaren*	*Ballantyne*	*Love*	*Paterson*	*Yorston*	*McDermid*	*Galloway*
								Ref: A Leishman (Falkirk)	Well's rearranged side prove too hot for feeble Dons on a sweltering day more suited to cricket. McFadyen's hat-trick is due to his fine placing for picking up crosses. John McMenemy rekindles memories of his famous father with his refined play. Motherwell now go 'carpet weaving'.										
7	A	ST MIRREN		4	W	1-0	1-0	Dowall 33	McClory	Johnman	Ellis	Wales	Craig	**McKenzie**	Murdoch	McMenemy	Dowall	Stevenson	Ferrier
	1/9		*10,000*	*10*	11				*Fotheringham*	*Hay*	*Ancell*	*Gebbie*	*Walker*	*Miller*	*Knox*	*Workman*	*McCrae*	*McIndoe*	*Meechan*
								Ref: D Reilly (Port Glasgow)	With their backs to the wall Well still carry danger in the breakaway. Against the run of play Dowall first times a Ferrier cross home. Saints pass up gilt-edged chances and winger Knox misses from three yards. 'The finest game seen at Paisley for some time,' says *Glasgow Herald*.										
8	A	HAMILTON		4	D	2-2	0-0	McFadyen 73, Ferrier 78	McClory	Johnman	Ellis	Wales	Craig	Telfer	Douglas	McMenemy	McFadyen	Stevenson	Ferrier
	5/9		*12,000*	*11*	12			*Wilson D 74, 88*	*Wright*	*Allan*	*Watson*	*Dougall*	*Hill*	*McKelvie*	*McLaren*	*Cox*	*Wilson D*	*Moffat*	*Howe*
								Ref: R Morrison (Falkirk)	Well's depleted front line misfires until McFadyen's header begins a late scoring flurry. Dave Wilson levels before Ferrier sends home a Douglas cross. Willie McAndrew's Acas fight to the end and Wilson grabs a late equaliser. John Thomson, Celtic's keeper, dies on same day.										
9	H	FALKIRK		4	W	4-1	2-0	Douglas 8, Stevenson 19, Ferrier 48,	McClory	Hunter	Ellis	Wales	Craig	Telfer	Douglas	McMenemy	McFadyen	Stevenson	Ferrier
	12/9		8,000	*12*	14			*Morgan 50* [McFadyen 65]	*Thomson*	*Scobbie*	*Hamill*	*Kennedy*	*Low*	*Gall*	*McGregor*	*Morgan*	*Miller*	*Stevenson*	*Brown*
								Ref: H Watson (Glasgow)	The pick of Well's goals is Stevenson's deft turning inside to wheel in a 20-yard drive. Sandy Hunter brings down Miller but Ferrier's protest prompts the Ref to consult both linesmen and change his penalty award to a free outside the box. McFadyen's many misses are hard to fathom.										

10	H	THIRD LANARK	3	W	6-0	4-0	McFadyen 5, 20, 29, 60, 85, Ferrier 40	McClory	Dowall	Ellis	Wales	Craig	Telfer	Murdoch	McMenemy	McFadyen	Stevenson	Ferrier
16/9		5,000	*6*	16				*Reford*	*Simpson*	*Warden*	*McFarlane*	*Denmark*	*McLellan*	*Lynas*	*McKenzie*	*Dewar*	*Blair*	*Breslin*
							Ref: D Reilly (Port Glasgow)	Versatile Willie Dowall fills in at right-back. Well overwhelm Thirds with 'machine-like precision'. Murdoch lifts one over and Ferrier hits the woodwork early on. Willie McFadyen makes amends for last week's misses, four of his five being headers from Ferrier crosses or corners.										
11	A	CLYDE	2	W	3-2	2-0	Ferrier 20, Douglas 42, Wylie 72	McClory	Dowall	Ellis	Wales	Craig	Telfer	Douglas	McMenemy	**Wylie**	McFadyen	Ferrier
19/9		*5,000*	*8*	18			*Farr 75, Boyd 90*	*Stevenson*	*McKay*	*Culbert*	*Knox*	*Gibson*	*Simpson*	*McGurk*	*Farr*	*Boyd*	*Mayes*	*King*
							Ref: P Craigmyle (Aberdeen)	'Stevie' and Clyde's Blair are in the Scotland side as Tom Wylie makes a promising debut. Ferrier first times a Wales cross for the first and Douglas threads through to unleash a high 20-yarder home. Wylie gets his own first, while Farr puts in a King cross and Boyd's shot creeps in.										
12	H	LEITH ATH	1	W	**7-1**	3-1	McFadyen 7, 15, 49,54, Douglas 40,59	McClory	Dowall	Ellis	Wales	Craig	Telfer	Douglas	McMenemy	McFadyen	Stevenson	Ferrier
26/9		3,000	*19*	20			*Nicol 30* [Stevenson 70]	*Boyce*	*Bruce*	*Forrest*	*McNeill*	*Reid*	*Crawford*	*Connolly*	*McColl*	*Nicol*	*Johnston*	*McWilliams*
							Ref: P Craigmyle (Aberdeen)	Leith keeper Boyce gains plaudits for his heroics but Well are rampant. McFadyen gets things going as he heads home a Douglas cross. Nicol nips in to score a surprise one. McFadyen gains goals from the exhibition play of Stevenson and Ferrier and Well go to the top on goal average.										
13	A	MORTON	2	D	2-2	1-2	McFadyen 15, 85	McClory	Dowall	Ellis	Wales	Craig	Telfer	Douglas	McMenemy	McFadyen	Wylie	Ferrier
3/10		*10,000*	*18*	21			*Graham 10, Black 40*	*Wilson*	*Maguire*	*Smith*	*Clunas*	*Bulloch*	*Ritchie*	*Shankley*	*Lyle*	*Black*	*Graham*	*McCartney*
							Ref: A Leishman (Falkirk)	During play, Well re-jig a front line which is already missing 'Stevie' (Scottish League in Belfast). Ellis boobs to let Graham in, but good work by McMenemy helps McFadyen to level. Black restores the lead. Craig handles in area but McClory saves penalty. McFadyen nets late cross.										
14	H	DUNDEE UNITED	1	W	5-0	2-0	McFadyen 27, 81, 88p, Douglas 30, 82	McClory	Dowall	Ellis	Wales	Craig	Telfer	Douglas	McMenemy	McFadyen	Stevenson	Ferrier
10/10		4,000	*15*	23				*McIntosh*	*Taylor*	*Penson*	*Milne*	*Gardiner*	*Watson*	*Radcliffe*	*Jackson*	*Bennet*	*Brant*	*Kay*
							Ref: T Dougray (Glasgow)	'Stevie' returns to torment the top division's newcomers. McFadyen hooks in a Ferrier pass from twelve yards to begin his hat-trick. Alan Craig goes off to have stitches in a cut eye. The wriggling 'Stevie' is brought down in the box and Scotland's top scorer McFadyen converts.										
15	H	HEARTS	1	W	2-0	1-0	McFadyen 37p, Ferrier 47	McClory	Dowall	Ellis	Wales	Craig	Telfer	Douglas	McMenemy	McFadyen	Stevenson	Ferrier
17/10		8,000	*10*	25				*Harkness*	*Herd*	*Anderson*	*Massie*	*Johnston J*	*Bennie*	*Johnstone R*	*White*	*Gardiner*	*Chalmers*	*Murray*
							Ref: P Craigmyle (Aberdeen)	As the 'Old Firm' stumble, Well go three points clear. Committed play results in several injuries before Ferrier coolly shoots, only to see Herd palm it. McFadyen slots the penalty home. With Well on top, McFadyen sends a cute pass to Ferrier who beats Harkness from a tight angle.										
16	A	COWDENBEATH	1	W	5-1	1-1	Ferrier 36, McFadyen 46, 51, 82,	McClory	Dowall	Ellis	Wales	Craig	Telfer	Murdoch	McMenemy	McFadyen	Stevenson	Ferrier
24/10		***3,000***	*11*	27			*Venters 23* [Stevenson 57]	*Edwards*	*Johnstone*	*Menzies*	*Glancy*	*Frame*	*Roberston*	*Hamil*	*Anderson*	*Paterson*	*Venters*	*Stewart*
							Ref: M Hutton (Glasgow)	Scott Duncan's Cowden are no pushovers and they open the scoring when Venters heads in from a corner. 'Stevie' shoots and Ferrier puts in the rebound to equalise. 'Stevie' has the best of the three goals after the break. McFadyen's hat-trick puts him out in front in the scoring charts.										
17	H	CELTIC	1	D	2-2	1-2	Douglas 25, Dowall 72	McClory	**Mackrell**	Ellis	Wales	Craig	Telfer	Murdoch	McFadyen	Dowall	Douglas	Ferrier
31/10		**25,000**	*3*	28			*Napier 4, 13*	*Kennaway*	*Cook*	*McGonagle*	*Geatons*	*McStay*	*Whitelaw*	*McGhee*	*Thomson*	*Scarff*	*Napier*	*Hughes*
							Ref: A Leishman (Falkirk)	Each side has two men away with Scotland as Kennaway debuts for Celts. Charlie Napier's first is a close-range shot, then he beats the whole defence to pick his spot. Douglas drives high into net after McFadyen had hit woodwork. Ferrier and McFadyen combine for Dowall to level.										
18	A	DUNDEE	1	D	2-2	0-2	McFadyen 55, 78	McClory	Dowall	Ellis	Wales	Craig	Telfer	Murdoch	McMenemy	McFadyen	Stevenson	Ferrier
14/11		*5,000*	*11*	29			*Campbell 30, Balfour 44*	*Marsh*	*Brown*	*Morgan*	*Symon*	*Gilmour*	*Blyth*	*Gavigan*	*Smith*	*Balfour*	*Campbell*	*Troup*
							Ref: D Reilly (Port Glasgow)	On a heavy pitch in constant drizzle, Dundee's 'dash' pays off as Campbell heads in a corner. Next Balfour turns and shoots home. McFadyen gets one back from twelve yards and then the equaliser from a McMenemy pass. Play turns 'hefty' as the Angus men hold out to defy Well.										
19	H	AYR UNITED	1	W	6-0	2-0	McFadyen 35, 41, 52, 70,	McClory	Dowall	Ellis	Wales	Craig	Telfer	Murdoch	McMenemy	McFadyen	Stevenson	Ferrier
21/11		5,000	*20*	31			[McMenemy 50, Craig 78]	*Hepburn*	*Robertson*	*Fleming*	*York*	*McLeod*	*McCall*	*McGillivray*	*Armoury*	*Merrie*	*Taylor*	*Fuller*
							Ref: W Holburn (Glasgow)	Ferrier hits the post and McFadyen the bar before Willie cleverly sweeps past Hepburn. His second is hotly contested and players come to grips. Alan Craig puts in a low fast drive from the edge of the area for a rare goal which is roundly cheered. Hepburn keeps the score to six.										

No	Date	Att	Pos	Pt	F-A	H-T	Scorers, Times, and Referees	1	2	3	4	5	6	7	8	9	10	11
20	H AIRDRIE		1	W	3-0	1-0	McFadyen 41, Ferrier 50, 59	McClory	Dowall	Ellis	Wales	Craig	Telfer	Murdoch	McMenemy	McFadyen	Stevenson	Ferrier
	28/11	6,000	*17*	33				*Paterson W*	*Crapnell*	*McQueen*	*Preston*	*Blake*	*Sharp*	*Paterson J*	*McDonald !*	*Armstrong*	*Law*	*Bertram*
							Ref: T Dougray (Glasgow)	An inspired McClory keeps early Airdrie attacks at bay but Armstrong hits Well's bar. A Wales through ball bounces off McFadyen into the net. Ferrier scores from a tight angle on the drop, then sends a swerving left-foot drive home. McDonald is sent off in 65 minutes after several fouls.										
21	H ST MIRREN		1	W	4-1	3-0	McFadyen 14, Moffat 17, McMen' 40	McClory	Dowall	Ellis	Wales	Craig	Telfer	**Moffat**	McMenemy	McFadyen	Stevenson	Ferrier
	5/12	9,000	*5*	35			*Gebbie 53* [Stevenson 58]	*Fotheringham*	*Hay*	*Ancell*	*Gebbie*	*Walker*	*Miller*	*Knox*	*Workman*	*Meechan*	*McIndoe*	*Rankine*
							Ref: J Hudson (Glasgow)	The crowd swells as Hamilton's game is called off. McFadyen touches in from a Ferrier shot. Back defending, 'Stevie' gathers, goes on a solo run and scores with a drooping shot. Twice McFadyen is upended and twice he misses the penalties – firstly into the keeper, then a yard wide!										
22	A THIRD LANARK		1	W	2-0	0-0	McMenemy 68, McFadyen 80	McClory	Dowall	Ellis	Wales	Craig	Telfer	Moffat	McMenemy	McFadyen	Stevenson	Ferrier
	12/12	*25,000*	*6*	37				*Waugh*	*Simpson*	*Carabine*	*Moreland*	*Clark*	*McLellan*	*Lynas*	*Jack*	*Dewar*	*McKenzie*	*Breslin*
							Ref: D Reilly (Port Glasgow)	Winger Lynas is off for 37 minutes and Thirds are unsettled. Their player-manager, Russell Moreland, sets up Breslin but his header hits a post after Ferrier twice hit the woodwork. McMenemy curls one in from a corner; then McFadyen pounces on a cross to wheel round and score.										
23	H QUEEN'S PARK		1	W	4-1	4-1	Moffat 7, McMen' 12, McFadyen 16,	McClory	Dowall	Ellis	Wales	Craig	Telfer	Moffat	McMenemy	McFadyen	Stevenson	Ferrier
	19/12	8,000	13	39			*Gillespie 14p* [Stevenson 29]	*Peden*	*Walker*	*Dickson*	*Gardiner*	*Gillespie*	*Grant*	*Crawford*	*Bremner*	*Dodds*	*McAlpine*	*McKenzie*
							Ref: A McLean (Rutherglen)	With the sun behind them, Well forwards run riot. Ex-Hamilton Willie Moffat opens as he nips in to edge home Ferrier's cross. Ellis barges Crawford and Gillespie's strong penalty hits back of net and rebounds out. 'Stevie' blasts against the bar as Queen's belatedly shut up shop.										
24	A RANGERS		1	L	**0-1**	0-1		McClory	Dowall	Ellis	Wales	Craig	Telfer	Moffat	McMenemy	McFadyen	Stevenson	Ferrier
	26/12	***55,000***	*2*	39			*English 20*	*Hamilton*	*Gray*	*McAulay*	*Meiklejohn*	*Simpson*	*Brown*	*Archibald*	*Marshall*	*English*	*McPhail*	*Fleming*
							Ref: P Craigmyle (Aberdeen)	In a clash of the league titans, a poor Well struggle against the wind as Davie Meiklejohn marshals Rangers. English's clever head-flicked goal underlines his strong input. With the wind, Well disappoint in the second half, while McMenemy ends limping and Ellis is helped off the field.										
25	H HAMILTON		1	W	3-1	0-0	Stevenson 47, McFadyen 53, Ferrier 58	McClory	Dowall	Ellis	Wales	Craig	Telfer	Murdoch	McMenemy	McFadyen	Stevenson	Ferrier
	1/1	13,000	*14*	41			*Wilson D 82*	*Wright*	*Allan*	*Watson*	*Dougall*	*Hill*	*Bulloch*	*Wilson F*	*Cox*	*Wilson D*	*McLuckie*	*King*
							Ref: D Reilly (Port Glasgow)	Acas show six changes for this Ne'erday derby at a wet and blustery Fir Park. In a second half scoring burst, Wales lobs for 'Stevie' to head in then McFadyen scores his 40th counter before Murdoch crosses in from the right for Ferrier to drive home. Dave Wilson nets in a breakaway.										
26	A FALKIRK		1	W	3-2	2-0	Murdoch 6, Moffat 36, McFadyen 51	McClory	Mackrell	Ellis	Wales	Craig	Telfer	Murdoch	Moffat	McFadyen	Stevenson	Ferrier
	2/1	*10,000*	*17*	43			*Miller 50, Morgan 73*	*Ferguson*	*Richardson*	*Hamill*	*Kennedy*	*Townsley*	*Hutchieson*	*McGregor*	*Stevenson*	*Morgan*	*Miller*	*Gall*
							Ref: A McLean (Rutherglen)	It's still stormy as 'Stevie' faces his brother John. Both sides are keen, despite tough games yesterday. Murdoch taps in a parry by Ferguson; then Moffat nods home from a free. Miller scores from a low cross but McFadyen replies immediately after. Morgan looks offside as he nets.										
27	H KILMARNOCK		1	W	4-0	2-0	Ferrier 34, 40p, 80, Wylie 48	McClory	Dowall	Ellis	Wales	Craig	Telfer	Murdoch	Moffat	Wylie	Stevenson	Ferrier
	9/1	6,000	*6*	45				*Bell*	*Falconer*	*Leslie*	*Morton*	*Smith*	*McEwan*	*Connell*	*McLeod*	*Maxwell*	*Duncan*	*Aitken*
							Ref: J Love (Helensburgh)	Both sides are understrength on another atrocious day. Killie's Maxwell heads against the bar. Bob Ferrier plays keepy-up and nets on the run. Murdoch is tripped in the box and Ferrier converts. Again Murdoch is brought down: Bell stops Ferrier's penalty but Bob nets the rebound.										
28	A ABERDEEN		1	W	1-0	0-0	McFadyen 67	McClory	Dowall	Ellis	Wales	Craig	Telfer	Murdoch	Moffat	McFadyen	Stevenson	Ferrier
	23/1	*12,000*	*8*	47				*Smith*	*Cooper*	*McGill*	*Fraser*	*Falloon*	*Ballantyne*	*Love*	*Adam*	*Armstrong*	*Beattie*	*McLean*
							Ref: W Holburn (Glasgow)	Dons held both of the 'Old Firm' here last month, but last week lost to Arbroath in the Cup. Moffat misses a 'sitter' then hits the post. Johnny Murdoch races down the wing and crosses for McFadyen to head in from close-in. He has now equalled Hugh Ferguson's 42 goals for Well.										

No	H/A	Opponent					Scorers											
29	A	LEITH ATH	1	W	5-0	2-0	Moffat 13, 18, 85, Wylie 60, 75	McClory	Dowall	Ellis	Wales	Craig	Telfer	Murdoch	Moffat	Wylie	McFadyen	Ferrier
	6/2	*3,000*	*20*	49				*Boyce*	*Allan*	*Lockie*	*McNeil*	*Reid*	*Crawford*	*Thomson*	*Laidlaw*	*Nicol*	*Coutts*	*Johnston*
							Ref: W Webb (Glasgow)	Leith are lively but can't finish despite playing Coutts, signed in midweek from Hearts. Flu victim 'Stevie' joins the injured McMenemy in the stand. Leith hit bar twice and post too, but Well take all of their chances and are two up by the time Leith's Allan goes off with a fractured arm.										
30	H	MORTON	1	W	4-2	1-0	Murdoch 7, 77, McFadyen 62, 70	McClory	Dowall	Ellis	Wales	Craig	Telfer	Murdoch	McMenemy	McFadyen	Stevenson	Ferrier
	17/2	3,000	*16*	51			*Lyle 66, Anderson 89*	*McArthur*	*McGuire*	*Smith*	*Clunas*	*Hunter*	*Ritchie*	*Shankley*	*Lyle*	*Black*	*Anderson*	*McCartney*
							Ref: W Webb (Glasgow)	Full strength Well are watched by shopkeepers and merchants on a Wednesday half-day. Murdoch counts with two headers, while McFadyen twice bears down on the keeper to net his goals. Lyle scores from a Ritchie free-kick and Anderson breaks away to score with an angled drive.										
31	A	DUNDEE UNITED	1	W	6-1	2-0	Murdoch 30, 35, McFad' 47, 49, 51, 78	McClory	Dowall	Ellis	Wales	Craig	Telfer	Murdoch	McMenemy	McFadyen	Stevenson	Ferrier
	20/2	*6,000*	*19*	53			*Taylor 57p*	*McIntosh*	*Taylor*	*Penson*	*Milne*	*Morris*	*Watson*	*Glover*	*Brant*	*Dyet*	*Kay*	*McGlynn*
							Ref: H McArthur (Airdrie)	Royal Scots abroad clamour for news of Well's results. United are fighting against relegation and Murdoch's two goals from close-in are hard on them. McFadyen seals his hat-trick with a solo run and chip over the onrushing McIntosh. Alan Craig handles and Taylor puts away the kick.										
32	A	HEARTS	1	W	1-0	1-0	Stevenson 42	McClory	Dowall	Ellis	Wales	Craig	Telfer	Murdoch	McMenemy	McFadyen	Stevenson	Ferrier
	27/2	*21,000*	*11*	55				*Harkness*	*Anderson*	*King*	*Massie*	*Johnston J*	*Bennie*	*Johnstone R*	*White*	*Battles*	*Smith*	*Murray*
							Ref: J Thomson (Hamilton)	Alan McClory saves from a great Battles drive and Well have two good chances early on. Both Alan Craig and Stevenson have head injuries attended to. Although 'Stevie' could have laid one off for McFadyen to equal the scoring record, he flashes it between keeper and post himself.										
33	A	CELTIC	1	W	4-2	2-1	Murdoch 14, 55, Stev' 39 McFad' 60	McClory	Dowall	Ellis	Wales	Craig	Telfer	Murdoch	McMenemy	McFadyen	Stevenson	Ferrier
	12/3	*30,000*	*7*	57			*Thomson 25, O'Donnell 65*	*Kennaway*	*Cook*	*McGonagle*	*Morrison*	*McStay*	*Geatons*	*Napier*	*Thomson*	*O'Donnell*	*Smith*	*Kavanagh*
							Ref: A Leishman (Falkirk)	With hope of the Double gone, Well make a push for the Flag. They press Celts hard and Murdoch runs Ferrier's corner into the net. Thomson equalises in off a post before 'Stevie' heads in from a corner. Willie McFadyen nods in from near the line to equal Celt McGrory's record 49.										
34	H	PARTICK TH	1	W	1-0	0-0	Stevenson 88	McClory	Dowall	Ellis	Wales	Craig	Telfer	Murdoch	McMenemy	Moffat	Stevenson	Ferrier
	19/3	7,000	*6*	59				*Jackson*	*Calderwood*	*Rae*	*Elliot*	*Donnelly*	*McLeod*	*Ness*	*McGourty*	*Wylie*	*Ballantyne*	*Torbet*
							Ref: R Morrison (Falkirk)	McFadyen is out injured and in his place Moffat is off form. Well have the bulk of possession but it's long-range tries from Ellis and Craig that threaten. Keeper Jackson and local man Donnelly hold the Well forwards until 'Stevie' shifts into the centre where he slides in to prod home.										
35	H	DUNDEE	1	W	4-0	3-0	Stevenson 25, Moffat 38,85, Wales 44	McClory	Dowall	Ellis	Wales	Craig	Telfer	Murdoch	Moffat	Wylie	Stevenson	Ferrier
	26/3	5,000	*9*	61				*Marsh*	*Morgan*	*Gilmour*	*McNab*	*McCarthy*	*Symon*	*Gavigan*	*Robertson*	*Balfour*	*Campbell*	*Troup*
							Ref: A Leishman (Falkirk)	Wylie is in for injured McFadyen and John McMenemy is being rested. It is a tight game until Well break through when 'Stevie' lifts the ball over a defender then lashes it in as it comes down. A rare Wales goal comes in a solo run from midfield and Well are looking good for the title.										
36	A	PARTICK TH	1	D	0-0	0-0		McClory	Dowall	Ellis	Wales	Craig	Telfer	Murdoch	Moffat	McFadyen	Stevenson	Ferrier
	2/4	*32,000*	*5*	62				*Jackson*	*Calderwood*	*Rae*	*Elliot*	*Donnelly*	*McLeod*	*Ness*	*McGourty*	*Wylie*	*Ballantyne*	*Torbet*
							Ref: J Hudson (Glasgow)	Sir Harry Lauder is in the Firhill stand as McFadyen returns, keen to break the goal record. It's not to be, as he looks unfit and his forwards have an off-day. Thistle's Ness heads against a post and Moffat steps in and wastes Ferrier's shot. It's only Well's third time without scoring.										
37	H	COWDENBEATH	1	W	3-0	0-0	Ferrier 53, McMenemy 55, McFad' 89	McClory	Dowall	Ellis	Blair	Craig	Telfer	Murdoch	McMenemy	McFadyen	Stevenson	Ferrier
	16/4	**2,500**	*12*	64				*Edwards*	*Johnstone*	*Russell*	*Robertson*	*Menzies*	*Campbell*	*Hamil*	*Frame*	*Paterson*	*Venters*	*Stewart*
							Ref: D Reilly (Port Glasgow)	A blank first half builds up tension, broken by Ferrier from a Murdoch cross. Russell deflects in McMenemy's shot. McFadyen is given every chance to score and break the record which he does dramatically at the death. The Fifers made it tough for Well, still, the title is all but won.										
38	H	CLYDE	1	W	3-0	2-0	McFadyen 15, 80, McMenemy 23	McClory	Dowall	Ellis	Blair	Craig	Telfer	Murdoch	McMenemy	McFadyen	Stevenson	Ferrier
	30/4	7,000	*13*	66				*Stevenson*	*Russell*	*Culbert*	*Gibson*	*Summers*	*Mayes*	*McGurk*	*Munro*	*Boyd*	*Smith*	*King*
	Home	Away					Ref: D Reilly (Port Glasgow)	Alan Craig is to have the game as his benefit. McFadyen stretches his new record first with a header and then a prod home. Before an open goal he blasts one against the bar. McMenemy scrambles a rebound home while lying prone. Clyde show no respect and battle till the end.										
Average	8,200	14,800																

Scottish Cup					F-A	H-T	Scorers, Times, and Referees	1	2	3	4	5	6	7	8	9	10	11
1	H	STENH'SEMUIR	1	W	7-2	4-0	Fer' 9, McM 11, Mur' 12,75, McF 14,63,	McClory	Dowall	Ellis	Wales	Craig	Telfer	Murdoch	McMenemy	McFadyen	Stevenson	Ferrier
16/1		3,400	*2:4*				*Cowan 62, Mooney 74* [Stevenson 60]	*Fraser*	*Turnbull*	*Prior*	*Cowie*	*Brown*	*Mooney*	*Knox*	*Sutton*	*Hart*	*Cowan*	*Robertson*
							Ref: T Small (Dundee)	In wind and heavy rain Ferrier opens with a walking pace goal from a tight angle then McMenemy crashes in a left foot drive. Murdoch and McFadyen grab doubles and 'Stevie' gets one but 'Muir are still game as Cowan blasts in a 35-yarder and a Mooney grounder beats McClory										
2	A	QUEEN'S PARK	1	W	2-0	2-0	Stevenson 7, Moffat 30	McClory	Dowall	Ellis	Wales	Craig	Telfer	Murdoch	Moffat	McFadyen	Stevenson	Ferrier
30/1		*58,000*	*14*					*Smith*	*Campbell*	*Walker*	*Gardiner*	*Gillespie*	*Grant*	*Crawford*	*Bremner*	*McLelland*	*McAlpine*	*McKenzie*
							Ref: P Craigmyle (Aberdeen)	The crowds on Hampden's slopes see a poor tie although Stevenson gets Well off to a great start with a header that trundles over the line. Wales is the best player afield and Moffat's head deflects his 30 yard pop away from Smith, onto bar then down and in off the keeper's neck!										
3	H	CELTIC	1	W	2-0	1-0	Murdoch 21, Ferrier 76	McClory	Dowall	Ellis	Wales	Craig	Telfer	Murdoch	McMenemy	McFadyen	Moffat	Ferrier
13/2		36,000	*5*					*Kennaway*	*Cook*	*McGonagle*	*Wilson*	*McStay*	*Geatons*	*Thomson*	*Smith*	*McGrory*	*Napier*	*Kavanagh*
							Ref: T Small (Dundee)	There is fighting behind one goal in Fir Park's record crowd before k.o. Willie Maley fields an unfit McGrory and it proves costly as he lasts only 30 minutes. As McGonagle dithers, Murdoch nips in to score. Kennaway's palm out breaks to Ferrier who nods home to win a hard tie.										
QF	A	RANGERS	1	L	0-2	0-1		McClory	Dowall	Ellis	Wales	Craig	Telfer	Murdoch	McMenemy	McFadyen	Stevenson	Ferrier
5/3		*88,000*	*2*				*Murray 26, McPhail 84*	*Hamilton*	*Gray*	*McAulay*	*Meiklejohn*	*Simpson*	*Brown*	*Fleming*	*Murray*	*English*	*McPhail*	*Morton*
							Ref: P Craigmyle (Aberdeen)	A huge Ibrox crowd sees early Well pressure come to nothing and Murray nets with a fast, rising shot that slithers from McClory's grasp. There's too much tip-tapping from Well's arguing forwards. McPhail slams home a late cross.' Fir Park attack a broken reed,' says the *Record*.										

			Home					Away					
		P	W	D	L	F	A	W	D	L	F	A	Pts
1	MOTHERWELL	38	18	1	0	72	11	12	5	2	47	20	66
2	Rangers	38	16	2	1	67	14	12	3	4	51	28	61
3	Celtic	38	13	2	4	64	24	7	6	6	30	26	48
4	Third Lanark	38	15	1	3	61	29	6	3	10	31	52	46
5	St Mirren	38	13	2	4	49	22	7	2	10	28	34	44
6	Partick	38	11	3	5	33	26	8	1	10	25	33	42
7	Aberdeen	38	10	6	3	33	15	6	3	10	24	34	41
8	Hearts	38	10	5	4	35	18	7	0	12	28	43	39
9	Kilmarnock	38	13	2	4	50	26	3	5	11	18	44	39
10	Hamilton	38	11	3	5	54	29	5	3	11	30	36	38
11	Dundee	38	9	7	3	38	26	5	3	11	23	46	38
12	Cowdenb'th	38	11	4	4	38	28	4	4	11	28	50	38
13	Clyde	38	10	5	4	37	24	3	4	12	21	46	35
14	Airdrie	38	10	5	4	45	28	3	1	15	29	53	32
15	Morton	38	10	4	5	54	31	2	3	14	24	56	31
16	Queen's Pk	38	9	2	8	36	38	4	3	12	23	41	31
17	Ayr	38	9	1	9	43	32	2	6	11	27	58	29
18	Falkirk	38	10	3	6	52	31	1	2	16	18	45	27
19	Dundee Utd	38	4	5	10	18	49	2	2	15	22	69	19
20	Leith	38	6	0	13	23	49	0	4	15	23	88	16
		760	218	63	99	902	550	99	63	218	550	902	760

Odds & ends

Double wins: (11) Queen's Park, Ayr, Aberdeen, St Mirren, Falkirk, Third Lanark, Clyde, Leith, Dundee United, Hearts, Cowdenbeath.
Double losses: (0)

Won from behind: (3) Queen's Park (a), Rangers (h), Cowdenbeath (a).
Lost from in front: (0).

High spots: League leaders since October.
4-2 win over champions Rangers in second game of season.
League and Cup victories against Celtic.
Team's goal record of 119 scored in league.
Willie McFadyen's record-breaking goals total.

Low spots: Losing to Rangers in league and Cup.
Some poor home attendances.

Five goals: (1) McFadyen.
Four goals: (4) McFadyen.
Hat-tricks: (5) McFadyen (3), Ferrier (1), Moffat (1).
Ever-presents: (2) Ellis and McClory.
Leading Scorer: McFadyen (52).

	Appearances		Goals		
	Lge	SC	**Lge**	SC	**Tot**
Blair, John	**4**				
Craig, Alan	**37**	4	**1**		**1**
Douglas, Tom	**8**		**7**		**7**
Dowall, Willie	**32**	4	**4**		**4**
Ellis, Ben	**38**	4			
Ferrier, Bobby	**36**	4	**13**	2	**15**
Hunter, Sandy	**1**				
Johnman, John	**7**				
McClory, Allan	**38**	4			
McFadyen, Willie	**34**	4	**52**	2	**54**
McKenzie, Tommy	**1**				
Mackrell, James	**2**				
McMenemy, John	**31**	3	**7**	1	**8**
Moffat, Willie	**11**	2	**8**	1	**9**
Murdoch, Johnny	**26**	4	**10**	3	**13**
Stevenson, George	**34**	3	**11**	2	**13**
Telfer, Willie	**37**	4			
Wales, Hugh	**36**	4	**1**		**1**
Wyllie, Tom	**5**		**4**		**4**
(own-goals)			**1**		**1**
19 players used	**418**	**44**	**119**	**11**	**130**

No	Date		Att	Pos	Pt	F-A	H-T	Scorers, Times, and Referees	1	2	3	4	5	6	7	8	9	10	11
1	H	KILMARNOCK			D	3-3	2-2	McMenemy 6, Murdoch 44, Ferrier 70	McClory	Dowall	Ellis	McKenzie	Craig	Telfer	Murdoch	McMenemy	McFadyen	Stevenson	Ferrier
	13/8		12,000		1			*Maxwell 16, 33, 65*	*Bell*	*Leslie*	*Milloy*	*Glass*	*Smith*	*McEwan*	*Connell*	*Sneddon*	*Maxwell*	*Williamson*	*Aitken*
								Ref: W Holburn (Glasgow)	Inspired by the unfurling of the League flag, Well have a whirlwind start. McMenemy opens after Murdoch had hit woodwork. Killie weather the storm and Connell hits a post before Maxwell levels. McFadyen is out of sorts and misses half a dozen excellent chances to win the game.										
2	A	ABERDEEN		10	D	1-1	0-1	Ferrier 73	McClory	Dowall	Ellis	Wales	Craig	Telfer	Murdoch	McMenemy	McFadyen	Stevenson	Ferrier
	20/8		*23,000*	*15*	2			*Moore 9*	*Smith*	*Daly*	*McGill*	*Fraser*	*Falloon*	*Dickie*	*Love*	*Beattie*	*Moore*	*Mills*	*McLean*
								Ref: H McArthur (Airdrie)	With new boys Mills and Daly, Dons are the more direct, scorning Well's pretty patterns. McClory performs heroics but is beaten by Moore's first-time volley. Keeper Smith now blocks from McMenemy and clears from McFadyen. Ferrier scrapes home the equaliser for a lucky point.										
3	A	DUNDEE		7	W	3-0	2-0	McFadyen 15, 77, McMenemy 35	McClory	Dowall	Ellis	Wales	Craig	Telfer	Murdoch	McMenemy	McFadyen	Stevenson	Ferrier
	24/8		*8,000*	*20*	4				*Marsh*	*Morgan*	*Gilmour*	*McNab*	*McCarthy*	*Smith T*	*Munro*	*Millar*	*Balfour*	*Robertson*	*Troup*
								Ref: G Pool (Edinburgh)	It's all Well in the first half as McFadyen opens from a scrimmage, then a 'Stevie' pass lets McMenemy net easily from close in. Dundee resume urgently and McClory is the busier keeper. McFadyen grabs another when McCarthy misses and Willie unleashes an unstoppable shot.										
4	H	CLYDE		7	W	1-0	0-0	Ferrier 75p	McClory	Dowall	Ellis	Wales	Craig	Telfer	Murdoch	McMenemy	McFadyen	Stevenson	Ferrier
	27/8		6,000	*14*	6				*Stevenson*	*Russell*	*Smith*	*McPhail*	*Wood*	*Summers*	*McGurk*	*Munro*	*Boyd*	*Mayes*	*McCulloch*
								Ref: A McLean (Rutherglen)	Hamilton and Cowdenbeath are the unlikely League leaders as Clyde here set about Well. McPhail's red head is conspicuous as he covers so much ground. Well gain control and Bob Ferrier's shot is going into an empty net when Russell palms it out. Bob converts for a deserved win.										
5	A	ST JOHNSTONE		4	W	1-0	0-0	McFadyen 52	McClory	Dowall	Ellis	Wales	Craig	Telfer	Murdoch	McMenemy	McFadyen	Stevenson	Ferrier
	3/10		*10,000*	*12*	8				*McLaren*	*Welsh*	*Clark*	*Mason*	*Ireland*	*Priestley*	*Sherlaw*	*Benzie*	*McBain*	*Ballantyne*	*Nicholson*
								Ref: W Holburn (Glasgow)	Far from Championship best, Well go under the cosh in Perth. McBain passes up a gift, Sherlaw misses from six yards out, and McClory has some fine saves too. Interplay by Ferrier and McMenemy allows McFadyen to pilot home easily. Only Well and Acas now remain unbeaten.										
6	H	HAMILTON		3	W	4-1	3-0	Murdoch 2, McFadyen 7, Ferrier 27, [McMenemy 54]	McClory	Dowall	Ellis	Wales	Craig	Telfer	Murdoch	McMenemy	McFadyen	Stevenson	Ferrier
	10/9		12,000	*5*	10			*Wilson D 87*	*Wright*	*Allan*	*Bulloch*	*Dougall*	*Hill*	*McLuckie*	*Wilson F*	*McLaren*	*Wilson D*	*Herd*	*King*
								Ref: J Hudson (Glasgow)	George Stevenson leads a rampant forward line, making three of the goals but striving in vain for one himself. Murdoch gives Well a dream start with a goal in 90 seconds. Dave Wilson rounds Ellis and nets a late consolation for Acas. Well are now unbeaten at home for three years.										
7	H	AYR UNITED		2	W	3-1	1-1	Ferrier 39, 89, Wales 62	McClory	Dowall	Ellis	Wales	Blair	Telfer	Murdoch	McMenemy	McFadyen	Stevenson	Ferrier
	14/9		3,500	*13*	12			*McGrath 30*	*Hepburn*	*Willis*	*Fleming*	*Taylor*	*McCall*	*Carmichael*	*Brae*	*McGrath*	*Merrie*	*Brannan*	*Ferguson*
								Ref: D Reilly (Port Glasgow)	A sparse midweek crowd applauds keeper Hepburn's astonishing saves as all the home forwards have a pop. In a rare breakaway Merrie's cross is headed in by McGrath but is cancelled out by Ferrier's low drive. Hugh Wales scores with a long shot and Ferrier nets at his third try.										
8	A	FALKIRK		3	D	2-2	0-1	McFadyen 62, McMenemy 86	McClory	Dowall	Ellis	Wales	Craig	McKenzie	Murdoch	Moffat	McFadyen	McMenemy	Ferrier
	17/9		*11,000*	*19*	13			*Dougall 13, 65*	*Thomson*	*Richardson*	*Hamill*	*Batchelor*	*Low*	*Murray*	*Dougall*	*Thompson*	*Calder*	*Hutchieson*	*Radcliffe*
								Ref: J Thomson (Hamilton)	Willie Orr's young winger Dougall is a thorn in Well's side and he drives home the opener. Missing Telfer and 'Stevie' (Scotland), Well must fight all the way and Ferrier hits the woodwork three times! Brockville waits in silence as McMenemy takes an age to trundle in a late leveller										
9	H	MORTON		2	W	**7-0**	2-0	Stevenson 8, Murdoch 30, McFad' 57, [McMenemy 65, Ferrier 67, 84, 90]	McClory	Dowall	Ellis	Wales	Blair	Telfer	Murdoch	McMenemy	McFadyen	Stevenson	Ferrier
	24/9		4,000	*15*	15				*Wilson*	*Bourhill*	*Miller*	*Clunas*	*Hunter*	*Ritchie*	*Shankley*	*Stewart*	*Lyle*	*Keyes*	*McLaughlan*
								Ref: H Watson (Glasgow)	Allan Craig is again rested but the Morton are overwhelmed. Stevenson opens from a Ferrier corner while Murdoch's flag kick goes straight in. Ferrier's hat-trick is a trio of his trademark left-foot thunderbolts. Keeper Wilson's brave performance wins him Fir Park's admiration.										

No / Date	Venue	Opponent / Att	Pos	Res / Pts	F-A	H-T	Scorers, Times, Referees	1	2	3	4	5	6	7	8	9	10	11
10	A	RANGERS	2	D	2-2	1-0	Murdoch 20, Ferrier 68	McClory	Dowall	Ellis	Wales	Craig	Telfer	Murdoch	McMenemy	McFadyen	Stevenson	Ferrier
1/10		***50,000***	*1*	16			*McPhail 55, 61*	*Hamilton*	*Gray*	*McDonald*	*Meiklejohn*	*Simpson*	*Brown*	*Archibald*	*Marshall*	*English*	*McPhail*	*Smith*
							Ref: W Holburn (Glasgow)	Well dominate the first half with deliberate, skilful play. Murdoch shoots home from ten yards out and Well hit woodwork three times. After the break Rangers' strong, forceful play allows McPhail to twice smash home. Ferrier's free-kick finds its way through for a deserved equaliser.										
11	H	QUEEN'S PARK	2	W	7-2	4-2	Fer'2p,3,Mur' 21,McF' 33,70,Stev' 57,	McClory	Dowall	Ellis	Wales	Craig	Telfer	Murdoch	McMenemy	McFadyen	Stevenson	Ferrier
8/10		6,000	*10*	18			*Hosie 15, Crawford 35* [McMenemy 58]	*Smith*	*Campbell*	*Walker*	*Gardiner*	*McCarthy*	*Grant*	*Crawford*	*Anderson*	*Morrison*	*Hosie*	*McKenzie*
							Ref: W Webb (Glasgow)	A trip on Stevenson gives Ferrier an early penalty and Bob follows with a smash past Smith. Hosie then pierces an uncertain defence to score, but visions of a sensation are dispelled by lethal Well finishing. An exhibition of 'carpet weaving' follows and McFadyen heads the seventh.										
12	A	HEARTS	4	L	0-2	0-1		McClory	Mackrell	Ellis	Wales	Craig	Telfer	Murdoch	McMenemy	McFadyen	Stevenson	Ferrier
15/10		*36,000*	*5*	18			*White 35, 65*	*Harkness*	*Anderson*	*O'Neill*	*Massie*	*Johnston J*	*Herd*	*Johnstone R*	*Coutts*	*White*	*Smith*	*Murray*
							Ref: W Jamieson (Paisley)	Well's unbeaten 24-game run ends in a ding-dong contest. Allan McClory stops White several times and sees an effort hit his post. He's at fault when White's shot bounces from his fingers and in. McFadyen's effort is offside before White nets again as the visitors now claim offside.										
13	A	CELTIC	6	L	**1-4**	1-2	McFadyen 20	McClory	Dowall	Ellis	Wales	Craig	Telfer	Murdoch	McMenemy	McFadyen	Moffat	Ferrier
22/10		*20,000*	*2*	18			*Thomson 9, Smith 34, Crum 52, 83*	*Kennaway*	*Cook*	*Hogg*	*Wilson*	*McStay*	*Geatons*	*Napier*	*Thomson*	*Crum*	*Smith*	*O'Donnell H*
							Ref: D Reilly (Port Glasgow)	'Stevie' is out and despite Dowall's return the defence is shaky. Thomson opens with a header from O'Donnell's cross but McFadyen is up to level. Smith's snappy header puts Celts ahead but Hogg has then to kick off the line. The home right is devastating and twice sets up for Crum.										
14	H	PARTICK TH	6	L	1-2	0-0	Ferrier 83	McClory	Dowall	Ellis	Wales	Blair	Telfer	**Ogilvie**	McMenemy	McFadyen	Moffat	Ferrier
29/10		4,000	*15*	18			*Ballantyne 60, Ness 66*	*Jackson*	*Calderwood*	*Cumming*	*Grove*	*McAllister*	*McLeod*	*Ness*	*McMillan*	*Boardman*	*Ballantyne*	*Torbet*
							Ref: P Craigmyle (Aberdeen)	The three-year unbeaten home record falls to lowly Thistle. Jackson is in brilliant form, helped by McAllister who twice clears off the line. Thistle emerge to probe at the weak Dowall and Ballantyne picks his spot, then Ness puts in from close range. Ferrier gets one from a melee.										
15	H	DUNDEE	5	W	6-1	1-0	Moffat 5, Ogilvie 50, McF' 62, 80, 82,	McClory	Mackrell	Ellis	Wales	Blair	McKenzie	Ogilvie	Moffat	McFadyen	McMenemy	Ferrier
5/11		5,000	*17*	20			*Roberston 87* [McMenemy 64]	*Marsh*	*Morgan*	*Gilmour*	*Symon*	*McCarthy*	*Smith T*	*Munro*	*Gullane*	*Balfour*	*Robertson*	*Troup*
							Ref: J Hudson (Glasgow)	A weakened side has only six Championship men in it. Moffat's high drive opens before Dundee's keeper is hurt in a collison and doesn't reappear after the break. Despite his hat-trick, McFadyen misses a tempting series of Ferrier crosses. John Blair excels in place of Craig.										
16	A	AYR UNITED	4	W	6-2	2-0	Ogilvie 9, McFad'35, 83, McMen' 53,	McClory	Mackrell	Ellis	Wales	Blair	Telfer	Ogilvie	Moffat	McFadyen	McMenemy	Ferrier
12/11		*4,000*	*16*	22			*Merrie 46, Carmich'l 89* [Ferrier 58,85]	*Hepburn*	*Robertson*	*Ure*	*Taylor*	*McCall*	*Carmichael*	*Tolland*	*McGrath*	*Merrie*	*Brannan*	*Ferguson*
							Ref: J Burdon (Glasgow)	Duncan Ogilvie gets his first goal for Well after Hepburn had pushed out a Ferrier shot. Well's second is McFadyen's rather than Ferrier's, as some reporters think. Ayr are still in with a shout until McMenemy shoots in from a crowded goalmouth. Well show Championship form here.										
17	A	AIRDRIE	4	W	4-1	0-0	McFad' 57, Ogilvie 66, Ferrier 70, 85	McClory	Dowall	Ellis	Wales	Blair	Telfer	Ogilvie	Moffat	McFadyen	McMenemy	Ferrier
19/11		*6,000*	*20*	24			*Thomson 72*	*Morrison R*	*Crapnell*	*McQueen*	*Blake*	*Morrison J*	*Duncan*	*Law*	*Davin*	*Armstrong*	*Thomson*	*Mooney*
							Ref: J Hudson (Glasgow)	Although McClory is early brought into action, it's Well who are on top. Ferrier is taken off but reappears with his leg bandaged. Nevertheless Bob crosses for McFadyen and Ogilvie to head in then coolly manages two by himself – first a walk-in, then a rebound from Ogilvie's shot.										
18	A	ST MIRREN	3	W	5-2	2-1	McFadyen 33, 62, 89, Ogilvie 42,	McClory	Mackrell	Ellis	Wales	Blair	Telfer	Ogilvie	Moffat	McFadyen	McMenemy	Dowall
26/11		*6,000*	*7*	26			*Gebbie 31, Knox 52p* [Moffat 46]	*Kenny*	*Hay*	*Ancell*	*Gebbie*	*Walker*	*Miller*	*Knox*	*Workman*	*McCrae*	*Rankine*	*McIndoe*
							Ref: A McLean (Rutherglen)	Ferrier and 'Stevie' are both out injured against strong-going Saints. Gebbie dispossess Blair to drive in the first but McFadyen levels after Moffat's 40-yard run. Ellis fells Rankine and Knox converts the pen. Back in his old berth, Dowall's cross hits the bar but McFadyen nets.										
19	H	THIRD LANARK	3	W	6-3	3-2	McFadyen 9, 36, 48, 60, 77	McClory	Mackrell	Ellis	Wales	Blair	Telfer	Ogilvie	Moffat	McFadyen	McMenemy	Ferrier
3/12		5,000	*11*	28			*Dewar 23, 87, Breslin 33* [Moffat 40]	*Taylor*	*Simpson*	*Warden*	*Waddell*	*Carabine*	*McLellan*	*Jack*	*Campbell*	*Dewar*	*Blair*	*Breslin*
							Ref: D Reilly (Port Glasgow)	Ferrier is back but it's McFadyen who brightens a dull day by going 'nap', his first when he connects with a cross at the second attempt. Thirds reply through Dewar after McClory was forced to parry a Breslin shot. Strangely, McFadyen also scored five in last year's Thirds game.										

SCOTTISH DIVISION 1

Manager: John Hunter

SEASON 1932-33

No	Date		Att	Pos	Pt	F-A	H-T	Scorers, Times, and Referees	1	2	3	4	5	6	7	8	9	10	11
20	A	EAST STIRLING		3	W	4-1	1-0	McFadyen 26, 66, Moffat 52	McClory	Dowall	Ellis	Wales	Blair	Telfer	Ogilvie	Moffat	McFadyen	Stevenson	Ferrier
	10/12		*4,000*	*18*	30			*Craigie 81* [Ferrier 80]	*Crawford*	*Buchanan*	*Fraser*	*Thomson*	*Crichton*	*McCabe*	*Latimer*	*Black*	*Craigie*	*Smith*	*Kemp*
								Ref: A McLean (Rutherglen)	George Stevenson returns to link with Ferrier and they open up 'Shire for McFadyen to open with a high shot. Kemp is fouled in the area and Fraser misses the penalty but it's to be retaken. McClory tips it over. McFadyen is then felled but Ferrier's penalty goes straight to the keeper.										
21	H	COWDENBEATH		3	W	2-0	2-0	Ferrier 3, McFadyen 29	McClory	Dowall	Ellis	Wales	Blair	Telfer	Ogilvie	Moffat	McFadyen	McMenemy	Ferrier
	17/12		3,000	*15*	32				*Crosskey*	*McDonald*	*Russell*	*Glancy*	*Adams*	*Campbell*	*Robertson*	*Finlayson*	*Renfrew*	*Venters*	*McCartney*
								Ref: W Webb (Glasgow)	Well try to keep the ball low in a gale and sleety rain. The game's hardly begun when McFadyen is brought down and Ferrier nets after his penalty is blocked. Both sides hit woodwork several times before McFadyen's pace takes him through to smack home. Willie Telfer is injured.										
22	A	KILMARNOCK		3	W	3-1	1-1	Ogilvie 30, Moffat 53, McFadyen 78	McClory	Dowall	Ellis	Wales	Blair	Telfer	Ogilvie	Moffat	McFadyen	Stevenson	Ferrier
	24/12		*8,000*	*10*	34			*McEwan 40p*	*Milliken*	*Falconer*	*Milloy*	*Glass*	*Smith*	*McEwan*	*Kenmuir*	*Williamson*	*Maxwell*	*Sneddon*	*Aitken*
								Ref: J Hudson (Glasgow)	Kenmuir goes off hurt and a defensive mix-up lets Ogilvie in to score, but Killie won't lie down. Blair pushes Maxwell and McEwan levels from the spot. Sneddon hits the bar and 'Bud' Maxwell hits the post, but Well come through to sneak two goals in a fiercely contested game.										
23	H	ABERDEEN		3	L	2-3	0-1	McGill 67 (og), Moffat 70	McClory	Dowall	Ellis	Wales	Blair	Telfer	Ogilvie	Moffat	McFadyen	Stevenson	Ferrier
	31/12		8,000	5	34			*Moore 30, 52, McDermid 61*	*Smith*	*Cooper*	*McGill*	*Fraser*	*Falloon*	*O'Reilly*	*Love*	*Beattie*	*Moore*	*Adam*	*McDermid*
								Ref: W Dawson (Leith)	The Dons' Paddy Moore is the star, his first goal a finely balanced hook shot. Well have to defend for a solid 30 minutes against a stiff wind. Moore dribbles round Ellis for the next, then McDermid counts with a 25-yarder. McGill's slice and Moffat's scrimmaged goal give late hope.										
24	A	HAMILTON		2	W	3-2	3-1	Stevenson 37, 38, Wales 39	McClory	Dowall	Mackrell	Wales	Blair	Telfer	Ogilvie	Moffat	McFadyen	Stevenson	Ferrier
	2/1		*16,700*	*7*	36			*Wilson F 30, McLaren 80*	*Wright*	*Allan*	*Bulloch*	*Dougall*	*Hill*	*Young*	*Wilson F*	*McLaren*	*Crawley*	*Herd*	*King*
								Ref: W Jamieson (Paisley)	Hamilton's defence defy wind and Well, and Wilson opens the scoring for them. Three goals in three minutes shoot Well in front, 'Stevie' with two 25-yard drives and Wales with a 20-yard shot that goes in off a post. Acas have wind advantage and McLaren puts in King's corner.										
25	H	FALKIRK		2	W	2-0	1-0	Stevenson 6, McFadyen 66	McClory	Dowall	Mackrell	Wales	Craig	Telfer	Ogilvie	Moffat	McFadyen	Stevenson	Ferrier
	3/1		6,000	*13*	38				*Thomson*	*Richardson*	*Hamill*	*Batchelor*	*Low*	*Hutchieson*	*Dougall*	*Morgan*	*Bartram*	*Anderson*	*Murray*
								Ref: J Hudson (Glasgow)	Allan Craig returns for his last game before going to Chelsea. Using the blustery wind, 'Stevie' shoots home a 20-yard left-footer then displays classy footwork, beating four men at one point. Ferrier drives across for McFadyen to head in. Mackrell shines against his former colleagues.										
26	A	CLYDE		2	W	3-2	2-1	Ferrier 16, McFadyen 32, Ogilvie 83	McClory	Dowall	Mackrell	Wales	Blair	Telfer	Ogilvie	Moffat	McFadyen	Stevenson	Ferrier
	7/1		*8,500*	*14*	40			*Mayes 12, Boyd 50*	*Stevenson*	*Russell*	*Smith M*	*McPhail*	*Wood*	*Smith J*	*McGurk*	*Mayes*	*Boyd*	*Howieson*	*McCulloch*
								Ref: W Jamieson (Paisley)	Dog-racing brings the benefit of having most of the ground covered. Mayes opens from point-blank range while McFadyen's shot is blocked but back-heeled in by Ferrier. McFadyen's solo effort is cancelled by Boyd's drive. Well hold out and Ogilvie, on hands and knees, nods in.										
27	H	ST JOHNSTONE		2	W	1-0	0-0	McFadyen 73	McClory	Dowall	Ellis	Wales	Blair	Telfer	Ogilvie	Moffat	McFadyen	Stevenson	Ferrier
	14/1		4,000	*6*	42				*McLaren*	*Welsh*	*Clark*	*Mason*	*Ireland*	*Priestley*	*Ritchie*	*Dickie*	*Fulton*	*Ferguson*	*Ballantyne*
								Ref: W Holburn (Glasgow)	Ben Ellis is back but Well toil in the strong wind and Saints' Dickie hits the bar. The home side come out with more aggression after the break and McFadyen tries his luck with a shot that's deflected in. Both sides now come close and Saints net, but it comes just after the final whistle.										
28	A	MORTON		2	W	2-1	1-1	McFadyen 15, Ferrier 48	McClory	**Crapnell**	Ellis	Wales	Blair	Telfer	Ogilvie	McMenemy	McFadyen	Stevenson	Ferrier
	28/1		*7,000*	*18*	44			*Keyes 35*	*McArthur*	*Morton*	*Bourhill*	*Bulloch*	*Hunter*	*Mooney*	*Clunas*	*Keyes*	*Lyle*	*Borland*	*Kay*
								Ref: W Jamieson (Paisley)	On a dangerously icy pitch Ferrier's header comes off the post but McFadyen slots in the rebound. Keyes replies by scrambling one over from a scrimmage. Ferrier's winner is a shot from the touch-line. Well are forced to defend as Crapnell impresses, twice clearing off his own line.										

No		Opponent	Div	Res	Score	HT	Scorers	1	2	3	4	5	6	7	8	9	10	11
29	H	RANGERS	2	L	1-3	1-1	Ferrier 38p	McClory !	Crapnell	Ellis	Wales	Blair	Telfer	Wylie	McMenemy	McFadyen	Stevenson	Ferrier
	11/2	**30,000**	*1*	44			*Fleming 20, 82, Smith 69p*	*Dawson*	*Gray*	*Russell*	*McDonald*	*Simpson*	*Brown*	*Main*	*Marshall*	*English*	*Smith*	*Fleming*
							Ref: J Hudson (Glasgow)	In a scrappy game Fleming is allowed to open with a soft header. McDonald handles a Ferrier shot and Bob converts the penalty. Even without Gray, Rangers still force the pace. English barges McClory and the keeper is sent off for clipping his heels. Smith beats Ferrier from the spot.										
30	A	QUEEN'S PARK	2	L	2-4	0-3	McFadyen 65, Blair 72	McClory	Crapnell	Ellis	Wales	Blair	McKenzie	Ogilvie	McMenemy	McFadyen	Stevenson	Ferrier
	25/2	*7,500*	*10*	44			*Crawford 4, 60, Dodds 29, 43*	*Smith*	*Campbell*	*Grant*	*Crawford*	*Anderson*	*Cooper*	*Gardiner*	*McCartney*	*Dodds*	*McAlpine*	*McKenzie*
							Ref: T Small (Dundee)	'Fast moving, go-ahead Amateurs spreadeagle the Fir Park defence,' runs the *Daily Record*. On a raw day Well are three goals down by the time Crawford beats three Well defenders to score one of his best ever goals. Two counters can't claw back the game and it's a disastrous loss.										
31	H	CELTIC	2	W	4-2	2-1	McFadyen 37, 39, 78, 84	McClory	Crapnell	Ellis	Wales	Blair	McKenzie	Murdoch	McMenemy	McFadyen	Stevenson	Ferrier
	11/3	17,000	*4*	46			*O'Donnell F 43, McGrory 80*	*Wallace*	*Hogg*	*McGonagle*	*Wilson*	*McDonald*	*Hughes*	*Thomson R*	*Napier*	*McGrory*	*O'Donnell F*	*O'Donnell H*
							Ref: H McArthur (Airdrie)	Fresh from drubbing Killie in the Cup, Well are desperate for points. Tom McKenzie retaliates, pushing Thomson but McClory smothers Napier's penalty. McFadyen puts two left-foot drives past Wallace before Frank O'Donnell replies. Willie gets two more opportunist goals.										
32	H	AIRDRIE	2	W	4-1	2-1	McMenemy 25, 31, McFadyen 69, [Ferrier 75]	McClory	Crapnell	Ellis	Wales	Blair	McKenzie	Murdoch	McMenemy	McFadyen	Stevenson	Ferrier
	25/3	4,000	*18*	48			*Connor 4*	*Morrison*	*Calder*	*McQueen*	*Blake*	*Crosbie*	*Thomson*	*Johnston*	*Harrison*	*Connor*	*Law*	*Mooney*
							Ref: M Hutton (Glasgow)	Turnberry's sea air seems to have done wonders for Well. Despite losing an early goal when Connor heads in, Well take control with two strong McMenemy drives. The story of the second period is one of the Well attack against the Airdrie defence, with McClory a mere spectator.										
33	H	HEARTS	2	W	5-1	3-0	Stevenson 30, Murdoch 32, Ferrier 42, [McFadyen 80, 86]	McClory	Crapnell	Ellis	Wales	Blair	McKenzie	Murdoch	McMenemy	McFadyen	Stevenson	Ferrier
	29/3	5,000	*3*	50			*Murray 77*	*Harkness*	*Pratt*	*O'Neill*	*Massie*	*Johnston J*	*Herd*	*Johnstone R*	*White*	*Dodds*	*Coutts*	*Murray*
							Ref: W Jamieson (Paisley)	George Stevenson takes the ball in the air and sweeps it in and heralds a return to top form. There's end-to-end raiding but Murdoch's left-foot drive and Bobby Ferrier's acute strike put the game beyond Hearts. Defensive slackness lets Murray in before McFadyen's late double.										
34	A	PARTICK TH	2	W	1-0	0-0	McFadyen 56	McClory	Crapnell	Ellis	Wales	Blair	McKenzie	Murdoch	McMenemy	McFadyen	Stevenson	Ferrier
	3/4	*20,000*	*8*	52				*Jackson*	*Calderwood*	*Cumming*	*Elliot*	*McAllister*	*McLeod*	*Ness*	*McMillan*	*Craigie*	*Watson*	*Torbet*
							Ref: T Small (Dundee)	The big holiday crowd sees a lively game but the defences dominate. McClory is nowhere as McMillan strikes a post and Well are now under severe pressure. Tom McKenzie's pace and control help build the move that ends with McFadyen cutely flicking Murdoch's pass in to win.										
35	H	ST MIRREN	2	W	3-0	2-0	Ferrier 23, Stevenson 43, McFad' 70	McClory	Crapnell	Ellis	Wales	Blair	McKenzie	Murdoch	McMenemy	McFadyen	Stevenson	Ferrier
	8/4	4,000	*10*	54				*Kenny*	*Hay*	*Ancell*	*Gebbie*	*Walker*	*Miller*	*McSorland*	*Workman*	*McCrae*	*Meechan*	*Phillips*
							Ref: W Dawson (Leith)	A dull game is brightened by its goals as the Cup-finalists ease up. Ferrier drives in from the bye-line at a seemingly impossible angle. 'Stevie' orchestrates the best moves and nets with a soft goal himself. A rare Saints attack ends with a Well breakaway and McFadyen left-footing in.										
36	H	EAST STIRLING	2	W	4-1	1-0	McFadyen 15, Ogilvie 58,75, Ellis 77p	McClory	Crapnell	Ellis	Wales	Blair	McKenzie	Ogilvie	McMenemy	McFadyen	Stevenson	Ferrier
	22/4	***2,000***	*20*	56			*Turnbull 55*	*Watson*	*Fraser*	*Black*	*Buchanan*	*Crichton*	*Thomson*	*Latimer*	*Smith*	*McAulay*	*Turnbull*	*Kemp*
							Ref: G Pool (Edinburgh)	With the Cup now lost and the League as good as gone, the most colourful aspect here is in the shape of fund-raising students. A Ferrier 'special' comes off the near post, then MacFdayen nets with a low drive. A powerful Ellis penalty completes the scoring after Black's foul.										
37	A	THIRD LANARK	2	D	1-1	1-1	Stevenson 36	McClory	Dowall	Crapnell	Wales	Blair	McKenzie	Ogilvie	**Johnston J**	McFadyen	Stevenson	Ferrier
	25/4	***2,000***	*13*	57			*McCulloch 35*	*Taylor*	*Simpson*	*Carabine*	*Blair*	*Clark*	*McLellan*	*Brown*	*Jack*	*McCulloch*	*McKenzie*	*Breslin*
							Ref: P Craigmyle (Aberdeen)	Both sides lose a player, Allan McClory having to go off in only 17 minutes with bad facial injuries. Dowall does well in goal but his fist-out is put into the net by McCulloch. A minute later 'Stevie' gracefully controls and shoots home from 30 yards. A lost point means no title this time.										
38	A	COWDENBEATH	2	W	4-1	1-1	McFadyen 20, 60, 67, Ferrier 85	McClory	Dowall	Crapnell	Wales	Blair	McKenzie	Ogilvie	Johnston J	McFadyen	Stevenson	Ferrier
	29/4	***2,000***	*17*	59			*Armstrong 10*	*Crosskey*	*McDonald*	*Gronbach*	*Glancy*	*Adams*	*Robertson J*	*Hamil*	*Campbell*	*Armstrong*	*Venters*	*Robertson A*
	Home	Away					Ref: H Watson (Glasgow)	Armstrong cleverly beats the Well backs and keeper to open. Venters twice hits the woodwork and Crapnell has to kick off his line before McFadyen equalises as Ogilvie's drive comes off the bar. The second half is a procession towards the Fifers' goal as Willie grabs a hat-trick.										
Average	7,400	13,100																

Scottish Cup			F-A	H-T	Scorers, Times, and Referees	1	2	3	4	5	6	7	8	9	10	11
1 A HAMILTON	2	W	2-0	2-0	Stevenson 10, McFadyen 32	McClory	Crapnell	Ellis	Wales	Blair	Telfer	Ogilvie	Moffat	McFadyen	Stevenson	Ferrier
21/1 *16,500*	*7*					*Wright*	*Allan*	*Bulloch*	*Dougall*	*Hill*	*McLuckie*	*Wilson F*	*McLaren*	*Crawley*	*Herd*	*King*
					Ref: H Watson (Glasgow)	Crapnell debuts on a sanded pitch. In a hectic contest 'Stevie' heads the opener. Dougall hits a post before McFadyen heads in from Ferrier's cross. Allan whips away Bob's legs, but Wright saves Wales' penalty. Crapnell then 'grasses' Herd, but he gets up to shoot wide from the spot.										
2 H MONTROSE	1	W	7-1	4-0	Wales 15, McFad' 20, 33, 35, 47, 69,	McClory	Crapnell	Ellis	Wales	Blair	Telfer	Ogilvie	McMenemy	McFadyen	Stevenson	Ferrier
4/2 2,967	*2:17*				*Stewart 65* [Ferrier 70]	*Gerrand*	*McDonald*	*Todd*	*Nicol*	*Burnett*	*Robertson*	*Sherlaw*	*Bennett*	*Stewart*	*Ross*	*Stoddart*
					Ref: J Hudson (Glasgow)	Although Stoddart hits a post early on, it's just about all Well and Wales spectacularly scores on the drop to open the floodgates. McDonald falls onto the ball but Ferrier's penalty is saved. With a first-half hat-trick, McFadyen then goes 'nap'. Well ease up after Todd has to go off.										
3 H DUNDEE	2	W	5-0	2-0	McFadyen 25, 46, Ellis 35p,	McClory	Crapnell	Ellis	Wales	Blair	Telfer	Ogilvie	McMenemy	McFadyen	Stevenson	Ferrier
18/2 8,000	*14*				[McMenemy 54, Ferrier 57]	*Edwards*	*Morgan*	*Gilmour*	*Symon !*	*McCarthy*	*Blyth*	*Munro*	*Guthrie*	*Balfour*	*Miller*	*Troup*
					Ref: H Watson (Glasgow)	A neat McFadyen header opens the scoring. A soft penalty is disputed by Dundee and missed by Ferrier. Left-back Symon is sent off for his tackle on Ellis. Well's Welshman then wallops in from the spot after Gilmour fouls Ogilvie. Ferrier then deftly finishes off a McFadyen cross.										
QF A KILMARNOCK	2	D	3-3	2-1	McFadyen 3, 23, Ferrier 80	McClory	Crapnell	Ellis	Wales	Blair	McKenzie	Murdoch	McMenemy	McFadyen	Stevenson	Ferrier
4/3 *20,685*	*11*				*Maxwell 20, 85, McEwan 79p*	*Milliken*	*Leslie*	*Milloy*	*Glass*	*Smith*	*McEwan*	*Liddell*	*Sneddon*	*Maxwell*	*Gilmour*	*Aitken*
					Ref: T Small (Dundee)	The right-wingers take the honours, Killie's young Liddell and Well's experienced Murdoch. Well lose their lead three times after McFadyen forced over from a melee to open. Blair handles and McEwan's pen brings Killie back into it. Ferrier replies but Maxwell's goal earns a replay.										
QF H KILMARNOCK	2	W	8-3	3-0	McF'12,28,51,90, Ellis40p, Les'73(og),	McClory	Crapnell	Ellis	Wales	Blair	McKenzie	Murdoch	McMenemy	McFadyen	Stevenson	Ferrier
R 8/3 23,846	*11*				*Maxwell 57, Glass 65,87* [Murd' 74,85]	*Milliken*	*Leslie*	*Milloy*	*Glass*	*Smith*	*McEwan*	*Liddell*	*Sneddon*	*Maxwell*	*Gilmour*	*Aitken*
					Ref: T Small (Dundee)	The large crowd sees the new Cup favourites as McFadyen opens from three yards. McEwan handles and Ellis is sure with his penalty. Killie get three after the break, Ferrier and McMenemy hit woodwork, Leslie deflects Murdoch's cross in and McFadyen gets his fourth on full-time.										
SF N CLYDE	2	W	2-0	0-0	McFadyen 82, Ferrier 85	McClory	Crapnell	Ellis	Wales	Blair	McKenzie	Murdoch	McMenemy	McFadyen	Stevenson	Ferrier
18/3 *25,000*	*13*					*Stevenson*	*Summers*	*Smith M*	*McPhail*	*Wood*	*Mayes*	*McGurk*	*Robertson*	*Boyd*	*Howieson*	*McCulloch*
(at Ibrox)					Ref: P Craigmyle (Aberdeen)	The sun shines on a poor crowd and a disappointing game. Allan McClory adds interest by protesting about his curling goal-line, which has to be repainted. It's anyone's game until Clyde's keeper fails to hold Murdoch's cross and McFadyen rushes in to open. Ferrier repeats the feat.										
F N CELTIC	2	L	0-1	0-0		McClory	Crapnell	Ellis	Wales	Blair	McKenzie	Murdoch	McMenemy	McFadyen	Stevenson	Ferrier
15/4 *102,339*	*3*				*McGrory 48*	*Kennaway*	*Hogg*	*McGonagle*	*Wilson*	*McStay*	*Geatons*	*Thomson R*	*Thomson A*	*McGrory*	*Napier*	*O'Donnell H*
(at Hampden)					Ref: T Dougray (Glasgow)	'Motherwell lack dash,' says the *Glasgow Herald* and it's the Well forwards who lose the Cup as they fail to shine during a first half controlled by Well. McFadyen looks lively but lacks support. Ellis and McKenzie bungle and Jimmy McGrory jumps in to win Celts 14th Scottish Cup.										

		Home						Away					
		P	W	D	L	F	A	W	D	L	F	A	Pts
1	Rangers	38	14	5	0	67	22	12	5	2	46	21	62
2	MOTHERWELL	38	15	1	3	66	24	12	4	3	48	29	59
3	Hearts	38	15	3	1	49	16	6	5	8	35	35	50
4	Celtic	38	13	3	3	47	18	7	5	7	28	26	48
5	St Johnstone	38	15	2	2	47	17	2	8	9	23	38	44
6	Aberdeen	38	13	4	2	63	19	5	2	12	22	39	42
7	St Mirren	38	12	3	4	48	23	6	3	10	25	37	42
8	Hamilton	38	11	5	3	54	31	7	1	11	36	47	42
9	Queen's Park	38	11	5	3	46	24	6	2	11	32	55	41
10	Partick Th	38	9	3	7	47	28	8	3	8	28	27	40
11	Falkirk	38	9	5	5	46	25	6	1	12	24	45	36
12	Clyde	38	12	0	7	42	29	3	5	11	27	46	35
13	Third Lanark	38	12	3	4	47	27	2	4	13	23	53	35
14	Kilmarnock	38	8	5	6	45	39	5	4	10	27	47	35
15	Dundee	38	9	6	4	34	27	3	3	13	26	50	33
16	Ayr Un	38	11	2	6	41	28	2	2	15	21	67	30
17	Cowdenbeath	38	9	3	7	44	38	1	2	16	21	73	25
18	Airdrie	38	9	2	8	37	34	1	·1	17	18	68	23
19	Morton	38	4	3	12	29	42	2	6	11	20	55	21
20	East Stirling	38	6	3	10	30	44	1	0	18	25	71	17
		760	217	66	97	929	555	97	66	217	555	929	760

Odds & ends

Double wins: (10) Airdrie, Ayr, Clyde, Cowdenbeath, Dundee, East Stirling, Hamilton, Morton, St Johnstone, St Mirren.

Double losses: (0).

Won from behind: (7) Ayr (h), St Mirren (a), Third Lanark (h), Hamilton (a), Clyde (a), Airdrie (h), Cowdenbeath (a).

Lost from in front: (0).

High spots: Reaching the final of the Scottish Cup for the second time. Joint League leaders, along with Rangers, in January.

Low spots: February losses to Rangers and Queen's Park end title hopes. Three successive league defeats also bring the end of Motherwell's three-year unbeaten home record. Losing Cup final to Celtic again.

Five goals: (1) McFadyen.

Four goals: (1) Mc Fadyen.

Hat-tricks: (4) Ferrier (1), McFadyen (3).

Ever-presents: (2) McClory, McFadyen.

Leading scorer: McFadyen (45).

	Appearances		Goals		
	Lge	SC	Lge	SC	Tot
Blair, John	**26**	7	**1**		**1**
Craig, Alan	**12**				
Crapnell, Jimmy	**11**	7			
Dowall, Willie	**25**				
Ellis, Ben	**33**	7	**1**	2	**3**
Ferrier, Bobby	**37**	7	**26**	4	**30**
Johnston, James	**2**				
McClory,Allan	**38**	7			
McFadyen, Willie	**38**	7	**45**	15	**60**
McKenzie, Tommy	**12**	4			
Mackrell, James	**8**				
McMenemy, John	**29**	6	**10**	1	**11**
Moffat, Willie	**16**	1	**6**		**6**
Murdoch, Johnny	**18**	4	**6**	2	**8**
Ogilvie, Duncan	**19**	3	**8**		**8**
Stevenson, George	**29**	7	**8**	1	**9**
Telfer,Willie	**27**	3			
Wales, Hugh	**37**	7	**2**	1	**3**
Wyllie, Tom	**1**				
(own-goals)			**1**	1	**2**
19 players used	**418**	**77**	**114**	**27**	**141**

No	Date		Att	Pos	Pt		F-A	H-T	Scorers, Times, and Referees	1	2	3	4	5	6	7	8	9	10	11
1	A	CLYDE				W	1-0	1-0	Ferrier 29	McClory	Crapnell	Ellis	Wales	Blair	Telfer	Dowall	McMenemy	McFadyen	Stevenson	Ferrier
	12/8		*10,000*		2					*Stevenson*	*Russell*	*Summers*	*McPhail*	*Wood*	*Mayes*	*Robertson*	*Wallace*	*Boyd*	*Howieson*	*McCulloch*
									Ref: T Small (Dundee)	The first-half cohesion and team-work shown by Well are enough to earn the points with Bob Ferrier shooting home first time. Willie Dowall is being tried out at right wing again but has to return to full-back when Crapnell is hurt. The Shawfield crowd unsportingly cheer his injury.										
2	H	ST JOHNSTONE		7		W	1-0	0-0	Stevenson 67	McClory	Crapnell	Ellis	Wales	Blair	Telfer	Dowall	McMenemy	McFadyen	Stevenson	Ferrier
	19/8		6,000	*17*	4					*Wylie*	*Welsh*	*Clark*	*Mason*	*Ireland*	*Ferguson*	*Tennant*	*Davidson*	*Stewart*	*Campbell*	*Dickie*
									Ref: W Dawson (Leith)	Well have Tommy Muirhead's Saints under sustained pressure, peppering the bar and posts with several long-range shots. John McMenemy swings over a pass to Stevenson who steadies himself and drives low into the corner of the net, helping to soothe the anxious home support.										
3	H	DUNDEE		3		W	1-0	1-0	McFadyen 8	McClory	Crapnell	Ellis	Wales	Blair	Telfer	Dowall	McMenemy	McFadyen	Stevenson	Ferrier
	23/8		6,000	*11*	6					*Marsh*	*Morgan*	*Gilmour*	*Symon*	*McCarthy*	*Blyth*	*Murdoch*	*Robertson*	*Mackay*	*Lee*	*Paterson*
									Ref: D Reilly (Port Glasgow)	Johnny Murdoch returns as part of a much changed Dundee outfit. Bob Ferrier's crisp cross is met by McFadyen with a diving header but keeper Marsh defies Well for the remainder of the game. Although Stevie rattles the bar with a rocket shot, it's a third consecutive 1-0 win.										
4	A	QUEEN OF SOUTH		2		W	5-0	2-0	McFadyen 5, 44, 55, 70, 80	McClory	Crapnell	Ellis	Wales	Blair	Telfer	Ogilvie	McMenemy	McFadyen	Stevenson	Ferrier
	26/8		*10,500*	*9*	8					*Smith*	*Savage*	*Culbert*	*Russell*	*Allan*	*Ferguson*	*Wales*	*Bell*	*McGowan*	*McDonald*	*McCall*
									Ref: M Hutton (Glasgow)	Promoted Queens had beaten Celtic on the first day of the league. McFadyen hits the bar before twice scoring from Blair passes. Willie's three second-half goals come largely from his providers on the left wing. 'Babes Well Spanked' says the *Motherwell Times* of a hot day in Dumfries.										
5	H	RANGERS		1		W	2-1	0-0	McFadyen 50, 85	McClory	Crapnell	Ellis	Wales	Blair	Telfer	Ogilvie	McMenemy	McFadyen	Stevenson	Ferrier
	2/9		**25,000**	*3*	10				*Stevenson 75*	*Dawson*	*Gray*	*Russell*	*Kennedy*	*McDonald R*	*Brown*	*Archibald*	*Stevenson*	*Smith*	*McPhail*	*Fleming*
									Ref: M Hutton (Glasgow)	Well go top after a battle of the giants with a fine first half, when Ferrier and Wales hit the woodwork. In a fair charge McFadyen bundles both keeper and ball over for the first. Gers' Stevenson shoots and McClory is beaten for the first time this season but McFadyen's fine shot wins it.										
6	A	HAMILTON		1		W	2-1	2-0	Ogilvie 11, Ferrier 28	McClory	Crapnell	Ellis	Wales	Blair	Telfer	Ogilvie	McMenemy	McFadyen	Stevenson	Ferrier
	9/9		*10,000*	*14*	12				*King 58p*	*Morton*	*Hunter*	*Bulloch*	*Dougall*	*Hill*	*Young*	*Park*	*McLaren*	*Wilson D*	*Crawley*	*King*
									Ref: J Hudson (Glasgow)	The heatwave continues as defensive blunders let Ogilvie and Ferrier in to score. McFadyen is herded out wide by Hill, while Ellis and Blair have their hands full with the Acas forwards. Blair downs Wilson and King converts the penalty. McLaren hits a post in the dying seconds.										
7	A	HIBERNIAN		1		W	2-0	1-0	Stevenson 26, McFadyen 83	McClory	Crapnell	Ellis	Wales	Blair	Telfer	Ogilvie	McMenemy	McFadyen	Stevenson	Ferrier
	13/9		*20,000*	*11*	14					*Blyth*	*Wilkinson*	*Urquhart*	*Langton*	*Watson*	*McFarlane*	*Walls*	*Wallace*	*Flucker*	*Halligan*	*Somerville*
									Ref: D Reilly (Port Glasgow)	His ball-control and spreading play make Stevie the best player afield and he opens with a header from Wales' free-kick. Hibs attack after the break but lack finishing power. The large midweek crowd have a long wait before McFadyen heads through a Ferrier cross for Well's second.										
8	H	ABERDEEN		1		W	4-1	2-1	McFadyen 11, 51, Stevenson 33, [Ogilvie 70]	McClory	Crapnell	Ellis	Wales	Blair	McKenzie	Ogilvie	McMenemy	McFadyen	Stevenson	Ferrier
	16/9		5,000	*10*	16				*Warnock 30*	*Smith*	*Cooper*	*McGill*	*Falloon*	*Gavin*	*Love*	*Benyon*	*Warnock*	*Moore*	*Mills*	*Gall*
									Ref: W Webb (Glasgow)	After McFadyen opens it's all Aberdeen and Gall heads against a post before Warnock deservedly levels. Well assert themselves more in the second half and although Moore hits a post, Dons fade out. Ref Webb blows for time with a good five minutes left and has to recall the teams.										
9	A	QUEEN'S PARK		1		W	5-1	2-1	McFadyen 33, 46, Ogilvie 44, 59, [Ferrier 70]	McClory	Crapnell	Ellis	Wales	Blair	Telfer	Ogilvie	McMenemy	McFadyen	Stevenson	Ferrier
	23/9		*20,000*	*4*	18				*Dodds 20*	*Smith*	*Campbell*	*Cooper*	*Gardiner*	*Lyon*	*Grant*	*Hosie*	*Anderson*	*Dodds*	*Bremner*	*Browning*
									Ref: P Craigmyle (Aberdeen)	A Dodd's flick opens for the on-form amateurs. Stevie hits a post before McMenemy earns a penalty but Ellis slams it against the bar. Ogilvie supplies for McFadyen's goal then snaps up one himself. The final goal is 'a thing of beauty' from Ferrier, 20 yards out near the by-line.										

No/Date		Opponent/Att					Scorers											
10	A	ABERDEEN	1	D	1-1	1-0	Stevenson 25	McClory	Crapnell	Ellis	Wales	Blair	Telfer	Ogilvie	McMenemy	McFadyen	Stevenson	Ferrier
25/9		*12,000*	*8*	19			*Moore 70*	*Smith*	*Cooper*	*McGill*	*Fraser*	*Falloon*	*Thomson*	*Benyon*	*Warnock*	*Moore*	*Mills*	*Gall*
							Ref: J Thomson (Hamilton)	Well are defending for most of the game on Aberdeen holiday Monday, Crapnell being outstanding. McClory is off for treatment and Ellis has to scramble away a Cooper lob. At close range Stevie heads in from a corner. Moore nods in a Cooper free-kick and Well drop their first point.										
11	H	FALKIRK	1	W	2-1	0-0	McFadyen 68, Stevenson 73	**Robertson**	Crapnell	Ellis	Wales	Blair	Telfer	Ogilvie	Johnston J	McFadyen	Stevenson	Ferrier
30/9		7,000	*11*	21			*Grant 60*	*Thomson*	*Nisbet*	*Hamill*	*Batchelor*	*Lowe*	*Shankley*	*Meechan*	*Dougal*	*Bartram*	*McNair*	*Grant*
							Ref: W Dawson (Leith)	Well have to battle all the way without McClory and McMenemy. Lowe is superb, giving McFadyen little room. Grant picks his spot to beat Robertson but this spurs Well on and McFadyen darts through to head in. Stevie runs through to volley in a dropping ball for the winner.										
12	A	KILMARNOCK	1	W	3-1	1-1	Stevenson 34, Ogilvie 66, McFad' 74	Robertson	Crapnell	Ellis	Wales	Blair	Telfer	Ogilvie	McMenemy	McFadyen	Stevenson	Ferrier
7/10		*20,000*	*5*	23			*Keane 30*	*Miller*	*Morton*	*Milloy*	*Glass*	*Smith*	*McEwan*	*Liddell*	*Williamson*	*Maxwell*	*Kelvin*	*Keane*
							Ref: H Watson (Glasgow)	Keane opens from close range before Stevenson drives in the equaliser. Well hold on for a critical ten minutes after the break and Ferrier's pinpoint cross is put in by Ogilvie. McFadyen, a revelation in his varied play, takes a Stevenson through pass in his stride to send in a blaster.										
13	H	HEARTS	1	W	2-1	1-1	Ferrier 41, Stevenson 75	Robertson	Crapnell	Ellis	Wales	Blair	Telfer	Ogilvie	McMenemy	McFadyen	Stevenson	Ferrier
14/10		12,000	*6*	25			*Johnstone R 38*	*Harkness*	*Anderson*	*McClure*	*Massie*	*Reid*	*Herd*	*Johnstone R*	*White*	*Battles*	*Smith*	*Murray*
							Ref: P Craigmyle (Aberdeen)	Hearts, beaten only once so far, get the opener in an engrossing epic of a game when Johnstone slaps one in. Ferrier's left-foot drive equalises before the break. Stevenson is in brilliant form but his winner comes when he gets a rebound from the ref, works his way forward, and scores.										
14	H	CELTIC	1	D	1-1	0-0	McFadyen 87	Robertson	Crapnell	Ellis	Wales	Blair	Telfer	Ogilvie	McMenemy	McFadyen	Stevenson	Ferrier
21/10		18,000	*13*	26			*Crum 75*	*Kennaway*	*Hogg*	*McGonagle*	*Wilson*	*McStay*	*Hughes*	*Dunn*	*Thomson A*	*Crum*	*O'Donnell F*	*O'Donnell H*
							Ref: T Dougray (Rutherglen)	Depleted Celts take on the only unbeaten side in Britain. Well storm in but can't put the ball in the net, Ferrier and Ogilvie both hitting the post. Crum nets from Wilson's free-kick before Ellis and Ferrier are hurt and all looks lost, but Ferrier lobs the keeper for McFadyen to nod in.										
15	A	PARTICK TH	1	W	4-1	2-0	McFadyen 41, 44, Ogilvie 57,	Robertson	Crapnell	Ellis	Wales	Blair	Telfer	Ogilvie	McMenemy	McFadyen	Stevenson	Ferrier
28/10		*20,000*	*20*	28			*Wylie 74* [Stevenson 72]	*Johnstone*	*Calderwood*	*Cumming*	*Elliot*	*McAllister*	*McLeod*	*Ness*	*Miller*	*Wylie*	*Ballantyne*	*Craigie*
							Ref: J Yeaman (Dundee)	Well have wind advantage and McFadyen firstly heads in a Ferrier cross then shoots home from a Stevie pass. Thistle remain aggressive but McMenemy breaks away with Ferrier to allow the unmarked Ogilvie in for the third. Stevie then runs 40 yards to shoot in a fine solo effort.										
16	A	DUNDEE	1	W	3-2	1-1	McFadyen 31, Ogilvie 52, 87	Robertson	Crapnell	Ellis	Wales	Blair	Telfer	Ogilvie	McMenemy	McFadyen	Stevenson	Ferrier
4/11		*20,000*	*13*	30			*Robertson 13, 59*	*Marsh*	*Morgan*	*Gilmour*	*Symon*	*McCarthy*	*Blyth*	*Murdoch*	*Mackay*	*Robertson*	*Lee*	*Kirby*
							Ref: T Dougray (Rutherglen)	Norman Kirby stars on his debut for Dundee, setting up both of Robertson's goals. McFadyen brings down a high ball and levels as Dundee claim for dangerous play. Ogilvie cuts in to head in firstly Ferrier's cross and then Telfer's. Ferrier manages to hit the woodwork three times.										
17	H	HIBERNIAN	1	W	2-1	0-1	McFadyen 48, Ferrier 53	Robertson	Dowall	Ellis	Wales	Blair	Telfer	Ogilvie	McMenemy	McFadyen	Stevenson	Ferrier
11/11		7,000	*15*	32			*Flucker 32*	*Blyth*	*Wilkinson*	*Urquhart*	*Langton*	*Crawford*	*McFarlane*	*Walls*	*Marshall*	*Flucker*	*Moffat*	*Malloy*
							Ref: J Yeaman (Dundee)	Remarkably Well press for almost the whole game but let Moffat in to set up Flucker to score. Robertson saves desperately to halt another breakaway before McFadyen levels at last with a low shot. Stevie and Ferrier carry the ball forward for Bob to blast in off Urquhart's leg.										
18	H	AIRDRIE	1	W	3-1	0-1	Ogilvie 51, McFadyen 55, 72	Robertson	Crapnell	Ellis	Wales	Blair	Telfer	Ogilvie	McMenemy	McFadyen	Stevenson	Ferrier
18/11		6,000	*16*	34			*Moore 44*	*Morrison*	*Calder*	*Shaw*	*Crosbie*	*Sharp*	*Todd*	*Ross*	*Grant*	*Moore*	*Collins*	*Mooney*
							Ref: W Dawson (Leith)	The Diamonds defend stoutly and Well can't finish despite their pressure. Sharp beats three men to set up Moore's opener. Well still dominate after the break and Ogilvie gets his head to Ferrier's cross. Stevie holds the ball up for McFadyen to drive in and then Willie manages another.										
19	H	ST MIRREN	1	W	1-0	0-0	Ferrier 67	Robertson	Crapnell	Ellis	Wales	Blair	Telfer	Ogilvie	McMenemy	McFadyen	Stevenson	Ferrier
25/11		6,000	*19*	36				*McCloy*	*Hay*	*Ancell*	*Workman*	*Wilson*	*Miller*	*Latimer*	*McAulay*	*Smith J*	*Smith W*	*Phillips*
							Ref: P Craigmyle (Aberdeen)	Although fielding a couple of juniors, Saints are hungry for the points and a dour struggle ensues. Ogilvie's corner is cleared, but only as far as Ferrier 20 yards out, and he shoots through a ruck of players to score. Willie McFadyen misses some great chances in his desperation to score.										

No	Date		Att	Pos	Pt	F-A	H-T	Scorers, Times, and Referees	1	2	3	4	5	6	7	8	9	10	11
20	A	THIRD LANARK		1	D	2-2	1-0	Ogilvie 31, McMenemy 47	Robertson	Crapnell	Ellis	Wales	Blair	Telfer	Ogilvie	McMenemy	McFadyen	Stevenson	Ferrier
	2/12		*8,000*	*17*	37			*McCulloch 66, Clark 73*	*McCormack*	*Carabine*	*Warden*	*Blair*	*Denmark*	*McLellan*	*Lynas*	*Clark*	*McCulloch*	*McKenzie*	*Breslin*
								Ref: P Craigmyle (Aberdeen)	It's looking good when Ogilvie puts in Ferrier's low cross and it seems safe when McMenemy shoots in a rebound from McFadyen. However, Willie misses a sitter and Thirds get one back through McCulloch. When Clark heads the equaliser and Crapnell is hurt, Well only just hold on.										
21	H	AYR UNITED		1	W	5-2	0-0	Wales 46, Ogilvie 55, 60, McM' 65, 89	Robertson	Crapnell	Ellis	Wales	Blair	Telfer	Ogilvie	McMenemy	McFadyen	Stevenson	Ferrier
	9/12		12,000	*4*	39			*Brae 72, McCall 88p*	*Wilson*	*Fleming*	*Ure*	*McCall*	*Currie*	*Holland*	*Robertson*	*Taylor*	*McGibbon*	*Brae*	*Rodger*
								Ref: T Dougray (Rutherglen)	Alex Gibson's Ayr are going really well but neither side makes progress till the second half when the wind helps take in a Wales lob. Ben Ellis plays on despite a collar-bone fractured in just five minutes. Even at four down, Ayr still fight and McCall nets with a penalty after he's fouled.										
22	A	COWDENBEATH		1	W	4-0	2-0	Ferrier 17, McFadyen 19, 65, 70	Robertson	Dowall	Crapnell	Wales	Blair	Telfer	Ogilvie	McMenemy	McFadyen	Stevenson	Ferrier
	16/12		***1,500***	*20*	41				*Scott*	*McDonald*	*Napier*	*McDonald D*	*Feeney*	*Bingham*	*Hamill*	*Cameron*	*Wilkie*	*McCurley*	*Robertson*
								Ref: W Dawson (Leith)	On a hard surface McFadyen ends his lean spell with a fine hat-trick but it's Ferrier's hard-driven shot that opens. McFadyen now heads in Ogilvie's cross before McMenemy rattles the bar. The points are won when Willie twice scores with hard angular drives but the score flatters.										
23	H	CLYDE		1	L	1-2	1-1	Blair 40p	Robertson	Dowall	**Sinclair**	Wales	Blair	Telfer	Ogilvie	McMenemy	McFadyen	Stevenson	**Johnstone C**
	23/12		7,000	14	41			*Johnstone 17, Carroll 55*	*Stevenson*	*Summers*	*Smith*	*McPhail*	*Wood*	*Mayes*	*Carroll*	*McNaughton*	*Robertson*	*Johnstone*	*Howieson*
								Ref: W Dawson (Leith)	Well are depleted, but it's still a shock when lowly Clyde end their unbeaten run. Clyde's Johnstone nets with a deflected shot but Blair's penalty levels it after Smith trips Ogilvie. Little Carroll skips in to put Clyde ahead and although each side hits woodwork, Well's run is ended.										
24	A	ST JOHNSTONE		1	W	2-1	0-0	McFadyen 53, Stevenson 85	Robertson	Wales	**Allan**	McKenzie	Blair	Telfer	Ogilvie	McMenemy	McFadyen	Stevenson	Dowall
	30/12		*10,000*	*8*	43			*Fulton 49*	*Wylie*	*Welsh*	*Clark*	*Mason*	*Moulds*	*Campbell*	*Tennant*	*Davidson*	*Fulton*	*Ferguson*	*Stewart*
								Ref: W Holburn (Glasgow)	Well's reshuffled side fall behind when Fulton shoots in a rebound. McFadyen levels when his cross goes in through the keeper's hands. Robertson is off to have a cut hand stitched but stand-in Dowall makes some fine saves before Stevie rises like a bird to head in the winner.										
25	H	HAMILTON		1	W	2-1	1-1	Dowall 42, McFadyen 60	**Walker**	Wales	Allan	McKenzie	Blair	Telfer	Ogilvie	McMenemy	McFadyen	Stevenson	Dowall
	1/1		12,000	*12*	45			*Park 2*	*Shevlin*	*Young*	*Bulloch*	*Cox*	*Hill*	*Murray*	*Park*	*Benzie*	*Crawley*	*Wilson D*	*King*
								Ref: T Small (Dundee)	Park's slanting shot finds the net early and weakened Well pick up even more injuries on a dull Ne'erday. Dowall's run up the left ends with a low drive into the net. Willie McFadyen is a mere passenger out on the left but he drifts in to head in McKenzie's cross, despite an eye injury.										
26	A	FALKIRK		1	W	3-1	1-1	Johnstone C 44, McFadyen 52, [Wyllie 56]	Walker	Wales	Allan	**Murray**	Blair	Telfer	McFadyen	McMenemy	Wyllie	Stevenson	Johnstone C
	2/1		*20,000*	*8*	47			*Bartram 25*	*Thomson*	*Nisbet*	*Hamill*	*Richardson*	*Shankley*	*Hutchieson*	*Batchelor*	*Anderson*	*Bartram*	*Hope !*	*Meechan*
								Ref: H Watson (Glasgow)	In a breakaway Bartram's shot goes in off Walker's hands. With a much weakened side, Well reply just before the break when Charlie Johnstone bangs one in. Charlie twice lobs in for McFadyen and then for Wylie to rush the ball in. Hope is sent off for a bad tackle on Blair.										
27	H	QUEEN OF SOUTH		1	L	1-2	1-2	Wyllie 7	Walker	Allan	Crapnell	Wales	Blair	Telfer	McFadyen	McMenemy	Wyllie	Stevenson	Johnstone C
	6/1		8,000	*7*	47			*McGowan 20, Cumming 35*	*Fotheringham*	*Savage*	*Culbert*	*Anderson J*	*Allan*	*Ferguson*	*Anderson W*	*Cumming*	*McGowan*	*McKay*	*Tulip*
								Ref: J Hudson (Glasgow)	Well open against giant-killing Queen's when Wyllie jabs in Johnstone's cross. Crapnell's mistake sets up McGowan's leveller, then Cumming puts Queen's ahead, the ball rebounding from the ref. His head plastered, McFadyen goes to centre in a desperate attempt to rescue the game.										
28	A	RANGERS		1	L	2-4	0-1	Stevenson 72, 88	Robertson	Wales	Ellis	McKenzie	Blair	Telfer	Wyllie	McMenemy	McFadyen	Stevenson	Dowall
	13/1		***70,000***	*2*	47			*McPhail 6, 59 Fleming 80, 86*	*Dawson*	*Gray*	*McDonald*	*Meiklejohn*	*Simpson*	*Brown*	*Main*	*Marshall*	*Fleming*	*McPhail*	*Nicholson*
								Ref: W Holburn (Glasgow)	Ellis is back but looks far from fit. His high boot catches Fleming and the huge Ibrox crowd are on his back even more. Well's offside trap fails twice as McPhail puts Rangers two up. Fleming's two are sandwiched between two by Stevie, his last a volley slammed in from 20 yards.										

No		Opponent	Pos	Res	F-A	H-T	Scorers, Times, Referees	1	2	3	4	5	6	7	8	9	10	11
29	H	QUEEN'S PARK	1	W	3-0	1-0	McFadyen 30, 63, McMenemy 85	Robertson	Allan	Ellis	Wales	Blair	Telfer	Ogilvie	McMenemy	McFadyen	Stevenson	Ferrier
	27/1	9,000	*14*	49				*Smith*	*Campbell*	*Dickson*	*Hosie*	*Stewart*	*McKelvie*	*Taylor*	*Bremner*	*Dodds*	*Anderson*	*McLelland*
							Ref: W Dawson (Leith)	Well pressure tells and Ferrier's free-kick finds its way to McFadyen who turns it in. McMenemy and Stevie both hit the post but it's Willie's toe-jab that brings Well's next. McMenemy slips past two men to tap in the third. Ogilvie has a fine return and Ferrier finds space to revel in.										
30	H	KILMARNOCK	1	W	2-0	2-0	Ferrier 24, Ogilvie 30	Robertson	Allan	Ellis	Wales	Blair	Telfer	Ogilvie	McMenemy	McFadyen	Stevenson	Ferrier
	24/2	5,000	*8*	51				*Miller*	*Anderson*	*Milloy*	*Glass*	*Smith*	*McEwan*	*Connell*	*Williamson*	*Gilmour*	*Kennedy*	*Keane*
							Ref: T Small (Dundee)	Without 'Bud' Maxwell, Killie struggle up front. Ogilvie's cross eludes everyone except Ferrier, who puts it past the stranded keeper. Ogilvie floats a corner straight inside the near post. McFadyen twice heads past an empty goal and Smith makes sure he doesn't get any more chances.										
31	A	CELTIC	1	L	**0-3**	0-2		Robertson	Crapnell	Ellis	Wales	Blair	Telfer	Ogilvie	McMenemy	McFadyen	Stevenson	Ferrier
	10/3	*20,000*	*11*	51			*O'Donnell H 30, 76, O'Donnell F 40*	*Kennaway*	*Hogg*	*McGonagle*	*Geatons*	*McStay*	*Hughes*	*Crum*	*Smith*	*McGrory*	*O'Donnell F*	*O'Donnell H*
							Ref: T Small (Dundee)	Opening exchanges are even until Crum gets the better of Ellis and then runs riot. His cross lets Hugh O'Donnell head in the first before his brother Frank takes a penalty after Blair had fouled Crum. Robertson saves it but Frank follows up. Hugh then shoots past stranded Robertson.										
32	H	PARTICK TH	2	L	2-3	2-0	Stevenson 11, Crawley 35	Robertson	Allan	Ellis	Wales	Blair	Telfer	Ogilvie	McMenemy	**Crawley**	Stevenson	Ferrier
	17/3	6,000	*13*	51			*Ness 63, Miller 65, Bain 72*	*Johnstone*	*Calderwood*	*Cumming*	*Elliot*	*Donnelly*	*McLeod*	*Ness*	*Miller*	*McLennan*	*Ballantyne*	*Bain*
							Ref: T Dougray (Rutherglen)	Stevie and debutant Crawley score easy goals as Well press. Stevie misses a five-yard sitter then Thistle break for Ness to head in. Miller follows with another headed goal, then Bain tricks Allan and shoots into the corner. Last season's stumble is repeated and the title hopes go.										
33	A	ST MIRREN	2	W	3-1	2-1	Stewart 35, McGillivray 43, [McFadyen 55]	Robertson	Crapnell	Ellis	Wales	Blair	McKenzie	**McGillivray**	McMenemy	McFadyen	Stevenson	**Stewart**
	20/3	*8,000*	*17*	53			*Knox 25*	*McCloy*	*Hay*	*Ancell*	*Gebbie*	*Wilson*	*Miller*	*Knox*	*Latimer*	*Smith*	*McGregor*	*Phillips*
							Ref: W Webb (Glasgow)	Knox blasts in the first but McMenemy passes for Stewart to score on his debut and McFadyen does the same for McGillivray before the turn. McFadyen's head glides home the third and McGillivray hits the bar. The omens look good for the Cup semi-final but Saints can play better.										
34	A	AIRDRIE	2	W	6-3	3-2	Stewart 1, 33, 63, McFad' 14, 65, 76	Robertson	Allan	Ellis	Wales	**Carlyle**	Telfer	McGillivray	McMenemy	McFadyen	Stevenson	Stewart
	24/3	*8,000*	*19*	55			*Law 8, Harrison 25, Ross 90*	*Wilson G*	*Crosbie*	*Shaw*	*Thomson*	*Sharp*	*Todd*	*Ross*	*Law*	*Wilson J*	*Harrison*	*Mooney*
							Ref: P Craigmyle (Aberdeen)	Stewart's early drive gets Well off to a flier but back come Airdrie when little Law rises to head in. McFadyen snatches a hat-trick while Stewart breaks during a spell of home pressure to complete his treble. Robertson is too late clutching Ross's shot as it's already over the line.										
35	H	THIRD LANARK	2	D	2-2	1-1	Stevenson 25, Ferrier 58	Robertson	Allan	Ellis	Wales	Telfer	McKenzie	Ogilvie	McMenemy	McFadyen	Stevenson	Ferrier
	7/4	4,000	*18*	56			*Howe 10, Clark 82*	*Taylor*	*Carabine*	*Harvey*	*Blair*	*Denmark*	*Waddell*	*Brown*	*Clark*	*McKenzie*	*McMillan*	*Howe*
							Ref: J Hudson (Glasgow)	Ferrier is back but Blair is still out as Thirds snatch the opener via Howe's head. Stevie replies with a 20-yarder high into the net. Well resume on the attack and Ferrier meets Ogilvie's cross in full flight to lead. Thirds gain a desperate point when Bruce Clark volleys home on the drop.										
36	H	COWDENBEATH	2	W	**6-1**	1-0	Wyllie 33, Crawley 49, 70, 86, [McMen' 62, Ogilvie 88]	McClory	Allan	Sinclair	Wales	McFadyen	Telfer	Ogilvie	Crawley	Wyllie	McMenemy	Stewart
	11/4	**1,500**	*20*	58			*Feeney 90*	*Scott*	*McDonald S*	*Mitchell*	*Wilkie*	*Napier*	*Bingham*	*Hamill*	*Renfrew*	*Feeney*	*McCurley*	*Glancy*
							Ref: T Dougray (Rutherglen)	In a meaningless game the doomed Fifers draw a paltry crowd. McClory makes a welcome return but McFadyen stands in for Blair. In a poor first half, Wyllie's headed goal brightens the miserable conditions. Crawley scores a hat-trick of strong drives and Feeney grabs a consolation.										
37	A	HEARTS	2	W	3-1	1-0	Stevenson 26, McFadyen 50, 84	McClory	Allan	Crapnell	Wales	Blair	Telfer	Ogilvie	McMenemy	McFadyen	Stevenson	Ferrier
	16/4	*14,000*	*8*	60			*Coutts 75*	*Harkness*	*Reid W*	*Hearty*	*Massie*	*Johnstone J*	*Miller*	*Johnstone R*	*Walker*	*Battles*	*Coutts*	*Munro*
							Ref: W Webb (Glasgow)	It's a Spring holiday evening and Blair is back for Well. Stevie gets the first with a typical low drive. McFadyen blasts in, then Coutts heads in one for Hearts. Allan is off hurt but resumes to help Well retake control and McFadyen heads home with fine judgment to finish the contest.										
38	A	AYR UNITED	2	W	3-2	1-1	McFadyen 38, 60, McMenemy 52	McClory	Crapnell	Sinclair	Wales	Blair	Telfer	Ogilvie	McMenemy	McFadyen	Stevenson	Ferrier
	21/4	*7,000*	*8*	62			*Mair 10, Rodger 67*	*Hepburn*	*Reid*	*Ure*	*Taylor*	*Currie*	*Holland*	*Mair*	*Brae*	*McGibbon*	*Brannan*	*Rodger*
	Home	Away					Ref: T Small (Dundee)	Perhaps minds are on the South African tour as Mair drifts in to open. Currie's slip lets McFadyen touch in the equaliser but Well pack their defence. After the break McMenemy first-times in from 25 yards then McFadyen scores after a solo run. Rodger pulls one back as Well dream.										
Average	8,600	16,300																

SCOTTISH DIVISION 1 (CUP-TIES)

Manager: John Hunter

SEASON 1933-34

Scottish Cup					F-A	H-T	Scorers, Times, and Referees	1	2	3	4	5	6	7	8	9	10	11
1	H	GALA F'DEAN	1	W	4-0	3-0	McFadyen 4, 20, 32, 89	Robertson	Allan	Ellis	Wales	Blair	Telfer	Wyllie	McMenemy	McFadyen	Stevenson	Ferrier
	20/1	3,013	*NL*					*Gardiner*	*King*	*Forrest*	*Robertson*	*Hamilton*	*McLaren*	*Carruthers*	*Sherlaw*	*Trantor*	*Johnston*	*Burns*
							Ref: W McCulloch (Glasgow)	Bob Ferrier is back on the wing but Gala's green strip recalls recent cup losses to Celtic. McFadyen's first is piloted in from Ferrier's carpet pass, his last from short range after McMenemy sets him up at the end. Well have eased up and content themselves with mere ball practice.										
2	A	PARTICK TH	1	D	3-3	3-1	McMenemy 3, 31, Ellis 35	Robertson	Crapnell	Ellis	Wales	Blair	Telfer	Ogilvie	McMenemy	McFadyen	Stevenson	Ferrier
	3/2	*33,000*	*17*				*Ballantyne 36, 79, McLennan 84*	*Johnstone*	*Calderwood*	*Cumming*	*Elliot*	*Donnelly*	*McLeod*	*Ness*	*Miller*	*McLennan*	*Ballantyne*	*Bain*
							Ref: T Small (Dundee)	It's frills from Well in the first and thrills from Thistle in the second before the round's biggest crowd. Well attack with eight men at times and McMenemy opens in text-book style. At 3-1 up Robertson fails to clear and Ballantyne crashes it in followed by McLennan's late equaliser.										
2R	H	PARTICK TH	1	W	2-1	2-0	Stevenson 2, McFadyen 16	Robertson	Crapnell	Ellis	Wales	Blair	Telfer	McKenzie	McMenemy	McFadyen	Stevenson	Ferrier
	7/2	16,000	*17*				*Miller 47*	*Johnstone*	*Calderwood*	*Cumming*	*Elliot*	*Donnelly*	*McLeod*	*Ness*	*Miller*	*McLennan*	*Ballantyne*	*Bain*
							Ref: T Small (Dundee)	The Wednesday half-holiday crowd are hardly in when Stevie darts through to score. McFadyen taps in the second when the keeper fails to clear. Thistle win a free-kick and Miller scrapes the ball over to complete a trio of scrappy goals in a raw cup-tie. McKenzie is out of position.										
3	H	EAST STIRLING	1	W	5-0	4-0	McFadyen 10, 14, 25, Ferrier 30, [Stevenson 75]	Robertson	Allan	Ellis	Wales	Blair	Telfer	Ogilvie	McMenemy	McFadyen	Stevenson	Ferrier
	17/2	5,200	*2:10*					*Edden*	*Scobbie*	*Geddes*	*Duncan*	*Brown*	*Thomson*	*Smith*	*Jack*	*Heeps*	*Miller*	*Kemp*
							Ref: P Craigmyle (Aberdeen)	Well's left wing pairing makes three of the first-half goals and Shire are toiling. Bob Ferrier's goal is the pick of the bunch, flashing in a spectacular volley from the edge of the box to leave young Edden helpless. Blair handles in the area but Brown blasts his penalty kick over.										
QF	A	ALBION ROVERS	1	D	1-1	0-0	McFadyen 75	Robertson	Crapnell	Ellis	Wales	Blair	Telfer	Ogilvie	McMenemy	McFadyen	Stevenson	Ferrier
	3/3	*16,155*	*2:5*				*McPhee 82*	*Crosskey*	*Waddell*	*Beath R*	*Donnelly*	*Bruce*	*Walls*	*McPhee*	*Beath J*	*Renwick*	*Browning*	*Barclay*
							Ref: H Watson (Glasgow)	The Coatbridge men look dangerous on the break and Well's finishing is poor. Robertson dives to save at Renwick's feet, then McMenemy hits the post at the other end. McFadyen breaks the deadlock from Ogilvie's cross but McPhee ties it when he heads in Barclay's corner-kick.										
QF R	H	ALBION ROVERS	1	W	6-0	4-0	McFadyen 10, 25, 33, McMenemy 23, Wales 55, Ogilvie 85	Robertson	Crapnell	Ellis	Wales	Blair	Telfer	Ogilvie	McMenemy	McFadyen	Stevenson	Ferrier
	7/3	11,000	*2:5*					*Crosskey*	*Waddell*	*Beath R*	*Donnelly*	*Bruce*	*Walls*	*McPhee*	*Beath J*	*Renwick*	*Browning*	*Barclay*
							Ref: H Watson (Glasgow)	The sun's out but a thin coating of snow covers the terracing as McFadyen takes a low Ferrier cross to net the first of his hat-trick. Sleet and snow bring semi-darkness as a Walls free-kick hits the bar. The sun's back out as Wales grabs a rare goal while Beath is in for the hurt keeper.										
SF	N	ST MIRREN	2	L	1-3	0-1	McFadyen 88	Robertson	Crapnell	Ellis	Wales	Carlyle	McKenzie	Ogilvie	McMenemy	McFadyen	Stevenson	Stewart
	31/3	*28,000*	*16*				*Knox 14, 63p, 67*	*McCloy*	*Hay*	*Ancell*	*Gebbie*	*Wilson*	*Miller*	*Knox*	*Latimer*	*McGregor*	*McCabe*	*Phillips*
		(at Tynecastle)					Ref: M Hutton (Glasgow)	Carlyle is in for Blair at the last minute and his foul on McGregor lets Knox open from the resultant free. Well hunt for an equaliser but Saints break and Carlyle pulls down Latimer. Knox converts the penalty then gets a third from a corner. Ferrier's omission is keenly felt as Well exit.										

		Home					Away					
	P	W	D	L	F	A	W	D	L	F	A	Pts
1 Rangers	38	16	3	0	65	18	14	3	2	53	23	66
2 MOTHERWELL	38	14	2	3	43	20	15	2	2	54	25	62
3 Celtic	38	12	5	2	47	20	6	6	7	31	33	47
4 Queen South	38	11	2	6	44	36	10	1	8	31	42	45
5 Aberdeen	38	12	4	3	55	12	6	4	9	35	45	44
6 Hearts	38	11	5	3	52	23	6	5	8	34	36	44
7 Kilmarnock	38	11	3	5	45	28	6	6	7	28	36	43
8 Ayr United	38	10	4	5	48	37	6	6	7	39	55	42
9 St Johnstone	38	11	3	5	43	19	6	3	10	31	34	40
10 Falkirk	38	12	3	4	49	31	4	3	12	24	37	38
11 Hamilton	38	9	5	5	35	30	6	3	10	30	49	38
12 Dundee	38	10	3	6	39	25	5	3	11	29	39	36
13 Partick Th	38	9	2	8	46	37	5	3	11	27	41	33
14 Clyde	38	8	5	6	36	29	2	6	11	20	41	31
15 Queen's Park	38	7	3	9	33	41	6	2	11	32	44	31
16 Hibernian	38	8	2	9	31	33	4	1	14	20	36	27
17 St Mirren	38	5	4	10	29	35	4	5	10	17	40	27
18 Airdrie	38	7	3	9	37	46	3	3	13	22	57	26
19 Third Lanark	38	6	6	7	38	41	2	3	14	24	62	25
20 Cowdenbeath	38	4	3	12	33	45	1	2	16	25	73	15
	760	193	70	117	848	606	117	70	193	606	848	760

Odds & ends

Double wins: (12) Airdrie, Ayr, Cowdenb'th, Dundee, Falkirk, Hamilton, Hearts, Hibernian, Kilmarnock, Queen's Pk, St Johnstone, St Mirren.
Double losses: (0)

Won from behind: (12) Queen's Pk (a), Falkirk (h), Kilmarn'ck (a), Hearts (h), Dundee (a), Hibernian (h), Airdrie (h), St Johnstone (a), Hamilton (h), Falkirk (a), St Mirren (a), Ayr (a).

Lost from in front: (2) Queen o' South (h), Partick Th (h).

High spots: Leading the league for six months.
Going seven points clear at the top in January.

Low spots: Losing the unbeaten record at Fir Park in December.
The Cup semi-final exit to St Mirren.

Five goals: (1) McFadyen.
Hat-tricks: (4) McFadyen (2), Crawley (1), Stewart (1).
Ever-presents: (1) Wales.
Leading scorer: McFadyen (38).

	Appearances		Goals		
	Lge	SC	**Lge**	SC	**Tot**
Allan, Willie	**11**	2			
Blair, John	**35**	6	**1**		**1**
Carlyle, Hugh	**1**	1			
Crapnell, Jimmy	**26**	5			
Crawley, Tom	**2**		**4**		**4**
Dowall, Willie	**9**		**1**		**1**
Ellis, Ben	**29**	7		1	**1**
Ferrier, Bobby	**29**	6	**9**	1	**10**
Johnston, James	**1**				
Johnstone, Charlie	**3**		**1**		**1**
McClory, Allan	**13**				
McFadyen, Willie	**37**	7	**38**	13	**51**
McGillivray, Charlie	**2**		**1**		**1**
McKenzie, Tommy	**6**	2			
McMenemy, John	**37**	7	**6**	3	**9**
Murray, Hugh	**1**				
Ogilvie, Duncan	**30**	5	**14**	1	**15**
Robertson, Jock	**22**	7			
Sinclair, Andrew	**3**				
Stevenson, George	**37**	7	**14**	2	**16**
Stewart, Willie	**3**	1	**4**		**4**
Telfer, Willie	**36**	6			
Wales, Hugh	**38**	**7**	**1**	**1**	**2**
Walker, Robert	**3**				
Wyllie, Tom	**4**	**1**	**3**		**3**
25 players used	**418**	**77**	**97**	**22**	**119**

Motherwell's third Cup final defeat, in 1939, left them with the reputation of being one of the best teams never to have won the trophy. Five months later Britain was at war.

SUBSCRIBERS	MOST IMPORTANT PLAYER
Gerard Brown	
Paul Carty	
Bob Clemenson	Allan McClory
Iain Crosby	
Scott Crosby	
Eddie Ferguson	Bob Ferrier
Graham Hamilton	Willie McFadyen
Fraser Hamilton	
William F Joyce	Willie McFadyen
Peter Laird	
Teresa Macdonald	
Bob Maxwell	
Martin Milligan	Bob Ferrier
James Mitchell	George Stevenson
Mackenzie Mitchell	Bob Ferrier
Jamie Nimmo	Willie McFadyen
Martin Nimmo	Willie McFadyen
Steven R Quither	Willie McFadyen
Stuart Reid	Willie McFadyen
Derek Samson	Willie McFadyen
Scott Smith	
Bill Stubbs	Willie McFadyen
Jim Tait	
Donald Taylor	Bob Ferrier
Alasdair Thomson	
John Sinton Ward	Willie McFadyen
Terry Willoughby	Ben Ellis